Cdr E.G. Martin OBE RNVR, painted by the war artist Stephen Bone in April 1944

The ROYAL OCEAN RACING CLUB

THE FIRST 75 YEARS

Ian Dear

ADLARD COLES NAUTICAL

LONDON

Published 2000 by Adlard Coles Nautical
an imprint of A & C Black (Publishers) Ltd
35 Bedford Row, London WC1R 4JH

ISBN 0-7136-5242-X

A CIP catalogue record for this book is available from the British Library.

Printed and bound by The Bath Press, Bath, U.K.

Production: Norman Hemsley
Design: Dick Vine

Contents

Acknowledgments

Where known, the owners of the illustrations have been credited. All reasonable efforts have been made to trace the copyright owners of those illustrations not credited. Copyright owners who have not been credited are invited to contact the Royal Ocean Racing Club. Many people, members and non-members alike, have helped to make this book possible, as have the club's secretariat who were infinitely patient in dealing with my incursions into their time. I hope I have been able, either in the text or in the photograph credits, to acknowledge all those who helped, as it is not possible to mention everyone by name here. However, I must single out the following who, though not currently RORC members, were of great assistance to me: Duke of Beaufort, Mrs van Busschbach-Bruynzeel, Mrs Molly Hewlett, Dr Norris Hoyt, Sandy Illingworth, David Mason, Sir Brooks Richards, John Spooner, Douglas L. Stein (Curator of Manuscripts, Mystic Seaport Museum), and Edward B. Watson (CCA archivist). Mrs Mary Pera and Dr Nick Greville took the trouble to read the manuscript, and provided helpful suggestions, and Mr Paul King kindly proofread the galleys. Lastly, I would like to thank Mystic Seaport Museum for supplying a copy of Norris Hoyt's photograph of Dick Nye in his bunk which appears on page 132.

Colour Illustrations

(for black-and-white illustrations see index)

frontispiece: painting of Cdr E.G. Martin OBE RNVR

Between pages 56 and 57
sketch of Sir Philip Hunloke
painting of the Fastnet Rock
painting of *Ilex*
painting of *Jolie Brise*
painting of *Bloodhound*
model of *Latifa*
painting of *Astrape*

Between pages 104 and 105
painting of *Yeoman III*
Clarionet and *Roundabout*
Noryema V
Frigate
Edward Heath at the helm of the fifth *Morning Cloud*
Don Street and his 17-ton (TM) *Iolaire*

Between pages 152 and 153
painting of *Lorelei* rescuing *Griffin V*'s crew during the 1979 Fastnet
Chris Dunning and his seventh *Marionette*
Peter Nicholson
Ted Turner
Mary Pera
Jonathan Bradbeer
Eddie Warden Owen
Graham Walker and his fourth *Indulgence*
Jamarella

Between pages 200 and 201
Desperado
Brava Q8
First Mumm 36 world championships
Zulu
start of 1998 North Sea Race
Assuage
Sydney 40

Author's Note

Chapter notes, which are to be found at the back of the book, are indicated in the text by an asterisk, thus*.

Chapter One

THE KING OF SPORTS

'WORK IS the curse of the sailing classes,' joked politician Edward Heath after his win in the 1969 Sydney-Hobart Race. But work, it seems, certainly didn't interfere with the pleasures of the founding members of what was to become the Royal Ocean Racing Club. Some had independent means, however tenuous, so that they could pursue a life afloat without having to be back in the office on Monday morning. Others, who ostensibly did work for a living, either belonged to the family firm or pursued their professions in so leisurely a fashion that today they would not have been tolerated in any business. A few were simply dedicated seamen who turned a penny wherever, and whenever, they could.

Typical of this last type was Joseph Weston Martyr, who in the early 1920s was living in New York with his actress wife. Martyr had gone to sea, aged 15, in square riggers before graduating to steamers. He subsequently became a gold miner in Africa, then a trader in the South Seas. In short, he was fairly typical of the breed of Englishman who sought adventure–and his fortune–in every corner of the globe.

In 1914 he was commissioned into the Sherwood Foresters (and later the Royal Engineers) and after witnessing the back of his batman's head being blown off by a shell on Vimy Ridge he ended the war on the verge of a nervous breakdown. Like other early members who fought on the Western Front, he remained deeply affected by his time in the trenches and the postwar business world of working in New York as a ship's broker virtually drove him over the edge.

During the early 1920s he began to scrape a living from writing. Having always loved the sea and ships, this is what he wrote about, and some of his

Weston Martyr

9

articles were published in the American magazine, *Yachting*, then edited by Herbert L. Stone. In 1924 he raced aboard *Northern Light in the Bermuda Race which the Cruising Club of America (CCA) had resurrected the previous year. The navigator lost the way and *Northern Light* came last, but the experience so filled Martyr with enthusiasm that when he returned to England later that year he wrote an article in *Yachting Monthly*, extolling the excitement and exhilaration of ocean racing, and challenging British yachtsmen to take it up.

'It is without question the very finest sport that a man can possibly engage in,' he wrote, 'for to play this game at all it is necessary to possess in the very highest degree those hallmarks of a true sportsman, skill, courage, and endurance.'

Ocean racing was not, of course, unknown in European waters. Depending on how one defines an ocean race, offshore competitions had been taking place right from the time yachting became an organised sport. But mostly they had been between large vessels run by a professional crew. Often the owner was not even aboard; if he was he would never have dreamed of taking charge himself. That was the job of the professional skipper.

But the First World War had fundamentally changed the environment for most yachtsmen. The super-rich ones still existed but they were mostly confined to the 'big class'. The average cruising *owner mostly skippered his boat himself, in the company of his wife and friends, perhaps helped by one or two paid hands. This type of owner had always been around but they had rarely competed against one another, and certainly not across many miles of open water.

In the next issue of *Yachting Monthly* Martyr warned that an American was building an ocean racing ketch with a view to challenging British yachtsmen to an ocean race in their own waters in 1925. 'She will be sailed by a crew of amateur yachtsmen, who know almost all there is to know about the deep-water racing game, and they will be in hard training after their passage across the Atlantic. Here is the gauntlet, already defiantly thrown, and about to fall on the floor of *our* area. Who is there to take up the challenge? Without a doubt we have the boats and the men willing to enter the lists. But are they *ready*?'

At the same time Martyr dropped Stone a cheerful letter from London. 'I am stirring up a great fuss about the lack of interest there is over here amongst yachting men concerning "The King of Sports–Ocean Racing"! Most people over here simply never have heard of it, and I am showing them they ought to be ashamed of themselves and that you Yankees are getting miles ahead of them at the game.'

He asked Stone to send him copies of Bermuda Race circulars that had been issued to all its participants which gave 'instructions regarding equipment and gear to be carried on the yachts, handicaps, etc. I intend to show them to people here so that they may see on what lines the race was arranged by you.'

Martyr's enthusiasm stirred a chord amongst a small coterie of yachtsmen. One of these was Evelyn George Martin, then cruising editor of *Yachting World*. Intrigued by what Martyr had to say, he and the editor of *Yachting Monthly*, Malden Heckstall-Smith, met Martyr to discuss the possibility of arranging an ocean race in British waters, and then approached a number of eminent yachtsmen, including Sir Ralph Gore Bt and the King's Sailing Master, Sir Philip Hunloke, to gain their support for the project.

In his biography[1] of Hunloke Lt-Commander Douglas Dixon relates that Martin and Algernon Maudslay–the proprietor of *Yachting World* and acting secretary of the Yacht Racing Association (YRA)–also discussed the merits of an ocean race. They met in the offices of *Yachting World* at 35 Albemarle Street in London's West End. At one point in the conversation Martin pulled a ten-shilling note from his pocket, placed it on Maudslay's desk, and asked if Maudslay also had one.

'I think so,' Maudslay replied, rather bewildered.

'Right!' said Martin. 'Put yours with mine. You be treasurer, and now we are the first two members of the Ocean Racing Club.' This story might be apocryphal but Maudslay did indeed become its first treasurer when the club was formed.

There was a good deal of discussion as to the course. Some wanted the Tuskar light vessel as the turning point; the well known cruising yachtsman Claud Worth, in a letter to *Yachting Monthly* in February 1925, suggested Vigo as the ultimate destination; but eventually, and after much argument, Martyr's original suggestion of a race around the Fastnet Rock, off the south-west Irish coast, was confirmed at a meeting at which were present Hunloke, then a senior vice-president of the YRA, Captain R.T. Dixon of the Royal Engineers, Maudslay, Martyr, Martin, Gore, and Heckstall-Smith.

After the meeting Martin and Heckstall-Smith issued a joint statement that 'in response to a demand for an Ocean Race to be held in British Waters this year' one was being organised. Its course was 'from Cowes round the Fastnet and back to Plymouth' and would be for yachts not exceeding 50ft LWL, which belonged to any nation represented upon the International Yacht Racing Union (IYRU) or which came from the United States[2].

There would be no entrance fee but it was proposed to open a subscription list to provide a suitable Challenge Cup and a replica which the winning owner would keep. Subscriptions were limited to ten shillings per individual and were invited 'because it is felt that many yachtsmen may welcome an opportunity of giving their support to the race.'

To make the necessary preparations an Ocean Race Committee was formed, comprising Martin, Heckstall-Smith and Martyr, with the first two acting as joint honorary secretaries and with Heckstall-Smith also acting as hon.

courtesy Sylvia Spice

E.G. Martin

1 *The King's Sailing Master*, published the year after Hunloke's death in 1947. Dixon became a member of the Ocean Racing Club in 1929

2 the USA did not at that time belong to the IYRU

measurer. At a meeting of the committee on 18th February 1925 it was agreed that the Boat Racing Association's (BRA) system of measurement would be used to obtain a rating for the competitors though it was to be 'modified and adjusted to meet the special requirements of an ocean race.' There was input on how this should be best done from the famous American yacht designer, John Alden, as well as from several British ones such as J.M. Soper and Charles E. *Nicholson, but the accepted version was the one put forward by Heckstall-Smith, who had produced the original formula in 1912. In Martyr's words, the *rule disadvantaged yachts designed for speed alone: 'low freeboard, long overhangs, unduly light displacement and absence of bulwarks, all features undesirable in sea-going craft, are penalized.'

There is a note in the club's archives written by Martin, dated 19th February 1925, which states that the King's harbourmaster of Plymouth Sound, Commander K.N. Humphreys RN, who became one of the club's first honorary members, had agreed to time the yachts across the finishing line, between a naval signal station on the mainland and North Drake Island buoy. He also arranged for the *lighthouse keepers on the Fastnet Rock to telegraph the committee the times each competitor rounded, a service which cost 14s. 2d, just over 70p in today's currency.

Martin's note also mentioned that the Royal Western Yacht Club, of which he was rear commodore at that time, 'has consented that the race should be sailed under its flag; and offered to make amateurs taking part in the race honorary members for the occasion, expressing a hope that they would make full use of the club and avail themselves of such comforts as it provides, at the conclusion of the race.'

The proposal to hold an ocean race caused a good deal of controversy, for such an event flew in the face of what was accepted common practice among those who cruised which was to shorten sail at night. Indeed, it was regarded as unseamanlike to do otherwise. 'At the risk of making an unpopular suggestion,' Claud Worth wrote in the correspondence columns of *The Field*, 'I venture to express a doubt which arises in my mind–are our latitudes suitable for a public ocean race?'

Then in June 1925 Worth responded to a query in *Yachting Monthly* as to why his new cutter, *Tern IV*, had not been entered for the Ocean Race by saying that if the course he had suggested had been accepted then he would have entered as Vigo would have immediately taken competitors away from the land. As it was the Fastnet course 'lacks the one great requirement of an ocean course. With the land close aboard for such a large proportion of the distance, a vessel might be entered on the chance of it being a light-weather race, as she could always give up and go in somewhere. As I pointed out at the time, any 12-metre or ex-15-

metre yacht would have had a 75 per cent chance of winning the race. Since then the [Ocean Race] Committee have had the humiliation of being obliged specifically to exclude all yachts built to an international rule and the racing men have been boasting, both verbally and in the journals, that but for their exclusion they could have beaten the cruisers at their own game.'

The reason the Ocean Race Committee gave for their ruling was to avoid drawing off entries from the West Country regattas. This could be so but Worth's criticism was probably the real cause. For Worth to call it a 'humiliation' seems excessive, but shows how strong was the undercurrent of hostility to the race.

Otherwise, the race was open to any fully-decked yacht which was within the lengths stipulated above, provided it was in full cruising trim which included a serviceable boat and suitable life-saving equipment. There were no restrictions as to the number of amateur hands which could be carried but 'no more paid hands will be permitted than can normally be accommodated in the fo'c'sle.'

The piratical-looking Ingo Simon at the helm of his converted Bristol Channel Pilot cutter, *Saladin*. He was in fact an opera singer

Sixteen eventually entered, but only seven started on 15th August and the original American challenger was not among them. Possibly Hunloke, informally at least, asked the Royal Yacht Squadron for the use of its line as the event thereafter was usually[1] begun from there. If he did his request was refused. Instead, the Royal Victoria Yacht Club at Ryde made their line available.

The entries were a mixed bunch, and were in no sense racing yachts as the term is understood today. Indeed, all but *Gull* had been built as working boats or along working boat lines. But though they all flew the flags of British yacht clubs they had an international feel about them: *Saladin*, a 33-ton Bristol Channel pilot cutter, was owned and sailed by a Basque Spaniard, Ingo Simon, 'a dark flamboyant character with a gold earring' who was an opera singer by profession; George Martin's *Jolie Brise* had originally been built as a French pilot boat; the 18-ton Camper & Nicholson designed cutter, *Gull*, of 1896 vintage, was owned and sailed by an Irishman, H.P.F. Donegan; and two of the other entries, Ray Barrett's *Banba IV* and Michael Tennant's *North Star*, were Norwegian Colin Archer-type ketches. The remaining two, the 14-ton cutter, *Fulmar*, and *Jessie L*, another Bristol Channel pilot cutter, were owned by the Royal Engineer Yacht Club (the Sappers) and C.J. Hussey respectively. Except for the last, they were all gaff rigged, and only *North Star* was new. Though no American boats were present, two Americans, R.F. Laurence and J.C. West, did participate, as members of *Saladin*'s crew.

1 but not always. In 1935 it began from Yarmouth; in 1939 from Ryde

photo Beken of Cowes

photo Beken of Cowes

photo Beken of Cowes

OPPOSITE PAGE, CLOCKWISE
Jolie Brise, the winner of the first Ocean
Race in 1925. She was built in 1912 as a Le
Havre Pilot Cutter. Her dimensions were: 56ft
LOA, 48ft LWL, 15ft, 9in. beam, 10ft, 2in.
draught. *Fulmar*, entered by the Royal
Engineer Yacht Club, finished second in the
first Ocean Race. Her dimensions were: 38ft
LOA, 34ft LWL, 12ft beam, 7ft draught.
Saladin came fourth in the 1925 and 1926
races, and second in 1929. Her dimensions
were: 49ft LOA, 43ft LWL, 14ft, 8in. beam,
7ft draught.
Gull finished third in the 1925 Ocean Race.
Her dimensions were: 44ft LOA, 37ft LWL,
10ft beam, 7ft draught.

THIS PAGE, CLOCKWISE
Banba IV finished last in the first Ocean
Race. Her dimensions were: 38ft LOA, 34ft
LWL, 12ft beam, 7ft draught.
Jessie L, the only bermudan-rigged boat in
the first Ocean Race, retired. Built in 1887
she was the oldest boat in the race. Her
dimensions were: 42ft LOA, 37ft LWL,
13ft, 4in. beam, 6ft, 6in. draught.
North Star motored across the finishing line
and was therefore disqualified from the first
Ocean Race. Her dimensions were: 49ft
LOA, 46ft LWL, 14ft, 6in. beam, 7ft draught.

photo Beken of Cowes

The weather was fine, the Solent calm, when the starting gun went at noon. *Gull* was the first to cross the line but in the light ENE winds, and adverse tide, all the entries were soon struggling to make headway as they sailed east-about around the Isle of Wight, the only restriction in the sailing instructions apart from having to leave the Fastnet Rock to starboard when rounding it. Aboard *Banba IV* Barrett even hoisted two topsails as water sails in an attempt to stem the tide, and eventually had nine sails set from her two masts and spinnaker boom, making her look not unlike a waterborne laundry line. This kept her ahead of the slower boats but after a night of being becalmed the three fastest ones, *Jolie Brise*, *Gull* and *Saladin*, caught a new breeze ahead of the rest of the fleet and had soon opened a commanding lead.

By Monday morning the wind had backed easterly and freshened nicely. Out in front *Jolie Brise* was off the Manacles at 0800 with *Gull* close behind. *Jolie Brise* with her spinnaker set was going like a train, and *Gull*, though festooned with mainsail, jackyard topsail, yankee-jib topsail, and a balloon staysail, found it hard to keep up with her. However, Donegan managed to close the gap to about ten minutes by cutting close to the Lizard and then making a snappy gybe. By contrast, Martin kept well clear of the promontory and then took a leisurely 16 minutes to reset his spinnaker.

By the time the leading two boats were heading into the open sea *Saladin* had dropped out of sight. Then the wind faded and *Jolie Brise* and *Gull* were left rolling horribly in the Atlantic swell. So violent was the motion that *Gull*'s topsail halyards parted. Given that she had a nine-hour handicap allowance over *Jolie Brise* this accident probably cost her the race. *Saladin*, borne along by a breeze of her own, caught up with the two leaders. The same breeze also brought *Fulmar* back into contention and by dusk all four were in sight of one another.

Next day *Jolie Brise* and *Saladin* surged ahead on a waft of wind that missed the others–*Fulmar*, on several occasions, drifted round in a full circle–and by the time *Jolie Brise* rounded the Fastnet at 1950 on the 19th she was over 12 hours ahead of *Gull*, which rounded at 0835 the next morning. Astern of *Gull* was *Fulmar* which rounded at 0920, and *Saladin* followed five minutes later.

Jolie Brise was becalmed between midnight and dawn but then the wind set in briskly from the SSW and for the next 16 hours she averaged 8.1 knots, and from the Longships to the Lizard 8.7 knots. 'It was sailing such as one gets but seldom in a lifetime,' Martin said afterwards. *Gull*, too, caught this freshening breeze and by late afternoon on the 20th she was lee rail under and Donegan, who was below making notes on the race, had a hard time of it. 'The cabin swing-table is doing its level best to assassinate me,' he wrote. 'I have been struck in the chest and chin, while the weighty box beneath is making frantic efforts to amputate one or both of my legs.'

H.P.F. Donegan, the owner of *Gull*

courtesy James D. Donegan

As night closed in the weather deteriorated but *Jolie Brise* was ahead of the worst of it though she encountered large seas off the Lizard; and her log records that by 0500 on the 21st the wind had risen to Force 7. On the approach of a particularly vicious-looking squall Martin dropped his loose-footed mainsail as he could not reef[1] it, but then the wind dropped and he reset it. Off Dodman Point he hoisted his spinnaker, gybed off Rame Head, and carried his spinnaker almost to the finishing line which he crossed at 1445. Not only did he take line honours in a time of 6days, 2hrs, 45min., but as the scratch boat won the Challenge Cup which he himself had donated for the first boat on corrected time.

Behind *Jolie Brise* the fleet was well spread out, so well spread that the three slowest were still flogging their way towards the Fastnet in a rising gale. The first of them, *North Star*, did not round the rock until the morning of the sixth day of the race, the 21st. *Banba IV*, having been forced to heave to in the night, followed close behind her; but once she had rounded she could not cope with the full force of the gale and her owner, Ray Barrett, decided to run for the shelter of Baltimore on the southern Irish coast. However, the wind then moderated and *Banba IV* reversed her course. But the weather had been too severe for the crew of *Jessie L*. They retired, put into Crosshaven under power before rounding the rock, but eventually turned up at Plymouth in time to take part in the after-race dinner at which the club was formed.

Fulmar was second to cross the line, at 1048, followed by *Gull* three-quarters of an hour later. There was then a long wait for Commander Humphreys before *Saladin* turned up at 1854. *North Star* finished at midnight, but was disqualified as a ferocious ebb tide provoked her tired crew into motoring across the line.

However, when *Banba IV* arrived the following evening her crew succumbed to no such temptation. When they ran out of wind they kedged off the pier on the eastern side of Drake Island just short of the finishing line and, while waiting for the tide to turn, went below to eat a well earned supper. As they were doing so the sound of cheering floated across the water from the dining room of the Royal Western then situated high up on the Hoe no more than half-a-mile away. To great acclaim the Ocean Racing Club had just been founded. Eventually, *Banba IV* crept across the finishing line at just before 0100 the next morning, but by then Humphreys had relinquished his vigil and so the yacht's finishing time was never officially recorded.

The race was pronounced a great success by its participants and in the euphoria that followed it *Gull*'s owner, H.P.F. Donegan, wrote a letter to Weston Martyr, who had crewed aboard *Jolie Brise*, which is worth quoting in full:

'I was exceedingly glad to get your breezy letter which was redolent of the salt sea, and may I say here that if my crew favourably impressed you, you in turn, made a very lasting impression upon us all, short though our opportunities were

courtesy Duke of Beaufort

Michael Tennant, the owner of *North Star*, aboard *Jolie Brise* in 1929 when she was owned by Tennant's friend, Bobby Somerset

1 'The sail was new,' Martin wrote afterwards, 'and I had determined that on no account would I reef it, and so had rove no reef pendants or lacings'

for sizing each other up. I must say, further, that we were all appreciative of the excellent types of sportsmen that now go to constitute the Ocean Racing Club.

'Take for instance these boys in the *Fulmar*. Under ordinary circumstances we, as traditional Irishmen, should have been in their wool after the finish, yet, we all fell round each other's necks with the truest spirit of comradeship and made merry on both ships. Martin, needless to say, shines out as a most excellent type. We were particularly pally with the crew of *Jolie Brise* later, and doubtless had *North Star* and *Banba* moored near Drake's Island, we would all have fraternized in the same way.

'I have raced a great deal and know the little petty feelings that sometimes prevail after the finish of an ordinary race. If one's boat has done excellently up to a point, and has then been pipped by horrible ill-luck by some rival, sometimes there is not a superabundance of joy. Contrast that with the congenial assembly in Plymouth, and do you not share with me the impression that the Ocean Race has merits beyond the most optimistic hopes of the originators, in that it brings out the best in us and creates a feeling of good fellowship amongst the competitors that no other class of racing is calculated to do so thoroughly and effectively.' There's little doubt that Martin was a popular winner and that Donegan's high opinion of him was well merited, and though there are no records extant to prove it, his election to become the club's first commodore was almost certainly unanimous.

It had been Weston Martyr who had triggered the idea of an ocean race and Martin gave him full credit for doing so. 'Weston Martyr,' he wrote afterwards, 'to whom in the first instance, the organisation of the race is due', and added that Martyr was 'the only man in the fleet who had sailed an ocean race before'.

But it was Martin who implemented Martyr's idea and saw the founding of the club through to fruition, and Martyr was the first to recognise this. 'But for the work done by Martin,' he wrote, 'I do not think we would have had any ocean race at all…we really elected Martin [to be commodore] because we felt that whatever he steers, be it boat or club, is bound to go ahead on a true and steady course at its maximum rate of speed.'

Indeed, Martin was the ideal candidate for the job. He was a very experienced yachtsman, and a first-rate seaman. A scion of the family which founded Martin's Bank, he had enough money—or, as one relation suspects, his mother gave him enough—not to have to work for a living. Born on 22nd March 1881, he was the son of a colonel serving in the Indian Army. As children, he and his brother were often left in the care of a friend who lived at Brixham.

He read medicine at Oxford where he was obviously regarded with affection by his contemporaries. He was 6ft, 5in. tall—one of his crew remembers him as

photo Beken of Cowes

'a huge man who wore black brogue shoes at sea and ashore did up the collar of his shirt with spun yarn instead of a stud'—and a pen portrait in *The Isis* magazine calls him 'this kindly giant', and goes on to describe a young man who is 'as gentle as he is strong' and whose clothes fail to fit him.

They're off! The start of the first Ocean Race, 15th August 1925

The same article listed Martin's many accomplishments. 'On the ski and on the piano, with the paint-brush and with the dissecting knife, he is equally at home.' He had a two handicap at golf and was a fine cricketer—he played for Oxford and Worcestershire—who bowled lightning yorkers, though his fielding was not of the same standard. He also played the violin, which on one occasion at least he took to sea with him, and when in the 1930s he had a book published on helmsmanship he wrote from first-hand knowledge that it 'undoubtedly is an art; and one which, to me, seems to be akin to that of the violinist.' He even tried his hand at acting and wrote articles on sailing for beginners in *Paris Soir*.

Despite this plethora of talents Martin is remembered as being a 'shy bachelor' who avoided female company. Brixham gave him an early love of the sea, and he and his brother, according to his sister Dorothy, 'made a start in seamanship as small boys' by going out with the Brixham trawler fleet, and his deep and abiding love of the working boat certainly stemmed from those days. However, according to *The Isis* article, 'his nautical instincts found their first outlet in Kensington Gardens where for some years his well-trimmed craft furrowed the stormy waters of the Round Pond.'

Between Eton and Oxford he spent three years 'during which he hardened his hands and weakened his heart with work in the shipyards', an early indication that his health was not good. Many years later he wrote a friend that at 19 he had had a condition known in those days as 'athletes' heart' which caused him giddiness if he moved suddenly. It may have been his health that prevented him from taking his final medical exams–though he was awarded a BA degree–and in later life he had prolonged bouts of illness.

As a young man he owned a whole string of sailing boats: a 4-ton cutter called *Swallow* was followed by a restricted one-rater, *Swallow II*, which was almost unbeaten in 1900. The same year he bought a 10-ton fishing cutter, *Hope*, which he owned until 1905 when he acquired a 35-ton cutter, *Chance*. After *Chance* came *Chance II*, an 86-ton auxiliary ketch, which was replaced towards the end of the First World War by a 37-ton yawl, *Conquest*.

In these later yachts Martin made some remarkable cruises for his day. After joining the Royal Cruising Club in 1905 he won its Challenge Cup two years running (1907–1908). He also owned two 6-metres at different times. In one of them, *Bunty*, he won the European Cup at Kiel in 1912, beating the Germans in the final race. He always remembered the total silence with which he was greeted by the spectators when, flying his winning flag, he sailed up Kiel Harbour and past the German High Seas Fleet.

At the start of the First World War he joined the RNVR as a sub-lieutenant and served in the Auxiliary Patrol, which had been formed from civilian vessels fitted out to combat U-boats around the British coastline. In November 1914 he was promoted to lieutenant and given command of a motor yacht called *Mayfair*. When this was sunk in April 1915 he joined the monitor, *Prince Rupert*, as its First Lieutenant. In 1917 he was promoted to lt-commander and posted to the Rescue Tug Service at Plymouth. For his wartime services with tugs he was awarded the OBE.

In 1920 he became commodore of the Royal South Western Yacht Club (which eventually merged with the Royal Western in 1961). In 1921, after unsuccessfully standing for rear commodore, he resigned from the Royal Cruising Club. 'Although it is impossible to be sure of the main reason for his resignation,' the RCC's history comments, 'it is surely more than a passing coincidence that, soon afterwards, he became a founder member and the first commodore of what we proudly know today as the Royal Ocean Racing Club.'

In 1923 Martin combined his love of working boats with that of sailing for pleasure by purchasing the 44-ton *Jolie Brise*[1], a Le Havre pilot cutter, from her French owner after he was given a half model of her by a pilot friend working out of the port.

By 1925, aged 44 and a confirmed bachelor, Martin was undoubtedly one of the country's most experienced deep water yachtsman with an ability to inspire and organise. Stone wrote of him as 'a thorough seaman, a man of long and

1 Robin Bryer tells her story in *Jolie Brise: A Tall Ship's Tale*

varied experience who knew the way of sea and sail'. He was a thoughtful man of few words who at the time the club was founded must have been at the height of his not inconsiderable intellectual and artistic powers.

The bonhomie the first Fastnet engendered did not encompass Ray Barrett, the owner of *Banba IV*. Barrett and his crew hailed from the east coast and there may have been some of the traditional antipathy towards those from the 'grander' Solent area. He was far from satisfied with the committee's treatment of him as it not only failed to measure his boat before the race but, he suspected, implied that he and his crew were beginners by allotting them the letter 'L' as their distinguishing signal.

In a two-page letter to the committee he described how *Banba IV* had sat idle at Gosport for ten days waiting for Malden Heckstall-Smith to measure her before the race began. Telegrams had flown to and fro, and Barrett had eventually been told that all the competitors would be measured at Ryde. Except for *Banba IV* they all were. When Martin had pointed out his omission the hon. measurer had turned back and 'in an extremely peremptory manner pushed aboard some instructions and informed me I should be measured at Plymouth on arrival.'

However, when *Banba* arrived at Plymouth Barrett was informed that her measurements would be taken from drawings supplied by the designer. If this was a sufficiently good method for measurement, Barrett tartly commented, 'it could have been done months ago.' He had, Barrett concluded his letter, enjoyed the trip but could only surmise that Heckstall-Smith 'considered that such an insignificant little body of genuine enthusiasts as the Crouch Yacht Club had no business to be represented in so important an undertaking as the Ocean Race.' To add insult to injury, someone, 'as a final master touch', had allotted *Banba* the letter 'L' as her distinguishing signal.

It is not known how the committee, when it met on 9th October 1925, dealt with this barrage of complaint, but it must have done so satisfactorily for Barrett shortly afterwards joined the club and sent a long letter of constructive ideas. However, the committee's allotment of the letter 'L' still rankled, for one of the suggestions he put forward was that some letters used as distinguishing flags might be omitted, and added, 'I may say I speak feelingly on this point'. As will be seen later, he must have been a touchy individual, though a devoted servant of the club.

What is known is that the 9th October meeting officially transferred the Ocean Race Committee's affairs to the newly formed Ocean Racing Club; appointed the club's first committee; confirmed the agreement, made at the inauguration dinner at the Royal Western in August, that the club's annual subscription would be £1, and that there would be no entrance fee; framed rules for the club; fixed a date for the race in 1926; voted that the YRA be asked for recognition; and considered the wording of the Deed of Gift for the Challenge Cup which had been donated by Martin.

There is a minor but interesting discrepancy between the minutes of that first meeting, and a letter Martin published in *Yachting World* immediately after the race which publicised the formation of the club. 'To be eligible for election,' Martin wrote, 'a yachtsman must be an amateur and have competed in one of the club's ocean races either as owner or crew', while the minutes state that to be eligible a yachtsman must have 'sailed the complete course.'

Probably all those who took part in that historic first race, or were concerned with organising it, were made members, but at the meeting on 9th October it must have been decided that in future a yachtsman would have to complete the course to qualify. Certainly, the owner and crew of *Jessie L* joined even though they had retired as did Hunloke, Heckstall-Smith, Gore, and the club's American representative, Herbert Stone, though none of them had been able to take part. Sir Philip Hunloke was elected the club's president, and Heckstall-Smith, Gore, Stone, and Martyr along with the club's officers, made up the club's first committee.

Those first minutes also record that Heckstall-Smith and Martin were to continue as joint secretaries, but during 1926 the job seems to have been shunted from one committee member to another. In March Gore signed a letter to *Yachting World* about the second Ocean Race as coming from the hon. secretary, and in August Martin wrote on one memo: 'Martyr ought to realize he can't chuck secretaryship at any moment he feels inclined–I have written asking him to continue over the race'. However, it appears that Martyr did 'chuck' being secretary as the task reverted to Heckstall-Smith alone who also continued as hon. measurer.

The accounts for that first year record that subscriptions for the Fastnet Cup amounted to £26.4s.6d and that members' subscriptions totalled £34–so there were 34 founding members. The amount spent on the four cups (the Challenge Cup, a replica of it for the winning owner to keep, and cups for the second and third) was £33, and the total expenditure of £47.19s.1d included the cost of an album of photographs of the entries still in the club's possession.

At some point, there is no record of exactly when, the club's seahorse crest was designed, the idea *originating from a wooden carving of a boat's badge Martin had made during the First World War. It was not an exact copy of the real creature (*Hippocampus vulgaris*) but an heraldic variation–dubbed *Hippocampus rorcus* by a future secretary, Alan Paul–which had its tail boldly curled the opposite way to that which nature had decreed.

Chapter Two

THE BLUE WATER BADGE

IN MAY 1926 the Council of the YRA accepted the Ocean Racing Club's application to be recognised as a yacht club and two guineas were duly removed from its meagre coffers for the annual subscription.

The next piece of correspondence in the club's archives is a letter of 28th July 1926 from Heckstall-Smith to Lloyd's Register of Yachts in Fenchurch Street. The club wanted the loan of William Meek, the Surveyor of Yachts for Lloyd's Register, to be available before the second Ocean Race to give advice on the ORC's measurement formula which was based on Lloyd's Rules. Lloyd's agreed, and after the race Meek was elected an honorary member and subsequently served as a technical adviser for over ten years. For the 1926 race a minimum LWL of 30ft was introduced, and the rating rule was altered as the measurement of sailing length and displacement had proved too complicated. The displacement factor was now omitted from the formula and replaced with a beam and depth one. It was this change which established the principle that, in the words of Douglas *Phillips-Birt, the club's first historian, the rule[1] 'should depend on measurements that may be obtained from a yacht lying afloat at a normal mooring. Neither absolutely calm water nor designers' certificates are required.'

The race began from the Royal Yacht Squadron's line on 14th August 1926, and was notable in several ways. The first yacht to be specially constructed for the event, *Hallowe'en*, made her appearance as scratch boat; the first woman to compete, Mrs Aitken Dick[2], came to the line in her 14-ton cutter, *Altair*; and the race's first foreign entry, the American schooner, *Primrose IV*, sailed across the Atlantic to take part. Other entries from the first race included *Jolie Brise*, *Gull*, *Banba IV*, and *Saladin*, and the Sappers also entered again–they've never missed a race–this time in the much faster 20-ton *Ilex*. Robert (Bobby)

1 it was this rule that the French adopted for their races and the Americans for their 1928 Bermuda and Transpacific Races

2 she never joined club

Somerset, the navigator in Michael Tennant's *North Star* in 1925, also entered the lists on his own account with the 34ft cutter, *Penboch*.

Interest mostly focused on the largest competitor, Colonel Baxendale's Fife-designed *Hallowe'en*, and on the American schooner. Built to the maximum limit of 50ft LWL, *Hallowe'en* was a sturdier version of a 15-metre and boasted a marconi rig and the then fashionable triple headsails; *Primrose IV*, owned by Frederick L. Ames of Boston, was an Alden design which had won line honours in the Small Class in the 1924 Bermuda Race. Two other Americans, Warwick Tompkins and Alfred Payne, were so keen to compete that they paid their own fares across the Atlantic on the off-chance of finding berths. Donegan heard about them and arranged for Tompkins to race in *Gull* and Payne in *Saladin*.

As was to happen so often in the future, the faster entries experienced light and variable breezes to the Fastnet Rock before the wind freshened, while the slower ones were hit by heavier conditions. By the evening of the third day *Banba IV* was hove-to in a southerly gale 60 miles short of the Rock and after rounding it even the experienced Martin hove-to under double-reefed mainsail and spent the next five hours 'playing wild music on a fiddle'. Some years later he wrote that though heaving-to might have been a wise move if he had been cruising 'it definitely lost us the chance of a place in the race'. But his crew, apparently, was an inexperienced one and he probably acted wisely.

Penboch and *Altair* also hove-to for a time and the log of *Saladin*, now preserved in the club's archives, noted after rounding the Rock on the evening of 17th August: 'Very bad sea, with rain squalls, great trouble in getting down reefs, as leech line got foul in reef cleat sheave. Bar now 29.45 and wind still rising. 2 reefs in mainsail, and small jib only set.'

Later the dial of *Saladin*'s log was washed overboard and at noon the next day the bobstay parted. Nevertheless, she kept going as did *Ilex* and *Primrose IV*. At one point *Ilex* lost three men overboard and was lucky to recover them all, while the American's balloon staysail was blown out. *Gull* sprang a leak, and her mainsail was also damaged and had to be replaced with a trysail. So bad did the leak become that Donegan decided to run for shelter.

After the race Tomkins gave a graphic description of this hair-raising run through mountainous seas which has gone down in the annals of ocean racing. 'The *Gull* was a plank-on-edge cutter of ancient vintage. She had a tremendous jackyard topsail, a terrific tiller, and a pack of wild Irishmen aboard her who flogged the life out of her....In thick weather we groped for Baltimore and when we got within what we estimated to be two miles and could not pick up the light we reluctantly gave up the heroic idea of beaching the *Gull* there, caulking her, and still finishing. (Yes, that's the sort of skipper and crew it was!)

We hauled off for Queenstown (Cobh). We were close-hauled under trysail and storm jib with the wind coming down now from about No'east and that delightful Irish coast altogether too close under our lee.

'The seas were breaching clean over the old packet, and the spitfire jib–though we didn't know it till daylight–was pulling the runner eyebolt right out of the counter. We passed the Stag Rocks and they weren't more than two hundred yards to leeward; on the darkest, wildest sort of night they were plainly visible and audible, great and terrifying founts of spray just to leeward.'

Donegan must have been furious at being forced to retire as the previous winter he had shown just how competitive he was. 'The ambition of all hands on Gull,' he wrote of the

The Alden-designed schooner *Primrose IV* at the start of the 1926 Fastnet. Owned by Frederick L. Ames of Boston, she was the first foreign boat ever to take part in the Fastnet Race. Note the squaresail she has hoisted

next race, 'is to save our time from *Jolie Brise* and beat *Fulmar* as we know we can. The day that *Saladin* will finish ahead of us will be a bad day to be out and crockery will get shifted. I am not afraid of any of our last year competitors, but doubtless we will have to reckon with new and unknown quantities. Whatever happens we must try and beat the yankee.'

Mrs Dick, who nearly lost one of her crew of four naval men overboard, also sought the shelter of Baltimore. For 48 hours no one knew where she was and before club officials received a cable from her two destroyers were dispatched to search for her.

Not surprisingly, the largest and most modern entry, *Hallowe'en*, won line honours and did so in such good time–3 days, 19hrs, 5min.–that her record was not broken until 1939. Despite her speed she could manage no better than third place behind *Ilex* and *Primrose IV*, proving, if proof were needed, that Fife had made no effort to take into account the ORC rule when he had built her. Indeed, one yachting journalist wondered if he had ever heard of it.

Jolie Brise finished a disappointing fifth, but as Martin had already that year crossed the Atlantic to take part in the Bermuda Race–in which he had won his class and come fifth overall, and had started a long tradition of RORC commodores taking part in the race–it is perhaps not surprising that he was not on top form.

If the 1926 Ocean Race had its rough moments, the 1927 one had few calm ones and goes down in the history books as one of the worst Fastnets ever. It had been a dreadful summer and heavy rain lashed the 15 boats as they crossed the start line on Saturday 13th August, though the wind was moderate. However, by the time they reached most southerly part of the Isle of Wight the sea was being whipped up by a strong so'westerly.

Ilex, Penboch, and *Altair* were all racing again, as was *Jolie Brise* which Martin had sold, after advertising her for some time, to Warren Ferrier and Dr. Brownlow Smith. New entries included two American schooners, Ralph St L. Peverley's *La Goleta* and Daniel Simond's *Nicanor*; an ex-10-metre, *Maintenes*, owned by a retired naval officer, Lt W.B. Luard, who was to become one of the club's best known members; the cutter-rigged *Spica*, owned by Mr and Mrs Hunt; and Conor O'Brien's *Saoirse*, described in the race programme as a

The Alden-designed schooner, *La Goleta*, one of the two American boats to enter the 1927 Fastnet and one of the only two to finish it. Her navigator was Alf Loomis (inset) who took part in, and wrote about, many of the club's races before and after the Second World War

square-rigged staysail schooner, and elsewhere as a 'sketch' or 'the smallest barquentine-rigged yacht afloat'. Her owner had sailed her around the world safely but the Ocean Race was to prove too much for her.

Nicanor was the boat to beat that year and even the crew of *La Goleta* held her in some awe. Before the race she recruited three Cowes yachtsmen who, it was supposed, would provide some local knowledge as well as extra muscle power. But it was they who were instrumental in *Nicanor* withdrawing from the race, for after advising the skipper to seek shelter they then refused to continue and went ashore. *Nicanor*, her crew reduced to five, left without them and reached within 100 miles of the Rock. But, short-handed as she was, she was forced to retire when her fore gaff broke.

Only two boats reached the Rock that year: *La Goleta*, which had been recently built in England, and the British cutter, *Tally Ho!*, a modified Falmouth quay punt owned by Lord Stalbridge. All the other entries were forced to retire. So foul was the weather that on the Monday night *La Goleta* hove to in the shelter of the Lizard while *Tally Ho!* anchored in Newlyn. But once started again the next morning they raced neck and neck to the Fastnet, *Tally Ho!* rounding it at 0120 on the Thursday morning with *La Goleta* close behind.

'The glass was now down to 29.3,' Lord Stalbridge later wrote, 'and we were palpably in the centre of a depression, large or small of course we had no means of telling, but I fear that standing into a lee shore in thick weather and a falling glass was not an act of great seamanship. However you cannot make omelettes without breaking eggs; we were out to win the Fastnet Race if we could, so we were out to take some chances, and luckily they came off.'

Alf *Loomis, aboard *La Goleta*, reckoned it blew Force 9 after the schooner rounded the Rock. An American yachtsman who was to become a veteran commentator of the ocean racing scene, he found it an unforgettable race for when he recalled it nearly two decades later he remembered every vivid detail.

'Only the skipper, Boyd, and a young American named Marshall Rawle touched the wheel that night. There were six of us on deck, sitting alert to anticipate a call for all hands. We had to gain five hours on *Tally Ho!* and there was no telling when either of us might be dismasted. At ten, the balloon fisherman was taken in as Peverley blanketed it with the mainsail...It was said that we bettered eleven knots in [the next] hour, and while I doubt it now I was ready to believe it then.'

What is certain is that the Americans averaged eight knots between the Runnelstone and the finish, but even this heroic effort did not save them their time for they crossed the line only 42 minutes ahead of *Tally Ho!*. They were within an ace of losing one of the *crew during the return passage from the Rock but he managed to hang on to some part of the boat and was hauled

aboard with a tackle. Martyr, who was on board, later wrote that 'he came back smiling too with his cigar still between his teeth. But the lower half of him was stripped and both his sea boots had gone.'

After it was all over William Meek reflected the anxiety of those on shore when he wrote to Heckstall-Smith that 'I almost wept for joy when I heard today that the heroic boys who manned the Ocean Racing Fleet had reported with numbers intact. Terrible indeed must have been the experiences through which they managed their little ships to safety.' He added that the race would 'go down in yachting history as one of the greatest ocean races ever sailed, an outstanding evidence of the bulldog tenacity of the Anglo-Saxon yachtsman and a triumph for the committee of the Ocean Racing club.'

The committee, however, were not entirely sure it was so much a triumph as a lucky escape and at a meeting on 9th December–at which it was also decided that as membership now numbered 73 the committee should be enlarged by an additional five members–it was proposed that the smaller boats should have a less onerous course. As further insurance against disaster the measurer

The start of the first Channel Race, 2 August 1928. Extreme left is *Mona Lisa*, the first German entry in the club's racing programme; and extreme right is *Jolie Brise*. *Spica*, owned by Mr and Mrs J.T. Hunt, is right centre. She won the event in 1930, 1932, and 1933

and two members of the committee would be 'empowered to refuse the entry of any boat which they did not consider fit to race' and the club's Special Regulations, which in the succeeding decades were to contribute so much to the safety of the sport, were altered. Certain safety equipment was already specified, but the dinghies carried aboard were now made unsinkable by having 'two 2-gallon petrol cans or buoyancy tanks of similar capacity, securely lashed in place', and these were now required to be inspected by the measurer before a race.

A further meeting held on 11th January 1928 agreed that the course for the smaller boats was to be from 'Cowes to Owers (26 miles) to Royal Sovereign (44 miles) to Cherbourg breakwater (100 miles), 2 miles along Breakwater[1], to the Nab (65 miles), to Cowes, finishing off the Royal Yacht Squadron (14 miles), a total of 251 miles'.

A plaintive letter from one member, Major Jerram, was also discussed, and showed that the club was going to have to get its act together. Jerram complained that all he ever heard from the committee was when they wanted

[1] after the 1929 race this part of the course was altered to 'round the Havre lightship'

money from him. Before the last Ocean Race he had written twice to the commodore and twice to the hon. secretary, asking for berths to be found for 'no fewer than six absolutely first class fellows' who wanted to take part. He had received no reply and had had to say so 'which made me feel pretty small both in their eyes and in my own', especially when he read afterwards that two of the entries had not started through lack of a competent crew. The committee agreed that a register should be started for those wanting to crew in the Ocean Race, and the club has run one ever since.

The tone of the minutes of these two meetings conveys that a landmark had been passed. For one thing a full time assistant secretary, Miss E.M. *Wield, was now employed and for the first time the minutes had been properly typed. For another, there was a feeling that the whole concept of ocean racing in British waters had been put to the test and had passed, though hardly with flying colours. The heady euphoric days of creating something entirely new were now behind the club, and the time had come for it to consolidate its position and improve its administration, which was well below par, as well as its bank balance which amounted to exactly nil.

photo Beken of Cowes

Penboch, the winner of the first Channel Race in 1928, the year this photograph was taken

The changes discussed at these meetings meant a redrafting of the rules which had to be ratified by the whole membership. In Martin's words, 'the first real' annual general meeting (AGM) was therefore convened at the Hyde Park Hotel on 15th February 1928.

It was chaired by Maudslay who began by saying the club was being reorganised and put on a proper basis. One of the matters the members had to decide was whether those who finished the lower division race should be eligible for membership. Donegan, about to be confirmed at the AGM as a committee member, thought not. 'The flag at present is a real blue-water badge,' he wrote, as he could not be present, 'and doubt if it will call for the same respect if it can be flown by competitors in a less sporting event.'

However, when it was pointed out that the race might provide as great a test of seamanship for the smaller boats as the Fastnet did for the larger a motion was passed to allow competitors in the Junior Ocean Race, as it was called, to apply for membership. The LWL proposed by the committee was between 30ft and 35ft for the Junior Ocean Race, while those entering the Fastnet had to exceed 35ft but not exceed 60ft on the waterline. However, after 'a certain amount of discussion' the minimum LWL limit for the Junior Ocean Race was agreed at 27ft.[1] For the first time entry fees were also introduced, and a sailing committee was elected.

Another matter to be considered was a letter Martin had written to Heckstall-Smith. It is worth quoting at length from it as it is one of the few surviving pieces of correspondence from those far-off days which touches on the motives and aspirations–and prescience–of the most important of the club's founding fathers.

Martin, who had been prevented through illness from attending either the January meeting or the AGM, began by offering his resignation as the club's commodore, writing that his place 'should be taken by someone who can take a far more active part in the club's affairs than I can do now–I have no boat, and am not likely to have one during the next two years I should think; and I have always felt that flag officers of clubs should be sea-going yachtsmen. This is particularly the case in regard to the ORC. I was elected commodore at a time when there was perhaps nobody else who could be chosen as conveniently, and that is another reason I think that I ought to tender my resignation at this time. The club is now really being thoroughly organised. It began in a small way. I was a good deal responsible for its arrangement, and such mistakes as may have been made are largely my fault–but if one cannot be both it is better to be enthusiastic than wise.

Robert Somerset, the owner of *Penboch*, in later life

'The club was started really at a moment's notice after our first dinner at the RWYC and with the knowledge that it would have to face considerable opposition–from people who as it happens have scarcely ever been out of sight land or taken a night watch. But it has grown, and there can be no doubt

1 lowered to 25ft at the 1933 AGM

that ocean racing is going to become a very important feature in yachting in the future. Thanks to your work on our rating rule the club formula has already become the standard one, and in a few years time I think that we may find the Americans and ourselves using exactly the same rule, and that yachts will be built to suit it. In this way our club has really taken the lead in organising ocean racing.

'The new race for the smaller class is to be held this year, and that I think will be very popular, and will indirectly increase the number of entries for future Fastnet Races. I feel that now with our enlarged committee and prospects, and revised organisation we are making a new start, and I should like to feel that the office of Commodoreship was held by someone who was an active yacht owner and would fly his flag afloat.'

Quite why Martin was without a boat–or ship as he and his contemporaries would also have called their yachts–is not known. Although 'of independent means' he was not a wealthy man and with the financial storms of the depression about to rage around everyone's head he may already have been feeling the pinch. However, his income was about to be supplemented with royalties from his first book *Deep Water Cruising* published later that year and it is equally probable that he was simply not very well.

After his letter had been read out an amendment was put forward asking him not to resign 'as his name is well-known in foreign countries and his reputation as a yachtsman is of great assistance to the club', and he agreed to stay. However, he obviously needed a back-up and Maudslay proposed that the owner of *Penboch*, Robert Somerset, be appointed the club's first vice commodore. This was seconded by Peverley and carried unanimously.

Appropriately, it was *Penboch* which won the first Channel Race, as it later came to be called, from 11 other entries in a hard fought contest, with Captain R.T. Dixon's *Lady Maud* second and J.H. Moltzer's *Mona Lisa* third, but the main interest in 1928 was again the Ocean Race and the two American yachts which had entered for it. The owner of one of them, Paul Hammond, wrote to Ralph Peverley, now a member of the enlarged committee, asking if he would like to take part in the Fastnet Race in Hammond's new 50ft schooner, *Nina*, designed by Starling Burgess. 'She is able and I think fast and I will be delighted to have you take her in the race as I cannot stay over as long as that.'

Hammond, a banker by profession, was one of the foremost yachtsmen of his day and at the time he built *Nina* he was vice commodore of the famous Seawanhaka Corinthian Yacht Club. Like *Saoirse*, no one was certain what to call his radically rigged ship. With her foremast shorter than her mainmast most yachtsmen, and that included Hammond, thought her a schooner. However, Sherman Hoyt, who eventually sailed her in the 1928 Fastnet, said this could not be so under the American Universal Rule to which she had been built. Perhaps the most accurate description of her was attributed to Alf Loomis who called her a two-masted cutter.

Whatever she was she was fast and Burgess had built her specifically to exploit the rule which governed that year's Transatlantic Race to Spain in which *Nina* had been entered. The rule was very similar to the club's rule and she not only won the Small Class in the Transatlantic Race with consummate ease, but went on to take the Fastnet Cup that year when she and another small class Transatlantic competitor, *Mohawk*, owned by Dudley F. Wolfe, sailed across to Cowes from Spain to join the other eight starters. One of these, *L'Oiseau Bleu*, owned by Leon Diot, was the first-ever French entry; another was *Amaryllis* in which Lt Mulhauser RN had cruised around the world and which, after being saved from a muddy grave by George Martin, was now owned by the Royal Naval College, Dartmouth.

But all eyes were on *Nina*. It was largely a windward race and, in Sherman Hoyt's words, she proved 'a love, a treat to sail', though his comments on his navigator, Warwick Tompkins, were less laudatory when the latter placed the *Nina*'s position 40 miles inside the French coastline. More navigational problems ensued at Plymouth. It was pitch dark and a moderate gale was blowing, and Hoyt could not find 'North Drake's Island' on the chart, where a buoy marked one end of the finishing line. Martyr, who was one of the crew, had to explain to him that the phrase meant the buoy was positioned to the north of Drake's Island and that Hoyt's efforts to find an island called North Drake would be without avail.

'I fear an interchange of remarks between my good friend, Malden Heckstall-Smith and myself was not in the best of taste,' Hoyt wrote later, 'for I asked when next they had American entries would they please print in parallel columns instructions in their language and in English as we spoke it'—not the first time nor the last that the Yanks and the Brits have found themselves divided by a common tongue.

Perhaps even more unfortunate than the language difference was the difference in attitude towards sport in general, for no sooner had he finished than Hoyt was being 'twitted' that '*Nina* in spite of her miraculous showing [she had won by over five hours on corrected time from *Jolie Brise*] was an undesirable if legal type of racing machine.' She was called a rule cheater by the ignorant, and the adverse comments which appeared in the British yachting press were given wide publicity by their counterparts in the United States.

Some yachtsmen, not all of them British—Ralph Peverley was one who denigrated such 'racing machines'—were deeply imbued with Grantland Rice's Victorian couplet that it mattered 'not that you won or lost—but how you played the game', and they firmly believed that boats like *Nina*, in trying to exploit the ORC rule, were inimitable to the spirit of true sportsmanship.

Common sense soon prevailed—Martin was one who spoke out against such nonsense—but while it lasted the storm of protest blew strongly. *Martyr rather provocatively called the Fastnet Cup the *Nina*'s Cup, and remarked that the only way for the British to win it back was to shoot Sherman Hoyt with the starting gun!

On 10th September 1928 Somerset informed Malden Heckstall-Smith that he and his father had purchased *Jolie Brise*. He also wrote that Hunloke—who must already have raised the possibility of a Royal Warrant for the club—had told him that the adverse publicity might stop the warrant being issued, a possibility Somerset deemed 'nonsense.'

The controversy did not dissuade Hoyt from taking up the offer of membership, which he accepted in November 1928. But he did point out in his letter of acceptance that it had put paid to the possibility of a Transatlantic Race in 1929, which he had discussed with the club before he had returned to the USA, as it 'would fall a flat failure'. He went on: 'It had not been our idea of British sportsmanship, nor personally can I believe the views expressed to be at all representative of it, to be accused of having built racing boats regardless of cost with the sole view of winning the Fastnet Race, to have their performances minimized as much as possible, and to find that we had created a sentiment in the minds of certain British yachtsmen that further participation of American entries in the Fastnet Race was at least undesirable even if not actually to be barred.'

Hoyt's letter was read out at a committee meeting held on 17th December 1928. It was decided that an official reply should be sent to him and at the AGM which followed the meeting he was unanimously elected the club's first rear commodore. 'We all hope,' Heckstall-Smith wrote to him, 'that you will accept the post, and we feel that you will be able to do much, both for the Ocean Racing Club and for deep-sea sailing in general, if you can spare the time that will be required to help things along on your side of the water.'

The committee also wrote officially to Hoyt, disassociating the club from the adverse comments in the British yachting press, which it called 'ill-informed, prejudiced, and even unsportsmanlike...The Ocean Racing Club perfectly realizes that *Nina* was not built to the Fastnet Rule, but for the Spanish Race; but they would like to take this opportunity to point out that, far from discouraging the building of boats to the rule, it is their great hope that before long this will be done both in America and in this country.' The AGM had, in fact, addressed this exact point. After one member, Brian Waite, asked if one of the objects of the club was to develop a certain type of yacht which would be built to the

club rule, it was unanimously agreed to add the sentence: 'It is the hope of the club that in promoting its races, and in the formulation of its rating rule, a type in which speed and seaworthiness are combined may be developed' to Rule 2. This outlined the object of the club as providing annually one ocean race of not less than 600 miles in length, and such other races as might be agreed upon.

On 23rd January 1929 Hoyt replied that he would be only too pleased to accept the post of rear commodore and that he would do all he could to further the interests of the club in the United States. He was true to his word for the Anglo-American breach was soon healed, and *Hoyt went on to compete in the 1931 (in *Mistress*) and 1933 (in *Dorade*) Fastnet Races and remained rear commodore until 1934.

Nina, at the start of the 1928 Fastnet, which she won. To windward of her is another American entry, the schooner *Mohawk*. *Nina* was skippered by Sherman Hoyt (inset) who in 1929 became the club's first rear commodore

However, the adverse publicity for ocean racing did not stop there, for in January 1929 an article, alternatively patronising and sneering in its tone, appeared in *The Daily Telegraph*. This implied that the Fastnet, having been won by an American, was now defunct and that it 'was intended for Corinthian yachtsmen, who had not much money to spend upon this particular race, but who looked forward to enjoying a week or so at sea and wanted to punch round the Fastnet for fun. Great sport, everybody will agree.' The article concluded by rubbishing the idea of a race to Santander, which was then in the air, calling it an unseamanlike enterprise.

The article was written by Malden's brother, Brooke, who signed it as secretary of the YRA which added unwarranted weight to his criticisms. This was a serious matter, for Heckstall-Smith's 'petty and unsportsmanlike attitude' against the club, as Hunloke described it, could easily have been construed by the public as representing the YRA's official view. A letter of protest, drafted by the committee, was passed to Hunloke in his position as senior vice president of the YRA for him to use as he saw fit, and Martin also wrote letters to *The Field* and *The Times*.

Despite the article, in February a sub-committee was appointed to make arrangements for the race to Santander. This had been proposed some time previously by the Real Club Maritimo who wanted the ORC to run it, but in another administrative glitch nothing had been done about it. The Spaniards became huffy and were about to approach the Royal Thames Yacht Club with the idea. Now it was agreed that the Large Class, for which the King of Spain was offering a Challenge Cup, should be for entries above 60ft LWL while the Small Class, for which the Queen of Spain was offering a Challenge Cup, should be for ones above 35ft LWL and not exceeding 60ft LWL. It was also agreed that the start would be from Plymouth on 26th August and that those completing the 450-mile course should be eligible for membership. The prize money provided by the Spaniards, some £950, was substantial by the standards of the day.

The Fastnet, which began on 14th August 1929, took place in largely moderate weather. There were no American entries but international interest was retained as two of the ten entries were French. Much of the comment on the fleet focused on the new bermudan-rigged 25-ton cutter, *Maitenes II*, which W.B. Luard had had Harley Mead design for him with the capture of the Fastnet Cup specifically in mind. However, Mead appeared not to have taken the ORC rule particularly into account and *Maitenes II* was not, in any case, sufficiently tuned to be a serious threat.

Another entry which aroused some comment, at least within the august walls of the Royal Yacht Squadron, was *Amaryllis*. When she turned up at Cowes before the start her naval officer crew were kindly treated by the Squadron which made them honorary members. One of them later recalled that they were introduced to 'a noble being in an armchair' by the secretary.

'These gentlemen are from the *Amaryllis*, sir.'

'Oh, yes, the yacht with the dirty sails.'

'She sailed round the world, sir,'

'Oh, well she *still* has dirty sails.'

It was a slow race and *Amaryllis* took a week to finish during which the coal stove capsized at about the same time as both primus stoves refused to work. Worse was to follow when the pensioner Chief Petty Officer who looked after the boat accidentally dropped his pipe into the heads. In attempting to grab the pipe, his teeth fell out and both articles disappeared down the pan. He tried fishing them out with a spoon which he dropped as well and the whole apparatus had to be stripped down by an engineer officer, a foul job, before the CPO could eat solid food again.

The race was won by *Jolie Brise*, Somerset noting in his log that when he rounded the Rock at 9pm on 17th August the lighthouse keepers signalled that he was the first to round, and he remained well ahead for the remainder of the race. The scratch boat, the 48-ton French yawl, *Guerveur*, owned by Baron de Neufville, crossed the finishing line so long after the others that her time was not officially recorded. But finish she did and at the dinner following the race

Tom Ponsonby at the helm of *Jolie Brise* during the 1929 Fastnet as she approached the Scillies. Relaxing beside him is Dick Maclean Buckley who served as the club's secretary for many years before becoming its admiral

courtesy Duke of Beaufort

both the owner and his wife were elected to the club, which made the Baroness the club's first lady member. Brian Waite, who had sailed in *Saladin*, recorded that when 'five-score lusty-voiced yachtsmen rose to sing "For she's a jolly good fellow"' she sat in her chair looking somewhat bewildered by the proceedings.

A few days rest and then Somerset, along with a number of that year's Fastnet entries, took part in the Santander Race, the club's first event to a foreign port. There were four entries in the Large Class and ten in the Small. The Large Class included Lord Stalbridge's three masted schooner *Cetonia* and the winner, *Maria del Carmen*, which, as *Meteor IV*, had belonged to the Kaiser before the First World War. It was to be nearly 30 years, when the first Sail Training Race was held in 1956, before such large sailing vessels were again seen racing together. Somerset, who was kept company by a Spanish submarine for most of the race, won the Small Class from *Ilex* and carried home the Challenge Cup which in due course became the club's Class II Points Trophy.

Another landmark in the club's history and been reached and successfully passed.

Chapter Three

ROYAL ASSENT

THE INCREASING popularity of the club prompted some unusual correspondence and requests. One man wrote to ask if he could enter his ex-Bristol Channel pilot cutter for the Fastnet under a 'nom de plume'. Martin told Miss Wield that as far as he knew there was no rule against this and speculated: 'I suppose he has either got a fussy wife, or perhaps he is a young man whom his parents do not like to go playing about with water.' Either way, the cutter never reached the starting line.

The club's administration was still below par as a letter from Maudslay to Somerset in June 1929 showed when he complained that the hon. secretary, Malden Heckstall-Smith 'is hopelessly bad at any correspondence'. Miss Wield, he said, did everything she could to keep the committee posted, but as many of the questions were technical ones, she could not answer all of them. Miss Wield was indeed having trouble for the same month she wrote to Somerset: 'I sent off a registered letter to Major H-S at Winchester in the hope that it would bring forth some sign of life!...What in the world am I to do if I can't get a reply from him and he won't come up to town!'

A more professional approach was obviously needed, and at the December 1929 AGM it was announced that Heckstall-Smith was stepping down but remained on the committee as the hon. measurer. He was replaced by Dick Maclean Buckley who had sailed with Martin in the first Ocean Race.

In October 1929 Somerset received a letter from the Comte de Chevriers, of the Club Nautique de la Rance at Dinard, enclosing a photograph of a Challenge Cup which King Edward VII had donated in 1906. It was for yachts rating 30 tons (TM) and above racing over a course from Cowes to the bay of St Malo, a distance of 165 miles. It had been competed for before the First World War but the event had since lapsed. Now the Club Nautique de la Rance

photo Beken of Cowes

Karin III was skippered by her owner, Edith Dorrien-Smith, in the 1930 Santander Race. She joined the club the following year, becoming the club's first woman owner. This photograph was taken in 1937

wanted to revive it, but the Comte had been unable to find details of the regulations governing the race, though it was known that the start had been supervised by the Royal Yacht Squadron and competitors had to conform with English handicaps. The Comte wanted to know Somerset's opinion about reviving the event. If it could be, and sufficient numbers entered, 'we would, of course, award very important prizes.'

Soundings were carried out and the Squadron's sailing committee's minute book noted that the committee 'were ready to start the race, but could not undertake any other responsibility in connection therewith'. The Ocean Racing Club therefore agreed to take over its organisation in England and to measure the yachts according to its rule. By doing so, as Phillips-Birt commented, the club 'implicitly adopted a fresh policy, and assured, though it may not have been realized at the time, its own future. Had the pure blue water school of thought controlled policy and a stringent attitude to what was an ocean race been maintained, the club might have failed altogether; or at the most remained a small and esoteric body on the fringes of yachting.'

The first Dinard Race, as it was to be called until *renamed in 1978, was won by Colonel Chambers' *Neptune*. Afterwards, Maclean Buckley wrote to Miss Wield that the least said about it the better. He had thought it 'a poor course' with 'a poor entry' and that it had been 'cold, rough and hard work', though it had not been 'too bad a match between JB [*Jolie Brise*] and *Neptune*'. Despite these jaundiced remarks the race, later organised in collaboration with the Dinard Yacht Club, became one of the club's most popular fixtures, though it was not listed as a club event until 1935 when those taking part became eligible for membership.

One of its attractions was a short course and, under normal conditions, a not very onerous one; another, in the mid-1930s, was a bar run by two 'absolutely ravishing' Russian girls. Yet another was Emily Verger[1] who organised the Dinard club's after-race dinner and always provided 'an unlimited number of

1 when Emily died in 1964 a plate was named in her honour and was awarded to the winner of Class I's 'A' Division

lovelies who acted as waitresses,' as one member recalled. 'She seemed to have the magic touch which, in an effortless kind of way, made anything happen.'

The same month as Somerset received the Comte's first letter, Hunloke told him that the club should apply to the Home Secretary for a Royal Warrant, and on 14th November Hunloke wrote to Martin–on Buckingham Palace writing paper–telling him to write in the following terms: 'Sir, I have the honour to request that you will put the following petition before HM the King. "With humble duty we the flag officers and members of the Ocean Racing Club humbly petition your Majesty that the Club may have the honour of becoming a Royal Yacht Club and thus become the Royal Ocean Yacht [sic] Club." I have the honour, sir, to enclose the list of officers, members, and rules of the club.'

It is curious that Hunloke, who at the beginning of the year had told Somerset that the adverse publicity the club had received might prevent a Royal Warrant being granted, should now advise it to apply for one. Anyway, it seems that his original doubts were correct for in January 1930 Somerset received the following reply from the Home Office: 'I am directed to inform you that your application of the 13th November on behalf of the Members of the Ocean Racing Club for permission to adopt the title "Royal" has been laid before the King, but the Secretary of State regrets that he was unable to recommend to His Majesty the grant of the desired permission.'

Despite this setback the club could be said to have survived its first four years fairly well and at last it had some money in the bank–£174 1s 0d. to be exact –but there were clouds on the horizon. Some members were not renewing their subscriptions and the club's finances were in a sufficiently delicate state for Martin to report at the end of year that there were insufficient funds even to consider sharing a *club room with the Royal Cruising Club which was looking for improved premises.

Lack of income prompted an emergency meeting, held at Cowes on 4th August 1930 after the third Channel Race. Although it had attracted a healthy number of entries, the weather had been so severe that *Spica*, which went on to win in 1932 and 1933, had been the only boat to finish. This eliminated the other crews as eligible candidates, but when Martin had pointed out that the club badly needed new members it was agreed to offer membership to those who had tried hard but had failed to complete the course. It wasn't a blanket invitation, but membership was offered to the owners and amateur crew of Dixon's *Lady Maud*–which had won the race in 1929 and was to win it again in 1931–*Freya II*, *White Heather IV*, *Altair*–now under new ownership–*Sirius*[1], and *Penboch*, which Somerset had sold to Dr Brownlow Smith, perhaps in part exchange for *Jolie Brise*. This brought in 34 new members and at long last solved

1 owned by F.R.G. Forsyth who donated the Forsyth Cup that year for the first boat to finish the race

the problem of one unfortunate, but dogged, applicant who had previously entered two Fastnets without managing to finish. Club funds were also boosted by £90 when, for the first time, life membership was granted to several foreign members.

However, the club's financial problems, combined with the low number of entries for the 1930 Fastnet—only nine were received—must have made the committee wonder exactly how secure the future of the sport was. True, the French were represented by Georges Baldenweck's new French cutter, *Ariel*, as were the Americans with Peverley's Dutch-built steel schooner, *Lelanta*, but it did not go unnoticed by the yachting press that again no American boat crossed the Atlantic to compete. However, the announcement at the 1929 AGM that the long-planned Transatlantic Race was definitely being held in 1931 must have been seen as boding well for the 1931 Fastnet.

The 1930 Fastnet was another tough affair with four of the entries retiring. Aboard *Maitenes II* was the young naval architect, Jack Laurent *Giles who later described the race as 440 miles of windward work, mostly in hard winds or gales and vicious channel seas, and 160 miles to leeward, mostly in a gale. Somerset's log shows that *Jolie Brise* encountered some moderate weather before rounding the Rock, and indeed was becalmed at one point. However, his comments are mostly of rising headwinds and a falling barometer with rain and fog, and it took him nearly a week to complete the course. But his victory was emphatic, for he won by six hours on corrected time from *Maitenes II*, and *Jolie Brise* still holds the record of being the only yacht ever to win the Fastnet three times.

The 1930 Fastnet was followed by another race to Santander which produced 13 starters for the Small Class, but only one for the Large. The race, and the Queen of Spain's Cup, was won by *Ilex*, with *Jolie Brise* second and *Neptune* third. Other entries included the Colombian-registered *Uraba III*, the first South American boat to enter a club event; and the 30-ton cutter, *Karin III*, skippered by Edith *Dorrien-Smith, who became, the following year, the club's first lady owner.

The success of the Santander Race, which one yachting correspondent predicted would soon overtake the Fastnet in popularity, raised, not for the first time, the possibility of running the Fastnet every other year if the Spanish race became established as an annual event[1]. However, as the Americans 'were coming over next summer'—a reference to the 1931 Transatlantic Race—it was decided to postpone any decision.

Ray Barrett, then rear commodore of the Crouch Yacht Club, must have still been working away in the background to make East Coast yachtsmen more involved in the sport, for at the last meeting of the year he was co-opted on to

1 the Spanish Civil War prevented this

the committee to form a sub-committee of East Coast yachtsmen to investigate the possibilities of holding a race from Burnham-on-Crouch to Cowes.

Nothing came of this idea but early in 1931 *Yachting Monthly* published a letter from Martin which announced that two North Sea Races were to be held that year, the Haaks for the Large Class and the Maas for the Small Class. Both events were to start from Burnham-on-Crouch and finish at Felixstowe. The Smith's Knoll, Haaks, and Maas light vessels were the turning marks for the Large class, a distance of 320 miles, while the Small class would proceed direct from the Smith's Knoll to the Maas, a distance of 260 miles. 'The Haaks is roughly rectangular,' wrote Martin, 'and the Maas triangular, and each may be expected to provide a test of the yachts upon all points of sailing, a feature which has been considered to be of great importance in planning Ocean Racing Club courses.'

But the two most important fixtures in 1931 were the Transatlantic and Fastnet Races. The former, organised jointly by the club and the Cruising Club of America (CCA), attracted ten starters including two British entries–*Maitenes II* and the ever-present *Ilex*. Six of the Americans then took part in the Fastnet, along with two French ones, and nine British (including *Maitenes II* and *Ilex*), a healthy increase in numbers over the previous year.

photo Beken of Cowes

However, the race was marred by the club's first loss of life when Colonel Hudson, the co-owner of *Maitenes II*, was washed overboard in storm force winds over the Labadie Bank.

This tragedy apart, both events proved memorable affairs and both were won by a 52ft yawl, *Dorade*. She was skippered and navigated by her 23-year-old American designer, Olin J. Stephens II. With him was his younger brother Rod who had designed her sail plan, rigging, and deck lay-out. Their father, Rod senior, vice commodore of the Larchmont Yacht Club and the boat's owner, was

Dorade at the windless start of the 1931 Fastnet. She revolutionised ocean racing when she won the 1931 Transatlantic Race and then the 1931 and 1933 Fastnet Races also aboard. Though Olin Stephens disagrees, Uffa Fox records that Rod senior's principal role was to stop any arguments between his sons!

Dorade, as Francis S. Kinney points out in his book *You are First*, was the product of a united family enterprise, for Rod senior shrewdly backed his sons in their early endeavours as yacht designers. This, and the arrangement Olin made with Drake H. *Sparkman, was all the foundation the brothers needed for their highly successful careers.

Rod senior had sold his anthracite business just before the 1929 stock market crash and when Olin's early designs (mostly 6-metres) proved successful he shrewdly decided to finance the construction of *Dorade*.

Like *Hallowe'en* before her *Dorade* was a sea-going development of the inshore racing yachts of her day–'narrow, deep, fairly light, and with generous overhanging length,' was Phillips-Birt's description of her, before adding that 'her boldly reduced keel[1] area and her generous length of overhang *Dorade* set the course of future offshore design and pointed clearly away from the earlier working boat tradition.'

What made the performance of the white-hulled yawl so phenomenal was that she not only won the 1931 Transatlantic Race on corrected time but also took line honours. Aboard the scratch boat, Paul Hammond's 72ft *Landfall*, was Waldo Howland. As he *remembers it, *Landfall* was approaching the finish at Plymouth when one of her crew spotted a small white yacht sailing towards them.

'Looks like *Dorade*,' he said.

'Don't even joke about such a thing,' Hammond replied.

But *Dorade* it was. By taking the most northerly great circle route she had beaten *Landfall* across the finishing line by over 45 hours and on corrected time had won by nearly four days from *Skål* a gaff-rigged cutter designed by Phil Rhodes. A launch sent out to greet *Dorade* after she entered Plymouth harbour passed her by as its helmsman, in glancing over the immaculate white yawl, supposed she could not possibly have just crossed the Atlantic, and went in search of a more battered-looking boat.

Dorade won the Fastnet just as convincingly and her crew were given a tickertape welcome along Broadway when they returned, a New York welcome which had never before been given to any yachtsmen. She was fourth across the finishing line, outsailing her larger rivals with an ease which made the yachting commentators realise that ocean racing would never be quite the same again.

After the race Malden Heckstall-Smith and George Martin met with Sherman Hoyt and Olin Stephens to discuss the possibility of amalgamating the club's rule, which had been revised for the 1931 season, with the CCA's. But the discussions produced no result and the ocean racing world had to wait nearly 40 years before an international rule eventually emerged in 1970.

1 Olin Stephens, who was made one of the club's few life honorary members in 1998, commented that he considered the keel 'moderate in length and area'

The year's expanded racing programme brought in 56 new recruits which included 22 life memberships at five guineas a time. One new member of note was Uffa Fox who later served the club as assistant measurer for the Solent district, though he declined to join the technical sub-committee. Others included Paul Hammond; the Stephens brothers and their father; and another seminal figure in the future of ocean racing, John Illingworth, a Royal Navy engineer lieutenant. He qualified for membership aboard the 42ft LWL *Viking*, owned by a fellow naval officer, Lindsay Fisher.

both photos courtesy Lady Mackworth

Many years later Illingworth vividly recalled the race in his autobiography, *The Malham Story*, and gave an authentic picture of what ocean racing must have been like in those early days. The cook was an ex-naval rating using a tiny coal-fired galley. 'Cooky was jolly good,' Illingworth wrote, 'and kept going in the worst weather, and used to dry our damp clothing in his little galley, which was filled with acrid smoke. The flow of filthy language from the galley was quite something, but Cooky never let us down.'

Viking at the start of the 1930 Fastnet. Georges Baldenweck's *Ariel* is astern of her. Inset: John Illingworth aboard *Viking* during the 1931 Fastnet

Illingworth then went on to describe the vagaries of sail handling in such an ancient tub. 'It was now blowing a moderate gale from the west: we had set small head sails, and handed the topsail and double reefed the gaff mainsail. The tanned mainsail was in Ratsey's heaviest canvas and reefing it was rather like reefing a sheet of plywood, so stiff it was. To get the sail down we used to lead the pennants to a drum on the anchor windlass on the fo'c'sle, and by engaging the low gear and putting stout hands on the handles we did manage to pull down the reefs.'

No wonder one of Illingworth's friends subsequently told him that Colin Archer designs went to windward in a seaway 'like a cow in a bog.'

At the meeting in *Plymouth after the race it was formally agreed that in future the Fastnet would be held during odd-numbered years only and that those eligible for it would be able to race instead as the Large Class in the Channel Race. 'The reason for this decision,' said *Yachting World*, 'is that the club feels that there would not be a sufficient entry to justify the event, and, further, that a contest of the nature of the Fastnet Race is too arduous to be endured each year.' But by letting the race lapse for a year the club was creating a situation 'even worse than that which it is trying to overcome', a prediction, as it turned out, that was only narrowly avoided.

The year ended on a satisfactory note when at a committee meeting on 5th November 1931 it was announced that 'His Majesty the King had been pleased to command that this club should henceforth be known as The Royal Ocean Racing Club', and a naval crown was added above the head of Martin's seahorse. At the AGM in December Martin opened the meeting by saying that he had heard that the King had been 'very pleased to give the warrant to the club, as it was a fine sporting organisation in which he took the greatest interest', and that he, Martin, had now applied to the Admiralty for a warrant to fly the blue ensign.

In January 1932 Ray Barrett reported that as 'there was great depression and as most of the big boats had been paid off' he doubted if there was any chance of running the *Haaks Race that year for the Large Class, though he hoped to muster enough entries for the Maas Race. Things looked bleak indeed. However, the scope for enlarging the membership was widened when in November 1932 the committee adopted a proposal put forward by one of the club's first members, Major Rose Richards, that 'persons who have both crossed the Atlantic and sailed in a Bermuda Race in a member's yacht shall be eligible for election.'

Rose Richards, then the owner of the 40-ton (TM) Shepherd-designed gaff cutter, *Lexia*, had in fact sailed across the Atlantic earlier that year to enter the Bermuda Race, as had Somerset in *Jolie Brise*. *Lexia* had finished ninth on corrected time, a credible performance. But *Jolie Brise* had not finished as she had been involved in a remarkable rescue of the crew of the American schooner, *Adriana*. Too large to enter the race the *Adriana* was sailing the course alone, against the best corrected time of the fleet, when she caught fire during the first night.

Somerset responded to her distress flares. His log, as all logs tend to be, was brief but to the point: 'lowered staysail and found schooner with sails all over the place. Came round to lie to leeward but seeing flames on deck ran along her lee side and crew jumped. Two missed one of them getting aboard through getting hold of bulwark, another being lost. Bump once moderately hard and narrowly avoid getting caught by rigging by heavy davits which I had not seen. Lay to and search for man lost round light buoys but no sign...Several other boats arrived at daylight. Petrol caught fire aboard about 10 minutes after getting crew. Masts finally fell and left schooner burnt to water's edge.'

Sherman Hoyt was aboard *Jolie Brise* as one of the mates and in his memoirs had the room to give a more dramatic account of the rescue. 'It was blowing hard with a considerable sea running as we drew alongside. With our headsails becalmed, *Jolie* took a shear and in spite of efforts to keep clear ranged into her, beam and beam, with a horrible crash and fouling aloft. We were at once boarded by her complement, some wildly hysterical, including their cook, a Peruvian Indian, stark-naked and brandishing a huge knife. With the tarred lanyards used in our old-fashioned rig to set up shrouds already on fire; with the confused mob on our deck crowded with both excited crews and, momentarily fearful of an explosion of what we erroneously assumed to be her gasoline fuel tank, we managed to get clear and pull away. Just as we did so, to my horror, I saw a man, hitherto obscured by the half lowered mainsail and boom sagged to the deck, appear around the mainmast and running to leeward, make a wild leap at us.'

The man, who had been attempting to keep the schooner steady while the rest of the crew escaped, fell short, and though Hoyt threw him a line he could not hold on, and was never recovered.

Shortly afterwards Somerset sold *Jolie Brise* and bought *Nina* from Paul Hammond. In February 1933 he set out for a Caribbean cruise but was forced into Bermuda when *Nina*, which had been laid up for a number of years, sprang a bad leak. Water was also coming in through her decks and her designer, Starling Burgess, was summoned, the leak was found, and the deck area was strengthened with knees. Somerset then continued his cruise, but still found *Nina* uncomfortable.

'Feeling very anxious for voyage to end,' he noted in his log on 4th March, just before reaching Nassau, 'as everything seems to go wrong and constant head winds in a ship one does not like are tiresome.'

Somerset's Rescue of *Adriana's* crew

BELOW: The start of the 1932 Bermuda Race. *Mohawk*, one of the entries, photographed from Robert Somerset's *Jolie Brise.*

FAR RIGHT: On the first night *Jolie Brise* approached the burning American schooner, *Adriana*, to make the dramatic rescue of her crew.

RIGHT: The cut in the side of *Jolie Brise* , caused by *Adriana's* boat davit.

For his skill and bravery Somerset was presented with a gold watch by the American President, Herbert Hoover. Somerset was also given the coveted Blue Water Medal by the CCA which Martin had been awarded in 1926 for his Transatlantic voyage in *Jolie Brise* to take part in that year's Bermuda Race. BELOW: *Jolie Brise* under repair in the Herreshoff yard, dwarfed by *Resolute* (left), and the J-class yachts *Yankee* and *Enterprise.*

ABOVE LEFT: *Adriana* the next morning, abandoned and still burning.

One of Somerset's crew, Waldo Howland, who had joined the club after competing in the 1931 Transatlantic and Fastnet Races, said later that Somerset 'never adjusted to *Nina*'s quicker motion and tendency to plunge; nor was her rig really handy for a small crew'; and instead of sailing on to England after his Caribbean cruise Somerset returned to New York and put *Nina* on the market.

At first 1933 threatened to be as quiet as 1932 and for some time there was only one starter for the Fastnet Race—the faithful *Ilex*. Then Rose Richards entered *Lexia* and Somerset agreed to skipper Charles E. Nicholson's cutter, *Flame*, which Nicholson had designed as far back as 1900 and which was now bermudan rigged. Then, no doubt much to the relief of the committee, it was announced that *Dorade*, this time skippered by Rod Stephens with Sherman Hoyt as mate, would enter again as would two other American entries, *Grenadier* and *Brilliant*.

The Fastnet course that year was altered so as to bring back the yachts to Cowes to enable them to take part in a series of coastwise races which had been planned in an effort to stimulate interest in racing offshore. The new course was westwards through the Needles to the Rock and then back to the Spithead forts leaving the Nab Tower to port, a distance of 720 miles.

There was also a new trophy for the race that year as Somerset had donated the Jolie Brise Cup with the idea of encouraging those entries which would not normally stand a chance of winning any other prize. Every owner allotted every entry except his own a time allowance which, in his opinion, gave it the best chance of winning. The mean of all these time allowances was then calculated and given to the yacht in addition to its ordinary time allowance.

It was largely a light weather race. *Flame*, which had her designer aboard, rounded the Rock first followed by *Dorade*, but though the Nicholson yacht finished six hours ahead of her the American yawl won easily on corrected time —by several months one journalist remarked sourly—with *Grenadier* second. What's more, *Dorade* won the Jolie Brise Cup as well, showing the other Fastnet entries still, and literally, under-rated her.

With the club's main event having attracted only six entries an inquest by the yachting press was inevitable. A leader in *Yachting World* commented that it was difficult to view the race as anything but a failure from the British standpoint, that the RORC rule was to blame as it had been drawn up to rate old cruising boats not new ocean racers, and that 'We now hear rumours that the last Fastnet Race has been sailed.'

Weston Martyr was scathing in his comments. 'I hear the Royal Ocean Racing Club is considering abandoning the Fastnet Race and substituting an event for Thames punts from Boulter's Lock to Maidenhead. Japanese lanterns may be carried in lieu of navigation lights. All punts must be equipped with at least one serviceable silk cushion for each member of the crew, with one portable wireless set, two gramophones, a sucking-bottle, and a certified wet nurse.'

The criticism was so widespread that in November 1933 the committee had to issue a press release denying the rumours that the club intended dumping its principal event. This must have been the nadir of the club's fortunes. If it was it did not stop the committee forming a technical sub-committee to look into discrepancies in the RORC rule. These had become apparent after the Royal Corinthian Yacht Club published the results of its competition held the previous year for boats designed to the Rule. Malden Heckstall-Smith and Charles E. Nicholson had been involved as judges and, as the introduction to the *published designs pointed out, the competition had put the club's rule on theoretical trial so it was important that any anomalies be ironed out.

Perhaps, too, the committee had taken *Yachting World's* comments to heart. For at the end of January 1934, when the sub-committee recommended an alteraton in the method of measurement of some of the formula's dimensions, a different rig allowance, certain restrictions on headsails, and a reduction in the time scale, these were all accepted.

The coastwise races were run again in 1934 but were poorly supported and were not repeated. By contrast, the Dinard, Maas, and Channel Races all attracted a healthy number of entries, though the Large Class for the Channel Race only produced two. The inaugural 251-mile Plymouth-Belle Isle Race, won by Gerald Potter's *Carmela*, was also held in conjunction with the Union Nationale des Croiseurs (UNC)[1], the club's French equivalent. It only had nine starters but later became a regular part of the club's programme. More popular was the 310-mile Heligoland Race which had replaced the Haaks Race in 1933, and which started from Harwich. It produced a fleet of 14 and was won by the smallest entry, the gaff-rigged *Isis*.

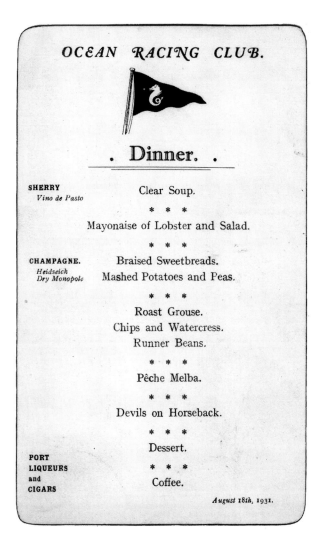

OCEAN RACING CLUB.

. Dinner. .

SHERRY *Vino de Pasto*	Clear Soup.
	* * *
	Mayonaise of Lobster and Salad.
	* * *
CHAMPAGNE. *Heidseick* *Dry Monopole*	Braised Sweetbreads. Mashed Potatoes and Peas.
	* * *
	Roast Grouse. Chips and Watercress. Runner Beans.
	* * *
	Pêche Melba.
	* * *
	Devils on Horseback.
	* * *
PORT LIQUEURS and CIGARS	Dessert. * * * Coffee.

August 18th, 1931.

Menu for the club dinner at the Royal Western Yacht Club which traditionally followed the Fastnet Race. It is dated 18th August 1931. Courtesy Seth Milligan who raced, aged 17, aboard George Roosevelt's *Mistress* that year

1 later renamed the Union Nationale de la Course au Large, or UNCL

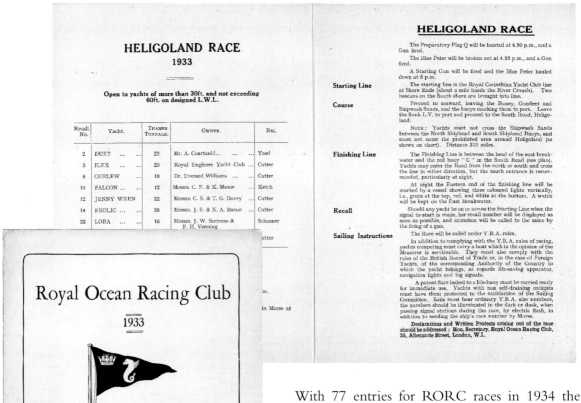

HELIGOLAND RACE
1933

Open to yachts of more than 30ft. and not exceeding 60ft. on designed L.W.L.

Recall No.	Yacht.	THAMES TONNAGE.	OWNER.	RIG.
2	DUET	22	Mr. A. Courtauld	Yawl
3	ILEX	20	Royal Engineer Yacht Club	Cutter
5	CURLEW	18	Dr. Everard Williams	Cutter
10	FALCON	12	Messrs. C. E. & K. Mason	Ketch
12	JENNY WREN	22	Messrs. C. S. & T. G. Davey	Cutter
14	FROLIC	35	Messrs. J. S. & N. A. Bacon	Cutter
22	LORA	16	Messrs. J. W. Scrivens & F. H. Venning	Schooner

HELIGOLAND RACE

The Preparatory Flag Q will be hoisted at 4.50 p.m., and a Gun fired.

The Blue Peter will be broken out at 4.55 p.m., and a Gun fired.

A Starting Gun will be fired and the Blue Peter hauled down at 5 p.m.

Starting Line — The starting line is the Royal Corinthian Yacht Club line at Shore Ends (about a mile inside the River Crouch). Two beacons on the South shore are brought into line.

Course — Proceed to seaward, leaving the Buxey, Gunfleet and Shipwash Sands, and the buoys marking them to port. Leave the Sunk L.V. to port and proceed to the South Road, Heligoland.

Nora : Yachts must not cross the Shipwash Sands between the North Shiphead and South Shiphead Buoys, and must not enter the prohibited area around Heligoland (as shown on chart). Distance 310 miles.

Finishing Line — The Finishing Line is between the head of the east breakwater and the red buoy " C " in the South Road (see plan). Yachts may enter the Road from the north or south and cross the line in either direction, but the south entrance is recommended, particularly at night.

At night the Eastern end of the finishing line will be marked by a vessel showing three coloured lights vertically, i.e., green at the top, red, and white at the bottom. A watch will be kept on the East Breakwater.

Recall — Should any yacht be on or across the Starting Line when the signal to start is made, her recall number will be displayed as soon as possible, and attention will be called to the same by the firing of a gun.

Sailing Instructions — The Race will be sailed under Y.R.A. rules.

In addition to complying with the Y.R.A. rules of racing, yachts competing must carry a boat which in the opinion of the Measurer is serviceable. They must also comply with the rules of the British Board of Trade or, in the case of Foreign Yachts, of the corresponding Authority of the Country to which the yacht belongs, as regards life-saving apparatus, navigation lights and fog signals.

A patent flare lashed to a life-buoy must be carried ready for immediate use. Yachts with non self-draining cockpits must have them protected to the satisfaction of the Sailing Committee. Sails must bear ordinary Y.R.A. size numbers, the numbers should be illuminated in the dark or dusk, when passing signal stations during the race, by electric flash, in addition to sending the ship's race number by Morse.

Declarations and Written Protests arising out of the race should be addressed : Hon. Secretary, Royal Ocean Racing Club, 35, Albemarle Street, London, W.1.

Royal Ocean Racing Club
1933

SAILING INSTRUCTIONS

:: For ::
1st
HELIGOLAND RACE

STARTING FROM BURNHAM-ON-CROUCH

Friday, 2nd June, 1933
at 5 p.m.

High Water at Burnham 7.30 p.m. British Summer Time.

Sailing Instructions for the first Heligoland Race

With 77 entries for RORC races in 1934 the committee must have been encouraged to think that, despite all the press criticism, the corner had been turned. By then the lease on the office at 35 Albemarle Street had expired, and from January 1934 committee meetings took place in one of the two rooms which Maudslay rented at 3 Old Burlington Street for £150pa. From December 1934 he allowed the club to use a room for £50pa. But there was still no serious thought of the club obtaining its own premises.

No less than five committee meetings as well as the AGM were held in the last quarter of 1934 as some important decisions had to be made. One was to elect new flag officers as the existing ones felt new blood was needed. There were no rules for appointing flag officers, or for appointing them for any fixed period. It was therefore decided the AGM would appoint the commodore, vice commodore, and rear commodore, each for a three-year term; the committee would appoint the treasurer, secretary, and measurer, for unspecified lengths of time. Members were invited to put forward their nominations for the vacant posts. When none was received the committee's candidates were confirmed as follows: Martin (admiral), Major T.P. Rose Richards (commodore), Captain A. Rosling (vice commodore), and W.H. Watkins (rear commodore).

Rose Richards had sailed in *North Star* in the first Ocean Race, and had then crewed for Somerset in the next three, first in *Penboch* and then aboard *Jolie Brise* in 1929 and 1930. He had also raced his own boat *Iolaire*–owned for over 40 years after the war by a current member, Don Street–in several Channel Races, and had won the first Maas Race in her before building *Lexia* in 1931. An experienced sailor, he was the ideal man to take over from Martin.

Initially Rose Richards had been reluctant to take the post but when no other suitable candidate could be found he had eventually agreed providing he had competent flag officers to help him. He proposed Rosling as vice commodore, for though only recently elected (in 1931), Rosling had raced with Rose Richards in the 1932 Bermuda Race and had proved to be highly competent. The new rear commodore, W.H. Watkins, who had joined in 1929, was also a keen racing man, having taken part in every Channel Race since 1930 in his 13-ton cutter, *White Heather IV*, winning it in 1934, and coming second in that year's Heligoland Race.

A decision also had to be reached on the five pages of suggestions submitted by John Illingworth. His idea of having an ocean racing championship trophy was one which found favour. This would be awarded to the yacht club which, through its entries in RORC races, accumulated the most points during the season. He also wanted the Fastnet regulations be changed to admit yachts of 35ft LWL as this would allow two of the club's yachts, *Iolaire* and *Thalassa*, to take part. This, too, was accepted and 35ft became a fashionable waterline length for an ocean racer as it optimized the owner's choice of RORC classes and events–and measuring a boat over 35ft cost two guineas instead of one!

This raft of business certainly gives the impression that the club was now on a firmer footing, especially when it was also decided to amend the clause in Rule 2 which stated the club's aim as being to provide annually 'one ocean race of not less than 600 miles in length, and such other races as may be agreed upon', to read: 'The object of the club shall be to foster ocean and long-distance racing in every way.'

But the matter which exercised the minds of the committee most at these meetings was the practical application of the club's scantling rule which required that 'yachts built subsequently to Dec. 11th 1929 to be classed at Lloyd's as cruisers, or to produce a certificate from the builders stating that their scantlings were at least equal to Lloyd's requirements.'

At the end of 1932 W.B. Luard had pointed out that it was unfair that British yachts built to Lloyd's scantlings had to compete against American yachts which might not be. The committee had been sympathetic but had felt it would be difficult to refuse yachts that had sailed all the way from America to race, and had declined to give a definite ruling. However, when William Meek suggested the phrase, 'Yachts entering for any of the club's ocean races must be of a strength equivalent to that required by Lloyd's for cruising yachts', the committee accepted it and Sherman Hoyt and Herbert Stone formed a small committee to issue certificates to American yachts crossing the Atlantic to compete in RORC events.

courtesy Duke of Beaufort

T.P. Rose Richards, commodore 1934–37, aboard *Jolie Brise* during the 1929 Fastnet Race. Bobby Somerset is standing behind him

This had appeared to settle the matter but in 1934 it was reported, though later denied by the owner, that an ex-15-metre called *Nanette III* had strained her deck during the RORC-organised Heligoland-Copenhagen Race. As a metre boat she did not, of course, meet Lloyd's cruiser scantling requirements and the comments the incident caused led Maclean Buckley to suggest that measurers be given more definite guidance on whether such boats should be allowed to compete in offshore races. Instead, the committee strengthened the relevant paragraph in the Sailing Instructions so that it read: 'The Measurer is empowered to refuse the entry of any boat which he does not consider fit to race.'

Shortly afterwards Somerset informed the committee that a Colonel C.F. King wished to buy *Nina* from him, but had asked for an assurance that she would be accepted by the RORC as an entry for their races. Meek pointed out that it was not possible 'because it might be taken as a statement that she was up to Lloyd's scantlings, which was probably not the case.' However, it was agreed that as she had already taken part in a club event entry to others could hardly be refused her. Maclean Buckley was told to inform Somerset that there was no reason why *Nina*'s entry should not be accepted with the proviso that the measurer always had the power to refuse entry to any yacht he did not consider fit to race. During this discussion two committee members commented that lightly constructed yachts should be accepted provided they were seaworthy as the scantlings rule was unenforceable!

This difference of opinion obviously got back to Laurent Giles whom King had commissioned to find him a suitable yacht for ocean racing. When King asked Giles if *Nina* was suitable, Giles, after examining her plans, replied that she could not be described as being of a strength equivalent to the Lloyd's scantling rules for cruising yachts. He must also have verbally mentioned the difference of opinion within the committee for King wrote him a letter on 14th November which showed that he was not a man who minced his words.

'My position with regard to *Nina* is that I expect an "honest" boat, irrespective of Lloyd's technicalities, and irrespective of the weakness or folly of the RORC committee, and rely upon you to see that I get one. You now suggest, apparently, that because two members of the RORC committee say that they are not interested in the observance of their own rules and because of their encouragement of a 15-metre [*Nanette*] you withdraw your previous opinion as to the work necessary to make *Nina* an honest boat. To quote your own words: "What can one say?"

'I am inclined to say three things: 1) that I don't think *Nina* is worth all the trouble. 2) that the RORC ought to change its committee pretty quickly. 3) that as a reasonable sport, big class ocean racing has been too much injured by the foolish policy of the RORC to be worth any real interest until it has been put on a proper basis. I do say one thing very definitely, namely, that I will not be interested in running any boat for the Fastnet which infringes the spirit of the rules in any way whatever–irrespective of what the committee of the RORC may encourage or permit other people to do. My feeling is growing stronger that unless and until the RORC put their house in order the Fastnet should be left severely alone. It would probably do no harm if somebody said so very loudly.'

photo Beken of Cowes

The Shepherd-designed *Lexia*, 50ft LWL, which Rose Richards entered for the 1931 and 1933 Fastnets and for the 1932 Bermuda Race

By the time he received this letter Giles had already written to Maclean Buckley asking if the scantlings rule was to be observed or not, adding that after *Nanette*'s alleged problems in the Copenhagen Race the technical sub-committee, of which he was a member, believed it definitely should be. He concluded: 'Further, there is evidence that the admittance of yachts of light construction and high ballast ratio on equal terms with yachts which conform to the scantling rule is a cause of well reasoned dissatisfaction and one likely to adversely affect entries.'

On 19th November Giles wrote again, enclosing a censored copy of King's letter–for some reason *Nina*'s name was deleted from it–and reiterating that he was convinced that the scantlings rule must be strictly adhered to. However, when asked, Meek stated bluntly that it '*is and has been* quite incapable of enforcement on economic and technical grounds'.

The committee circumvented this impasse by agreeing that the purpose of the scantling rule was to prevent unfair and unpopular competition by yachts of ultra light construction rather than to ensure the seaworthiness of an entry –which in any case it could not do. It therefore deleted the scantlings rule and in May 1935 introduced the technical sub-committee's proposal for a scantlings allowance formula which could be deducted from a yacht's rating.

*King, meanwhile, went off and bought himself a 32-ton gaff yawl called *Rose* which he entered for the 1935 Fastnet. He finished the race, was elected a member that October, and as he almost immediately joined the committee he presumably must have revised his opinion of it.

Sketch by Lord Albemarle of Sir Philip Hunloke, the King's sailing master, at the helm of *Britannia*. He was the club's first admiral

Painting of the Fastnet Rock by Admiral Richard Beechey (1808–1895) which hangs on the clubhouse's main staircase. It was donated to the club by Sir Owen Aisher

Painting by Frank Wagner (1931–1996) for the Royal Engineers of the 40ft LWL *Ilex* at the Fastnet Rock.
Built by Camper & Nicholson in 1899 the Royal Engineers raced her as a gaff-rigged yawl between 1926–1930,
as a gaff cutter 1931–34, and as a bermudan cutter from 1935. She is still afloat today

A painting of *Jolie Brise* by Gregory Robinson (1876–1967). Entitled 'Off the Fastnet Rock', it hangs, appropriately, in the club's Jolie Brise Room

A painting of the 45ft LWL *Bloodhound*, the winner of the 1939 Fastnet Race, by Charles Bryan. It hangs in the hall of the clubhouse and was donated by Lady Wyatt in memory of her husband, Sir Myles Wyatt

The model of *Latifa* which was donated to the club by Jack Salem. It stands in the clubhouse hall

Astrape, designed by Brooks Richards and launched in 1939. She won the Britannia Cup in 1947

courtesy Sir Brooks Richards

Chapter Four

THE DESIGN REVOLUTION GATHERS PACE

THE 1935 programme was smaller than the previous year with only six races being held. But it started promisingly when, for the first time, seven German yachts raced across the North Sea to take part the Heligoland Race. The 19 starters were divided into three classes and for the first 24 hours they were borne along by a moderate gale which blew from dead aft. The bigger yachts which had small spinnakers set them with reefed mainsails; those without small spinnakers set large ones until something carried away.

The Kriegsmarine's 65ft gaff-rigged ketch, *Asta*, took line honours by maintaining an average speed of 10.7 knots, and *Rose*, the second boat to finish, averaged 9.4 knots. But, as with *Isis* in 1934, the smallest yacht in the race, the Class III double-ended German ketch, *Hajo*, won on corrected time.

Another Transatlantic Race, this time to Norway and American run, brought across to Europe *Stormy Weather*, a 40ft LWL yawl owned by Philip LeBoutillier, designed by Olin Stephens and skippered by brother Rod. Slightly bigger than *Dorade*, and beamier, too, she won the race convincingly and then sailed to the Solent to join a fleet of 13 British yachts and three French ones for a Fastnet which Alf Loomis said afterwards was 'the most strikingly successful' so far.

Apart from *Stormy Weather* other first-time participants were the Royal Air Force with a sloop called *Emmeline*, one of nine yachts sporting a bermudan rig, still something of a novelty for larger yachts. Another first-time service entry was the Admiralty's *Tai-Mo-Shan* which had been sailed from Hong Kong the previous year by a group of naval officers. Five of the entries were new. One was the new French cutter, *Isis*, built for Georges Baldenweck; another was *Trenchemer* which had been constructed in Scotland from an Olin Stephens

design which he had submitted to the 1932 Royal Corinthian Yacht Club competition. *Trenchemer* therefore became the first yacht to be constructed to the RORC Rule, a fact which should have reflected great credit on her owner, Walter *Bell, but the circumstances in which she was built do not.

'I did not hear of it,' Stephens wrote later, 'until the boat had been completed and launched to float rather deep on her designed waterline. Construction had not been authorized nor had the construction drawings been followed as she was built of steel, rather heavily, though the design was for wood. So I felt that the owner was unreasonable in writing me for help in a rather accusatory mode. In the end I helped him to lighten the rig and expressed the hope that being deep might not hurt her and she turned out rather well.'

She did indeed for she came second on corrected time in the 1935 Fastnet and was still afloat thirty years later before being lost with her then owner, Robert Somerset, in a tragic accident. But it was another new yacht, the 45ft LWL cutter, *Foxhound*, which was perhaps the most significant from the club's point of view. Designed by Charles E. Nicholson for Isaac *Bell, an American living in England, she showed the way forward for those ocean racing in European waters. She had not been designed specifically to the RORC rule but had been constructed with it very much in mind. She and her near sisters *Bloodhound* and *Stiarna*, which appeared the following year, rated under the IYRU rule at about 12 metres. In the words of Phillips-Birt they were 'beautiful seagoing yachts, capable of going almost anywhere in the world that their draught permitted, while having a brilliant performance, and at the same time providing their crews with the amenities of life for a long

Trenchemer in 1935 and (inset) Walter Bell at her helm during the 1935 Fastnet Race

photo Beken of Cowes

period. For a little loss in smooth-water weatherliness, compared with a 12-metre, they gained the oceans of the world.'

The Fastnet start that year was from Yarmouth which shortened the course to 585 miles and in a race where the wind remained moderate *Stormy Weather* won convincingly by over six hours on corrected time. The new scantlings allowance worked well so that the scratch boat, *Kismet III*, described as an ex-15-metre with a 12-metre rig, could only manage fifth place on corrected time, though she was the first to cross the finishing line at Plymouth. A successful Fastnet was followed by an equally successful Belle Ile Race to finish a season which was a minor turning point in the club's history. Not only had the Fastnet been given new vigour but the other fixtures had attracted a substantial number of entries; and 15 clubs had competed for the championship *trophy donated by Illingworth and his cousin, Guy Napier Martin, who owned *Thalassa*, with the Royal Yacht Squadron emerging a clear winner.

courtesy Mrs D. van Busschbach-Bruynzeel

The Heligoland Race, especially, augured well for the future for it proved European yachtsmen's growing interest in the sport. The French had been competing in RORC events for several years and in 1934 the first Dutch yachtsman to enter an RORC fixture, Kees Bruynzeel, had taken part in the Heligoland Race and became a member in 1936. Now the Germans had decided to enter the arena in force and from then on they proved themselves doughty competitors. Soon the secretary was reporting that the RORC rule had been adopted for some German classes, and that two yacht clubs in the Netherlands were also adopting it.

However, as the smallest boat had now twice won the Heligoland, and as the largest, *Asta*, would have had to have averaged over 13 knots to win, there was something wrong with the time allowance system then being used and Ray *Barrett and Malden Heckstall-Smith put their heads together to produce a time-on-time system, known as the Time Correction Factor (TCF), instead of the old time-on-distance one.

The increased popularity of the sport, both in Britain and Europe, put additional pressures on the club, and in October 1935 it was decided that as the post of hon. secretary—which was soon to be combined with that of treasurer when Maudslay resigned at the end of the year—was now a full time job and that Maclean Buckley had to be paid an adequate salary.

The commodore, Rose Richards, also believed that the club's offices at Old Burlington Street were much too cramped, and that perhaps the time had come 'to take the plunge and have a proper clubhouse'. He had already received

Kees Bruynzeel, the first Dutch member, aboard his yacht *Goodewinde* in 1935. He owned many famous boats, including *Zeearend* in which he won the 1937 Fastnet Race guarantees amounting to £200 to help the club overcome the inevitable financial deficit which would occur if this step was taken.

A small sub-committee was formed to find a clubhouse and one was soon located above a shop at 2 Pall Mall Place which provided a club room, a bar (later the dining room), a library, two bedrooms for male members, quarters for a steward, the usual cloakroom facilities, and a bathroom. The premises were occupied in February 1936 and a house warming party held at which a future secretary, Alan Paul, was impressed to see Alfred Mylne, William Fife and Charles E. Nicholson standing in one corner with their heads together. Later a house committee was formed and given the task of creating interest amongst members in the clubhouse and of trying to make it the international head-quarters for the sport.

This was a large step to take and a bold one. An inauguration fund was started to defray some of the costs but the subscription had to be raised. Having a clubhouse also brought problems as to how it should be run. Initially, lady members and lady guests were given unfettered access to the club room and the bar—and the bathroom—but then 'in the light of three weeks experience of running the club house' restrictions were imposed. This found little favour with Miss M.E. Wiles, the part owner of the 9-ton *Coquette*, who objected strongly, and the restrictions were lifted.

courtesy Christopher Nicholson

According to Charles E. Nicholson's son, John Nicholson, Malden Heckstall-Smith is dressed here as 'The Dictator'. Note the club sea-horse and crown on his turban

1 the first all-female crew to take part in an RORC Race was when Nick Greville found himself with two boats at the time of the 1969 Mersea–Ostend Race. He skippered *Trocar* and his wife, Shirley, the 30ft Rustler, *Scalpel*, with five women crew

It should be mentioned here that, unlike many London clubs—or yacht clubs for that matter—men and women have always been equally eligible to join the RORC and it has had few lapses into discrimination. When the present clubhouse was first occupied women members were not allowed to use the bedrooms and there was some grumbling when they were. Rather more surprisingly, they were not allowed to crew[1] aboard the club yacht—which had its first female bosun, Margaret Carnell, in 1976—until 1973 and did not hold their first dinner until 1991.

In April, H.S. Rouse, a former commodore of the Royal Hong Kong Yacht Club, offered the club the Hong Kong Cup which the committee decided should be raced for by a new Cruiser Class in the next Fastnet. In non-Fastnet years it was to be awarded to the boat in the Cruiser Class which won most places in RORC events.

The increase in workload caused by the club's steady expansion led Maclean Buckley, who was in poor health, to resign in April 1936–he was soon persuaded to return–and his remark that 'he did not see how the club could hope to pay a secretary adequately or, in the ordinary way, to cover his expenses' showed that however successful it had been in establishing ocean racing, financially the club's future was still far from secure.

One way to help the finances was to increase the membership, and at the 1936 AGM, when membership stood at around 475, the introduction of provisional membership was approved. This allowed candidates to use the club house for a limited period while waiting to qualify. If they failed to qualify, their membership lapsed and they would then have to apply for an extension. Over the following years various forms of membership, including *cadet and veteran memberships, were also introduced and there was a scheme to take 'unknown quantities' on weekend sailing trips and passage-making. This enabled owners to size up the capabilities of individuals, gave novices some chance of testing out their skills, and allowed dinghy sailors an opportunity to race in larger boats.

At the same time as introducing provisional members the rules were tightened so that an owner had to satisfy the committee that a candidate for full membership was a competent member of the amateur crew. High spirits, rowdiness, call it what you will, after races, particularly after the Fastnet, was also raised in committee and it was felt that unless 'the tendency to make an excessive uproar after races was checked the club might find itself unwelcome at clubs around the coast', though it was agreed that only public opinion would be the sole effective restraint.

The Plymouth-Benodet and the Falmouth-Clyde Races were added to the fixture list in 1936. It was a year which produced the largest-ever entry for any RORC event with 37 yachts taking part in the Channel Race, 21 in the Small Class and 16 in the Large. 1937 saw the introduction of yet more fixtures–the Southsea-Brixham, Ijmuiden-Solent, Plymouth-La Baule, and St Nazaire-Benodet Races were all held for the first time–and there were a healthy number of starters in the established ones. The Fastnet had 29, by far the largest the race had so far attracted, and was the showcase for the revolution in design that was taking place.

courtesy Christopher Nicholson

Charles E. Nicholson, one of the greatest yacht designers of his age and a long-time supporter of the club

Among the starters were many types. It was also a truly international field, with entries from Germany, Holland, France, and the United States, and these brought out the punters. The most fancied, at 8-1, were *Bloodhound*, *Maid of Malham*, and *Ortac*; 10-1 was offered on the American entry **Elizabeth McCaw* and on Michael Mason's 53ft LWL Fife-designed yawl, *Latifa*; while *Zeearend*– which had been designed to the RORC Rule by Olin Stephens for Kees Bruynzeel–and *Stiarna* were quoted at 12-1.

Bloodhound and *Latifa* had both been built the previous year and had already proved themselves. Sherman Hoyt, no mean judge of a boat, thought *Latifa*, which had won the Plymouth-Benodet Race in 1936, the finest all round ship he had ever sailed in ocean passages or races, while *Bloodhound* became perhaps the best known ocean racer of all time. She replaced Isaac Bell's *Foxhound* after Bell had decided he wanted the rating advantage of a yawl. Instead of having *Foxhound*'s rig altered he sold her and Nicholson built him the slightly larger *Bloodhound*. She had immediately showed her speed by winning the Large Class in the 1936 Channel Race in which high winds and seas, combined with heavy rain, had caused 17 retirements out of the 37 yachts which had taken part.

Both *Bloodhound* and *Latifa* had been built, as Phillips-Birt later observed, with 'offshore racing and the RORC rule as the principal consideration, and they make, apart from their subsequent records which placed them amongst the greatest names in the RORC fleet, one of the highest tributes to the rating rule. They were that ideal combination of beauty, speed, seaworthiness, and habitability that rating rules have always sought to encourage but so rarely have achieved. To these two names should be added the earlier *Trenchemer*, and *Bloodhound*'s near sister *Foxhound*. These were the type of yacht that had been dreamed of when the RORC rule was founded.'

Nevertheless, it was the 35ft sloop, *Ortac*, which Phillips-Birt believed was unquestionably the boat of the year in 1937. Designed for the rear commodore, C.F. King, by the comparatively unknown Robert *Clark–who gave her the first pulpit to be fitted to a yacht–she won the Plymouth-La Baule Race and over the season accumulated enough points to win the Trenchemer Cup for the Class I individual points championship.

However, from today's perspective it was perhaps the appearance of Illingworth's **Maid of Malham* which was to prove more important. Not having played polo for some years, by 1936 Illingworth had saved up enough money–and plucked up sufficient courage–to build a 'flat out' 35ft ocean racer which had encouraged several other members, including King, to do the same. He discussed his ideas with both Fife and Mylne before opting for Jack Laurent Giles, who, with Robert Clark, represented the new generation of young[1] designers. He left the hull lines to Giles but laid out the yacht's interior

1 after one meeting of the technical sub-committee Charles E. Nicholson was heard to say: 'The trouble with these young men is that they think they know everything; the trouble with us old ones is that we know we do'

Colonel King and *Ortac*'s pulpit

Ortac's pulpit, the first ever fitted to a yacht, and *Ortac*'s owner, Colonel C.F. King, the club's vice commodore in 1939. Up to that time the lifelines on all boats finished at the stemhead, leaving any crew member working in the bows with little protection from being swept overboard. These photographs were supplied by Austin Farrar who remarks that 'The pulpit started as a sketch on my drawing board when I was working with Robert Clark on *Ortac*'s design in 1937. Colonel King saw the sketch and said he would have it; and Morgan Giles, the builder, made it under protest, saying it would spoil the yacht's appearance. He relented when he saw it fitted'

exactly as he wanted it, which provoked Giles into saying, laughingly, 'you buggers with fixed ideas are awful.'

Illingworth's specifications for the rigging prompted Giles to observe, rightly as it turned out, that it would make the foredeck look like a goods station shunting yard, though Illingworth wrote that he learned a lot from these early mistakes and used it to good effect in later yachts he owned. The double head-stays, which *Ortac* also had, were fixed at the masthead; and the hollow mast, instead of being tapered, was much the same diameter its entire length above deck to take more powerful foresails[1]. It was also set further aft which created a smaller, high aspect ratio mainsail and a shorter boom. As Phillips-Birt observed: 'with their generous overhangs and cut-away keels [*Ortac* and *Maid of*

1 the club allowed the use of double spinnakers in 1937-8

Malham] were in the new line of development which set the course for subsequent offshore design. On the smaller boats they had the influence that the *Trenchemer* and *Foxhound* types had on the larger.'

In the *Maid*'s first race, to Torbay, held in June 1937 to celebrate the coronation of George VI, she won her class; and but for being becalmed off the Eddystone Light when she had time in hand she might have won that year's Fastnet. As it was the bigger yachts ahead of her managed to finish before the calm descended, and the race was won by Bruynzeel's *Zeearend* by 2hrs, 17min. on corrected time from *Stiarna*, with Illingworth taking third place.

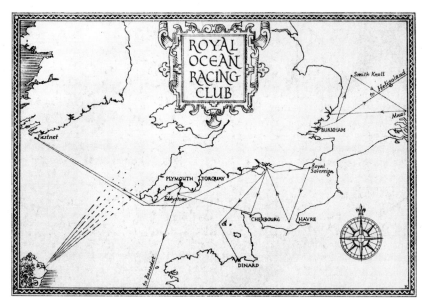

The drawing with which the front of the 1937 club programme was decorated

'I had just read the famous book of Uffa Fox,' Bruynzeel later wrote of his memorable victory, 'who mentioned the now well-known principle: if your course is going to windward, you should make your longest tack towards an expected wind change.'

As the north-west wind was forecast to back, Bruynzeel stuck to a westerly course which brought him outside the Scillies. The wind backed as predicted and Bruynzeel found himself rounding the Rock with the biggest boats.

Though the term for flag officers had now been increased to four years, Rose Richards stated at the end of 1937 that while he had greatly enjoyed being commodore he was looking for a replacement. Neither the vice commodore nor the rear commodore were willing to replace him and 'as he considered that there could be no more suitable man' than the owner of *Latifa*, he had asked Michael Mason, who had accepted.

A man of tremendous, battered, physique, whose body was tattooed with the exotic wildlife he loved so much—he apparently also had a magnificent Medusa's Head whose locks cascaded down his back—Mason was, like Weston Martyr, one those quintessential Englishmen who sought adventure and fortune in foreign places. His many talents—it was said that he spoke 11 languages —included a deft touch with the pen, and he wrote several travel books as well as a couple of novels. He was destined for a career in the Army but after Sandhurst, and claiming the Army's heavyweight boxing championship title, he lived in Arctic Canada for three years where he worked as a tracker, prospector, lumberjack and bootlegger.

He then took to exploring, and his adventures in places like the Sahara Desert and Cape Horn gave him sufficient material to launch his writing career. One of his books, *Where the Tempests Blow*, tells how he and his first wife explored and charted the still-unknown waters around the islands of Tierra del Fuego. His wartime adventures, related later, were equally exotic.

For the 1938 season yachts taking part in RORC fixtures were divided into an Open Class, a class for fast cruisers, and a third for cruisers. The Open Class, whose points championship *Maid of Malham* won that year, would race, as previously, without any restriction on the numbers of sails carried, but both the Fast Cruiser Class, or Class A, and the Cruiser Class, or Class B, would be restricted in the number of light weather sails they could have aboard.

It was the last full season before the war started and the club's busiest to date. The fixture list was the longest ever, though the Maas Race had to be cancelled because of the weather. It began with the annual Heligoland Race, and was followed by the Falmouth-Kingstown and the Kingstown-Clyde. Then on 14th July the first leg of a series of Baltic races began from Dover and ended at Kristiansand—it was won by Jack Rawlings' *Erivale*, a new Robert Clark design —and there were also the usual Channel and Dinard events. After the latter, yachts raced to Ile de Bréhat and from there back to Brixham.

But from the club's point of view the most important event in 1938—though it would not have appeared so at the time—was the construction of the 24-ton (TM) gaff-rigged cutter *Griffin* for the club's admiral, George Martin, and Herbert West. West, Martin's stockbroker and friend, had sold *Patience*, which Martin had skippered in the 1931 Fastnet, in 1934 and had not replaced her, while Martin had not owned a boat—at least not one large enough to appear in Lloyd's Register of Yachts—since he had sold his 2-ton *Minx* in 1928.

During one winter in the early 1930s Martin had indulged in his passion for working boats by shipping as mate aboard a Thames barge, and had written a *book about his experiences. He had then bought one of his own called *Memory* which he restored and then worked. He was still working her and living aboard her in 1938 when the yard of Harry King and Sons at Pinmill began the construction of *Griffin*. Martin's correspondence with West make it plain that she was to be built with comfortable cruising, and easy handling, in mind, which was almost certainly why he chose to have her gaff rigged. Commenting on Martin's choice Charles E. Nicholson later wrote that Martin was 'not only a great seaman but also an artist. Both these fine qualities may explain his preference for the gaff mainsail, which I know is very sincere.'

Griffin, the first club boat

The 24-ton (TM) gaff cutter, *Griffin*, was designed by W.E. Forster for H.E. West and E.G. Martin. In 1945 West presented her to the club in

memory of Martin. Her dimensions were 37ft, 8in. LWL, 11ft, 8in. beam, draught 5ft, 8in. Here she is seen being launched from her builders, Harry King & Sons of Pinmill in 1938; lying alongside, possibly at Dartmouth, date unknown; and well reefed down at the start of the Brixham-Santander Race in 1952

Perhaps, as John Bush–who was to run *Griffin* as the club yacht in the immediate postwar years–has pointed out, Martin may have been influenced by the old East Coast bargee who remarked: 'If I were a gen'leman, which I ain't, or rich, which I aren't, I'd never go to windward no not never.'

West, who financed the yacht's construction, had been really quite ill and Martin thought that a summer afloat would restore him to full health. With his medical background Martin was able to offer sound advice for recuperating, and 'whether we sail much or merely potter,' he wrote West in January 1938, 'I shall have enough to keep me fully occupied, for there is nothing I love more than caring for a ship–I have had several splendid ones, but never one to sail in which was the child of my own imagination as the *Griffin* is. Technically it is a most interesting problem to take a boat of her size and do all one can to make her easy to handle.'

By then he had obviously had enough of working *Memory*. 'For the time being at any rate,' he wrote the following month while aboard her, 'I have had my fill of this barge life. The number of days one spends at sea are so very few compared with those one spends in the docks getting knocked about and chivvied from place to place by steamers and lighters. There is no peace. Moreover the sense of adventure has passed.'

In his next letter he wrote that *Memory*[1] was sailing on Wednesday without him and that 'I feel a little sad at the break for I am very fond of her but she is in the hands of a splendid skipper, and from now on I must give my whole mind to the *Griffin*.' Thereafter Martin wrote from Alma Cottage at Pinmill and his letters were full of enthusiasm for his new venture. During April and May he 'watched every detail of her building and directed it', and his meticulous descriptions of *Griffin*'s construction and cabin plans show the artist in the man. She was launched at the end of May and soon afterwards Martin began to live aboard her. He found the experience a delightful one and encouraged the philosophical bent which had always been part of his character.

'I cannot help feeling that people have some influence upon the things with which they are most intimately associated,' he wrote West. 'Fiddles especially seem to respond to the minds and temperaments of those who use them constantly–and so do ships. But ships, strangely enough, seem to be born with characters of their own–every sailor feels that, and no one has expressed the feeling so well as Conrad.'

Work continued throughout June and July, with West making the occasional visit. But Martin continued to write almost weekly and he makes the usual complaints about delays and workmen making a mess, and there is a constant stream of requests about what food West should bring with him. The fitting and running of the radio also caused problems–'a voracious monster' was Martin's

1 *Memory* survived the war years, despite having the blazing engine of a downed German fighter land on her deck in June 1943

description of it as its consumption of power was excessive. After further delay because of bad weather, Martin sailed for the West Country in August with his nephew Rynn Stewart. West had planned to go, too, but decided he was not well enough and though, when he arrived in the West Country, Martin kept urging him to join him it is evident that he never did go aboard.

In mid-October, having shipped aboard his old professional skipper, Sydney Briggs, from *Jolie Brise* days, Martin headed back to Pinmill to lay up *Griffin* and Briggs proved the ideal companion. 'He is very quiet,' he wrote West, 'hates going ashore, seems to be more cheerful in bad weather at sea than at any other time, & doesn't mind being away for months.' As if the last attribute needed explanation, Martin added: 'His marriage is not a great success I think.'

In November 1938 Maclean Buckley found that, according to the new rules, Martin's time as admiral also expired after four years. 'The committee may want to alter the Rule back again, or nominate George for re-election, or try someone else,' he wrote Somerset. If it wanted someone else, would Somerset be prepared to have his name put forward? Somerset's reply was by return and was unequivocal. 'I would very much prefer not to be Admiral of anything...I have forgotten all the racing talk and don't know one boat from the other which is the least that must be expected from an Admiral.'

A committee meeting on 10th November approved Mason's suggestion that King George VI should be asked to be the next admiral. If the King refused then Martin would stay on. On 12th November Maclean Buckley wrote to Martin: 'Dear George. It's like this. The committee would like to re-elect you as their Admiral in preference to anyone else—with one exception. Mike Mason suggested that we ask the King and the committee agreed that if he would do it this would be a good thing, but no nonsense with any second-raters, Princes, Dukes and the like...The committee cannot very well tell the club what they are trying to do, but would hope that if H.M. will not play you will continue as our Admiral, or that if he will you would make room for him. This seems to be asking rather a lot of you, but I expect you will do it because your only competitor is a highly respected gentleman.'

From Pinmill Martin wrote West that he would 'consider it to be a great honour to resign in favour of such a successor—meanwhile being willing to keep the job warm—so I have sent the Commodore notice of my resignation "to take effect at such time as may be convenient to him and the Committee". If the King accepts there could be no more honourable end to my official relations with the club.'

The Keeper of the Privy Purse's answer to the club's request, dated 8th December, was not only swift but totally unexpected. 'I am commanded by the

King to inform you that His Majesty as been graciously pleased to grant his Patronage to the Royal Ocean Racing Club.'

Mason was obviously mortified by this unexpected turn of events. 'The enclosed, when it arrived this morning, annoyed me exceedingly,' he wrote Maclean Buckley. 'I think "Patronage" is the foulest word in the English language.'

However, 'on cooling down a bit' he had discovered that King George VI was Patron of several royal sailing clubs but admiral solely of the Royal Yacht Squadron; and that he was admiral of the Royal Motor Yacht Club only because he had been Duke of York when he had accepted the position. 'I feel the committee will be annoyed with me, and quite rightly so,' Mason confessed. 'I should have left the thing alone. I'll apologize to them. Anyway, we can now elect George Martin as Admiral for life–or I think we should.' However, at the AGM Martin was unanimously elected Admiral for a further four years and in due course the present Sovereign succeeded her father as the club's Patron.

In March 1939 Maclean Buckley was replaced as secretary by Alan Bird, but stayed on as treasurer. He was also appointed technical secretary as Bird did not have the required knowledge. Bird's appointment spurred the new vice commodore, C.F. King, to announce that it was time to take stock of the club's position and that if its rapid development was to continue individual members of the committee must take on more responsibility. Instead, discretion was given to an inner group which became known as the flag officers' committee.

The threat of war was already casting a long shadow. *Heligoland was now a fortified area so, at the request of the Germans, the finish was at Weser; and the Maas Race was replaced by one from Harwich to the Solent. Some committee members thought the Weser Race should be cancelled as they believed the local Harwich population might create incidents when the German entries arrived there. Feelings amongst the committee ran high and one member said he would not race if it was held. But held it was and was won by *Helgoland*, one of the nine German entries.

By 5th August, when the Fastnet started, it must have been obvious that war was inevitable. However, this did not prevent the Germans entering *Roland von Bremen*, which had competed in the 1937 race, and two new Kriegsmarine entries, *Walkure* and the 60ft LWL yawl *Nordwind*. There were no American entries, but the Dutch were represented by a new de Vries Lentsch bermudan cutter, *Olivier van Noort*, owned by Albert Goudriaan, and by the 1937 winner, *Zeearend*, and the French by Georges *Baldenweck's 40ft LWL *Aile Noire*.

The entries were divided into three divisions which the *Royal Artillery Journal* described in terms its predominently horse-minded readers would understand: Open Division: steeple chasers; A Division: genuine hunters; B Division: cobs. For those unacquainted with equestrian terminology, cobs meant that B

courtesy Frances Macdonald

Annual RORC dinner at the Cafe Royal, December 1937 with Michael Mason presiding at the top table. The group nearest the camera are the Hunt family who raced *Spica*. D.N.B. Hunt also skippered *Ilex* in many races during the 1930s. Kathleen Hunt was the club's assistant secretary during the late 1930s.

1 Kathleen Hunt   2 Mrs E.W.F. Hunt   3 J.T. Hunt   4 Mrs J.T. Hunt   5 E.W.F. 'Bunch' Hunt

Division was for the real old hookers of the type that had taken part in the first race–clumbungies they were called by some of the yachting press.

A Division's five entries included *Griffin* which was sailed by George Martin. Of the British yachts in the Open Division, three were new designs from Robert Clark: the 42ft LWL yawl *Lara*, built for the Lloyd's underwriter, Kenneth Poland; the 50ft LWL sloop, *Benbow*, built for Ted Gore-Lloyd, who was to be the club's vice commodore from 1947 to 1950; and that year's winner of the Dinard Race, *Mary Bower*, a near sistership of *Ortac*.

Other new entries included *Golden Dragon*, owned and designed by H.S. *Rouse, and Tom Ratsey's Fife-designed *Evenlode*, but it was the tried and tested modern designs–*Bloodhound*, *Zeearend*, *Roland von Bremen*, and *Latifa*–which carried away the prizes, *Bloodhound* winning on corrected time from *Zeearend*, with *Roland von Bremen* third, and *Latifa* fourth, while *Nordwind* broke the course record held since 1926 by *Hallowe'en*. At the after-race dinner *Roland von Bremen*'s skipper made a speech about how the Germans intended to win the 1941 Fastnet. No one present was left in any doubt what he was alluding to, and when the German crews gave the Nazi salute as *Nordwind*'s skipper was handed his trophies they were roundly booed.

The inaugural Plymouth-La Rochelle Race proved to be the last club event for six years, and *Bloodhound*, crewed by Rod Stephens and Ducky Endt, trounced the rest of the fleet. Both men indulged in their favourite tipple during the race and at the dinner that followed it Isaac Bell stood up and said solemnly that in all good conscience he was not able to sign the race declaration. Consternation! He couldn't do so, he said, because during the race he had used not one engine but two–pause for effect–one of which was powered by milk and the other by gin!

Loomis, who had crewed aboard Michael Mason's *Latifa* in the Fastnet, detected a trend in ocean racing which he did not like. There was, he wrote in *Yachting World*, too much organising. 'You had short races for short boats, long races for long boats, narrow races for narrow boats, all of them ordered by a central authority [was he referring to the RORC by any chance?] which seemed to me to be on the fringe of becoming domineering, autocratic, and egoistic.' This tendency, coupled with super-refinement of material and technique would result in ocean racing blowing up 'with a loud bang and return us all to leisurely, non-competitive cruising.'

But his strictures, which were published in June 1940, must have fallen on deaf ears as by then the only loud bangs club members could hear were the infinitely more lethal ones of high explosive bombs and shells.

Chapter Five

THE RORC AT WAR

WHEN WAR broke out on 3rd September 1939 the secretary left to join his regiment and the following week the general committee met to interview E.W.R. ('Pete') *Peterson for the post. Peterson had joined the previous year and had offered to fill Bird's place while hostilities lasted. His offer was accepted unanimously and with gratitude.

At the end of 1939, during the annual dinner at the Café Royal, which traditionally followed the AGM, Michael Mason, now a lieutenant RNVR, announced to the 144 people present that the club would be kept open; that the annual dinner would continue to be held; that the annual subscription would be reduced to one guinea; that the position of vice commodore, vacated by C.F. King, would be left unfilled; and that the remaining flag officers and the committee would remain in office until peace returned.

In a gesture which showed that, even in the extreme circumstances of war the club was determined to retain and nurture its international connections, the committee decided that the membership of foreigners, 'particularly *Germans', who could not pay their subscriptions while hostilities lasted, should not lapse and that, for the duration of the war, the members of certain other yacht clubs should be granted honorary membership–though they were not given the facility of cashing cheques in the club! Later, this invitation was extended to the members of certain yacht clubs abroad who were serving in the British forces in Britain. Temporary membership was also granted to serving naval officers of all Allied nations stationed in the country.

After Dunkirk the CCA awarded its coveted Blue Water Medal to all British yachtsmen who had taken part in the evacuation. Three representative British clubs, the Royal Cruising Club, the Royal Ocean Racing Club, and the Little Ship Club, were chosen to receive the medal, and the RCC, as the counterpart of the CCA, became its permanent custodian. Hugh Tetley, a member since 1926, who had chaired the club's committee meetings during 1939, and continued to do so for much of the war, represented the RORC at the presentation of the medal by the American Naval Attaché at Lincoln's Inn.

During the early months of the war, the club, in collaboration with its French equivalent, UNC, had helped to raise funds on behalf of dependants of the French Navy. After Dunkirk and the Fall of France in June 1940, the fund was enlarged to become the 'Allied Navies War Comforts Fund' for the men serving in the Dutch, Norwegian, Polish, Belgian, and Free French Navies, and appeals for donations to it were sent to yacht clubs and the yachting press.

'These men are "Orphans of the Storm"', Peterson wrote in *Yachting Monthly* in November 1940, 'cut off from their friends, with no one to take any personal interest in them...It is felt that this fund to help Allied seamen will make a special appeal to yachtsmen, so many of whom have enjoyed the hospitality of Norwegian, Dutch, French, Belgian and Polish waters.'

From the funds the appeal raised the club had 200,000 cigarettes manufactured and distributed to Allied naval personnel. On the packets were printed the club seahorse, the flags of six Allied nations (UK, France, Netherlands, Norway, Poland and Greece) whose navies were fighting alongside the Royal Navy, and messages of good wishes in the languages spoken by the recipients.

On 1st October 1940 the club's flag officers and committee held an 'At Home' party for representative officers of the various Allied navies, together with the officers of those yacht clubs to whom the RORC had already extended honorary membership and the hospitality of its clubhouse. It nearly proved to be a wake for on the night of 15th November 1940 the building received a direct hit from a bomb cutting the house in two and demolishing the staircase and one end of the club room. It killed the new steward, though his wife and the house-maid survived after being trapped in the rubble.

The club's records and trophies as well as some furniture, including the round table which is in the dining room of the present club house, were salvaged by Peterson and Ted Gore-Lloyd. They also rescued much of the contents of the wine cellar and carried them discreetly away on a blanket-covered stretcher. Onlookers lifted their hats respectfully as the two men manoeuvred the 'body' out of the ruins. Afterwards Peterson sent a telegram to the commodore: 'Clubhouse bombed. Steward killed. Wine saved.'

The destruction of the clubhouse brought a lament from one of the yachting journals. 'No longer can its members and friends foregather in that pleasant first floor room in Pall Mall Place, like an oasis in a desert of streets, and mundane things, there to forget wars and rumours of wars in sane talk about ships and sails; the next Fastnet; the owner of *Ortac*'s venture in design; new rules, and the like. The RORC shook the yachting community by its innovations. Its rule evolved a new type of vessel; but its club-house was as individual as its method of handicapping, though in a different sense. It was an old house in the heart of clubland, but the RORC had an atmosphere completely different from any other club.'

Hopefully, the writer concluded, the same atmosphere would be recaptured in the new premises then being actively sought. It was.

The loss of the clubhouse did not prevent 80 members turning up for annual dinner at the Café Royal on 21st December. As all three flag officers were absent on active service the dinner was chaired by Tom Thornycroft. It was the first of several annual ones at which distinguished naval officers were entertained. On this occasion it included the Second Sea Lord, Admiral Sir Charles Little—whose speech took place while bombs were exploding all around the restaurant—and the admirals commanding the Dutch, Free French, and Polish naval forces.

The first mention of the present clubhouse at *20 St James's Place appeared in the committee minutes of February 1941 when consideration was given to the offer of the Royal Thames, which had already extended its hospitality to RORC members, to set a room aside for them. After much debate, it was decided to decline the Thames' offer; and though St James's Place was thought too expensive, it was agreed that negotiations should be continued while looking elsewhere, though any possible premises should be 'no further west than the "In and Out"[1] club'. The pros and cons of finding suitable premises were argued endlessly. Those opposing such a move warned that any new clubhouse would also be bombed—and sure enough in April 1941 St James's Place was hit by an incendiary bomb.

The search for new premises was spurred on by a letter from the Royal Thames in June 1941 which stated that in future it would not be able to offer free hospitality for more than a month to the members of any club who had been bombed out of their premises, but that temporary membership was available for one guinea per month. An extension to the end of August was negotiated after which members had to make do with something called the Goat Club.

However, when the agents for St James's Place realised they could put the habitable part of the building into tenantable repair, and recoup the expenses against war damage, they agreed to more reasonable terms. They redecorated and otherwise made habitable the undamaged part of the house, and granted the club a lease at an initial rent of £150pa. It was to commence on 25th December 1941 and to extend for the duration of the war on a yearly basis, and for two years after the cessation of hostilities.

1 the Naval and Military Club, 94 Piccadilly

courtesy Mrs Molly Hewlett

Barraclough, who reached the rank of Commodore during the war, with his wife outside Buckingham Palace in 1946 after receiving the CBE

At the time of the agreement the house was still a sorry sight as part of the top floor was burnt out and a tarpaulin covered the remains of the roof. However, the rest was made comfortable. The curtains and pelmets were bought from the previous incumbent for £30, and members helped to scrounge furniture from various sources. One, Captain E.M.C. Barraclough RN, borrowed six bunks and mattresses from the General Steam Navigation Company which had been taken out of some of the company's ships when they were converted to minelayers. They were erected in cubicles in one of the two bed-rooms and members using them were charged 5s. a night. The other 'a small private bedroom' cost 7s.6d a night.

Another acquisition was the painting by the nineteenth century artist, Edward William Cooke, of the Dogana, the Customs House of Venice, which now hangs above the fireplace at 20 St James's Place. As related to Nick Greville by Peterson it was acquired in a most unusual way. The same stick of firebombs which damaged No.20 had destroyed the house next door, No.21. Peterson and Ted Gore-Lloyd, who had first found No.20 for the RORC, went to view the damage. They found firemen stacking furniture and furnishings taken from both houses, most of it ruined by smoke and water. The firemen, when asked what they were going to do, said they were going to gut No.21 and burn the heap of furniture.

Was No.20 salvageable?

'Oh, yes, if a roof were put on it.'

Peterson and Gore-Lloyd then spotted the painting amongst the condemned pile and one of them picked it up and put it inside the front door of No.20. After the clubhouse had been given its tarpaulin roof and had been cleaned up by members the painting was hung on the staircase, and later over the fireplace. After the war the owner came to view her old house. Asked if she wanted the painting back, she said she did, but then changed her mind. 'No, it has been here for some time and you should keep it.'

The news that the club had new premises was cheered to the echo when it was announced by Michael Mason at the annual dinner in December 1941, as was a stirring speech by the Russian Naval Attaché even though not a word of it was understood.

Equipping and furnishing the new premises cost £800–an appeal for £500 of this was sent to members–and before the year's end a cook and a steward, Owen Hinton, had been engaged as well as a housekeeper, Helen *Cattenach, and three cleaning staff. It was a large commitment, especially in wartime, and was, as Phillips-Birt rightly commented, an act of faith by the committee and one which has been of permanent benefit to all members who followed them.

The first committee meeting, to draw up the house rules, was held at the new clubhouse on 25th February 1942. The bar rules shed light on the drinking restrictions imposed on members. No doubles were to be served; ordinary gin (ie gin other than Plymouth or Hollands) was only to be used for cocktails or with Vermouth, etc.; *The Rule of Four* was to be strictly observed, that is members could not order a round of more than four drinks at any one time; and bottles could not be purchased to take away and could only be served at mealtimes.

'Pete' Peterson was the club's secretary throughout the war and became rear commodore after it. He is seen here raising his rear commodore's pennant aboard *Latifa* in 1946

The wartime years were, for Peterson, a constant struggle to obtain food and alcohol, and much of his time must have been consumed in trying to find adequate amounts of them. For example, in November 1941 his request for cider from a West Country firm of brewers for the new premises was politely but firmly turned down–'Unfortunately the apple crop this season was practically a failure and our stocks are almost depleted'–and in September 1942 he asked a Mr Freeman for help in acquiring a further supply of Plymouth gin. 'We have extended honorary membership to the Royal Naval Sailing Association and to officers of the Allied navies,' Peterson explained. 'You will realise how important it is to us, therefore, to be able to produce Plymouth[1] at all times.'

The same month Peterson wrote asking a fellow lawyer if his Inn had any wine to spare and in October he contacted the brewery which supplied the club with beer asking for an increase from two firkins to four. 'I realise that the times are extremely difficult but this club has a very special character,' he wrote by way of mitigation, adding that there was no doubt that the members preferred draught beer to the bottled variety.

[1] this was slightly disingenuous of Peterson as the RNSA had only been given use of the club premises if they could produce their own quota of Plymouth Gin!

Food was equally hard to get and in May 1943 he was trying to obtain a supply of salmon and game from a supplier in Scotland. 'We do about thirty lunches a day and a dozen dinners and, as you can imagine, supplies are very difficult. I should like to get hold of about 14lbs of salmon a week; and, if I could get grouse or other game, could take five brace when the time comes. Can you help me?'

In June he was asking Owen Aisher (Sir Owen from 1981), a future admiral of the club, if he could let the club have any soft fruit for bottling. Also, 'I understand that we can consume about 56lbs of apples a week and if we could have, say, a cwt a fortnight during the Autumn and Winter we should like it.'

Then in July he was admonishing the Moray Firth Fishing Company: 'This is the second week in which no kippers have arrived. Will you kindly inform me whether you intend to supply kippers or not.'

The Company replied, regretting none was available. From what Martin said in a letter from Scotland–where, as a lt-commander RNVR, he was running a highly successful Deep-Sea Rescue Tug Service at Campbeltown–it seemed they rarely arrived at their destination anyway, at least not in an edible condition. 'I sent you and my brother each a box last year,' he wrote West, 'yours was stolen and my brother's were so long on the journey that he had to bury them unopened.'

In the early days of the war, when they were available, kippers were a tradeable commodity. During the season he would get five boxes from Buckie, Peterson wrote Martin in November 1943, use one box in the club, sell two boxes to individuals, and sell the rest to members 'at so much a pair, and very welcome they were.'

Apart from a shortage of food and drink, there were problems with the American soldiers who occupied the Stafford Hotel close to the club. In November 1942 a GI drove into the railings around the house; and in July 1943 Peterson wrote plaintively to the officer commanding US Army troops in London asking if the 'marching of American soldiers up and down St James's Place, and the shouting of orders to them, for periods of an hour and upwards several days in the week could be carried out at a further distance than at present; for instance, in Green Park. We should be grateful also if the soldiers who are billeted in the Stafford Hotel could be reminded that there are other people living in the vicinity who find the practice of shouting from the street to the upper windows of the Stafford Hotel, and vice versa, somewhat trying.'

The following month he felt obliged to write to the Superintendent at Savile Row police station asking if the police could do something to 'discourage the excessive number of young women who are attracted to St James's Place by the existence of the American Army billet. They hang about and are becoming rather a nuisance. An even more serious matter is the use made of this Place by a more professional type of woman.'

In June 1942 those members too old to join the armed forces were presented with an opportunity to help with the war effort, and many of them jumped at it. Admiral Sir Lionel Preston, who commanded the Small Vessels Pool which had done such prodigious work during the Dunkirk evacuation, asked for a list of yachtsmen who would be available in the event of emergency to man coastal vessels, and to provide what was known as runner crews to deliver small vessels around the coast. Several members, including Peterson, a future secretary, Alan Paul, and Owen Aisher volunteered.

Recruitment of these crews was often organised by Peterson, and the arrangements were made without fuss. 'Dear James,' he wrote James Bacon in September 1942, 'Can you help ship a harbour launch from Harwich to Chatham on Saturday, the 12th September? She is steam. The rest of the crew will consist of Tetley and Tom Thornycroft. I shall sign on as skipper as I am on the spot. You can be mate and navigator. Let me know as soon as you can.'

On 23rd July 1942 the club was officially opened by King Haakon of Norway whose son, Crown Prince Olaf, had accepted life honorary membership the previous February. The King performed the ceremony before a crowd of distinguished guests which included A.V. Alexander, the First Lord of the Admiralty, Admiral of the Fleet Sir Roger Keyes, and the club's admiral, George Martin. After the speeches, in appreciation of naval officers from the occupied countries being offered honorary membership of the club, the representative of the Royal Netherlands Navy presented the club with a set of six tankards engraved with the Dutch naval crown.

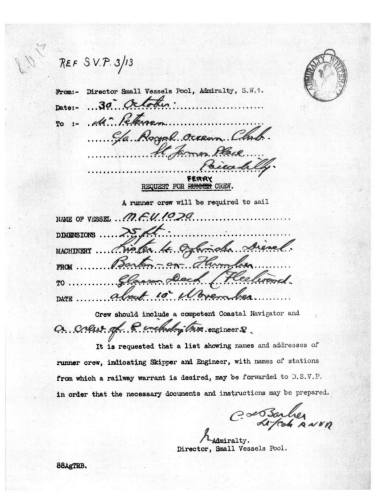

Form sent by the Admiralty requesting volunteers for ferry crew

Martin, especially, was delighted by the new premises. 'There is a sort of distinction in the house which I have seen in only one other club–the Arts Club in Dover Street,' he wrote to Peterson afterwards, and then added prophetically: 'If anything could be done to ensure the future of the club I believe that the move into our new quarters will be more effective than anything else.'

In November 1942 Martin proposed that King Haakon take his place as admiral, but the committee's unanimous opinion was that Martin should not retire. Instead, the Norwegian monarch was asked to accept life honorary membership, which he duly did. Martin announced this at the annual dinner in December 1942, held that year at Grosvenor House. When Sir Lionel Preston proposed the toast to the club he spoke of the good work being done by older members as runner crews, and said that he believed the club had evolved a new rule, where the age of the crew varied in inverse ratio to the length of their boat!

Close relations with the CCA were maintained during the war years when in the spring of 1943 a resolution was passed by the Americans that, while the war lasted, honorary membership would be extended to all RORC members visiting the United States. The club promptly reciprocated by inviting CCA members to use the club house whenever they were in London.

This portrait of King Haakon VII of Norway has been signed by him and was almost certainly presented to the club when he opened its present premises in July 1942

In September 1943 Lt-Colonel Tom Trevor, one of the war's most distinguished Commando leaders and a member since 1939, suggested that the club promote a competition for the design of an ocean racing yacht among British Prisoners-of-War, and offered to support such a competition with a donation of £20 provided the total prize money amounted to £100. The committee supported this proposal and the secretary was instructed to draft conditions for the *competition and to settle details with the British Red Cross and the St John's Prisoner-of-War Department.

In the autumn plans began to be made for the most ambitious annual dinner yet with Peterson writing to Hunloke and Lord Iveagh to try and obtain 40 brace of pheasant which, along with other game, was free of the strict food regulations then in force, though the price of it was controlled.

The new First Sea Lord, Admiral of the Fleet Sir Andrew Cunningham, was the guest of honour at the dinner which was again held at Grosvenor House and attended by 200 members and their guests. Martin, who had been flanked on either side by two admirals of the fleet, wrote afterwards that it had been a great success. He had told Cunningham all about the Fastnet Race 'and the sort of seamanship the members learn, and I think he was rather impressed, and revised his known opinion that yachting is all chromium plate, plate glass windows and stewards.'

Cunningham, in replying to Martin's toast of the Royal Navy, said he thought the Navy owed a debt of gratitude to the RORC both for the way in which the club had endeavoured to promote international understanding, and for the valuable training of handling small ships which it had given to so many young men. He also paid a tribute to the work of the runner crews, mentioning that members of the club had either formed part of or had supplied the whole crew in over 200 separate deliveries, sometimes to places as far distant as the Faroes and the Mediterranean[1].

At an informal ceremony during a house dinner in May 1944, with Prince Olaf of Norway present, Lt C. Vernon Porter presented a parchment scroll to the club on behalf of the CCA which was received by the chairman of the committee, Hugh Tetley. The scroll recorded the fact that the CCA had unanimously elected the present and all future commodores of the RORC to permanent honorary membership of the American club. The club reciprocated in November 1944 when Peterson asked Ralph Hawkes, who was going to the United States, to present to the CCA an illuminated resolution of the committee making the CCA commodore an ex-officio honorary member.

When it became obvious that the war could not last much longer, the committee began to prepare for the resumption of racing. In November 1944 some of the club's rules were *rewritten; and a questionnaire was posted to members and to other yachtsmen about their postwar plans for racing. Then in March 1945 it was announced there would be no alteration to the existing rating rule and time scale without 18 months' notice being given before the start of the racing season in which any alteration was to take effect.

On 26th April 1945, at a meeting held at the club, the Association of Service Yacht Clubs (ASYC) was formed, the aim of which was to foster the sport of yachting in all three services and to act as the representative and co-ordinating body for all service yacht clubs. The same month the Gunner representative

1 some members also helped to sail fleet minesweepers from the USA

on the club's committee, Colonel Maurice Hope, wondered what affect the development of modern electrical aids to navigation such as radar would have on the sport. He thought they should be banned; F.B.R. Brown, one of the club's founder members and a talented amateur designer, disagreed. The subject evoked such interest that at the end of the year there was an after-dinner debate about it, the idea being to give the committee a lead when the time came to formulate a rule about electronic aids. Opinion was sharply divided but there was general approval to use any device which helped towards safety at sea, but that all others should be banned. It was a subject which continued to exercise the committee for several decades.

~

It is a remarkable fact that by the end of 1943, the club, out of a total of about 600 members, had 200 serving in the Navy, 160 in the Army and RAF, and 30 or 40 working as runner crews. One or two, like Lt-General Viscount Gort, who led the British Expeditionary Force to France in September 1939, were already well known military figures and after the war a handful of others were thrust into the limelight when their war experiences were made known. For example, the distinguished lawyer, Ewen Montagu, who joined the club in 1937 before serving in naval intelligence, became a best-selling author when his book, *The Man Who Never Was*, was published and subsequently filmed. Major Millis Jefferis, a member since 1938, and Major 'Blondie' Hasler, Royal Marines, who joined in 1939, were two others whose exploits were made public. Jefferis ran a highly secret outfit, MD1. This developed experimental weapons such as the limpet mine and the sticky bomb, and its story was later told in a book called *Winston Churchill's Toyshop*. Hasler, of course, found fame as the leader of *The Cockleshell Heroes*[1], the party of Marine canoeists he led to raid German shipping near Bordeaux, whose story was published under that title and later filmed.

Among those who served their country behind the front line were a number who were able to make a substantial contribution solely because of their technical expertise. Uffa Fox designed air-dropped lifeboats; Camper & Nicholson, represented on the club's list by Charles E. Nicholson, his son, John Nicholson, and his nephew, Charles A. Nicholson, did sterling work developing, building, and repairing small craft for the Navy; Robert Clark worked for the Admiralty on small boat design; Bobby *Somerset served with Vospers Ltd, producing MTBs and other fast surface craft; Iorys Hughes helped

RM Museum, Eastney

Major 'Blondie' Hasler who led the daring canoe raid on German shipping on the Gironde. After the war he made a name for himself racing his 30sq.metre *Tre Sang*

1 Hasler's biographer (see *Blondie* by Ewen Southby-Tailyour) records that Hasler, who wrote the operational orders for the raid in the clubhouse, disliked the title and vainly tried to have it altered

to design the Mulberry harbours that made the Normandy landings possible; and Laurent Giles, whose firm was disbanded during the war, helped develop canoes for the Special Boat Sections–including a motorised submersible version developed by Hasler which was nicknamed the *Sleeping Beauty*–and high speed dispatch vessels for the British Secret Intelligence Service (SIS) which were built to look like French or Spanish fishing vessels. He also worked for the Royal Corps of Naval Constructors–he called it 'Obstructors'–where he designed the HDML 45ft picket boat and that maid-of-all-work the MFV (Motor Fishing Vessel).

In America Sparkman & Stephens, with Olin Stephens at the helm, grew to 50-60 people. It designed small naval vessels, submarine chasers, a midget submarine and a giant tanker, and a floating bridge for the US Army. Rod Stephens was responsible for the design of the famous amphibious truck called a DUKW. He designed it in 30 days and spent the rest of the war improving it and instructing the military in its use. By 1945 25,000 had been built and such was their success that Rod was awarded the Medal of Freedom, one of America's highest civilian awards.

Of particular interest, too, was the wartime work of RORC members who were well suited to clandestine operations because of their navigational skills, and their knowledge of the sea and the French coastline. One of these was C.F. Mason, known to his friends as 'Cutty'. Mason's talents were sufficiently diverse for him to have composed a number of songs, and written an opera and several books including one on ocean racing (*Deep-Sea Racing*). During the war his skill as a seaman was put to good use in the Small Vessels Pool which included an epic voyage to Iceland in a Watson lifeboat which was needed there by the Royal Air Force for rescuing downed air crews. But his 'wonderful knowledge of the coasts and harbours of Europe and an uncanny skill in pilotage' also led him to be part of a clandestine submarine operation to capture a French fishing trawler from Guilvinec which he then sailed to Newlyn, no doubt for the use of the SIS, or the Special Operations Executive (SOE) which specialised in sabotage and subversion. He crewed aboard *Erivale* from 1947 to 1952, before joining Selwyn Slater's *Uomie*. He died aboard her, aged 63, during the 1956 North Sea Race.

Because of his naval background, and his knowledge of Brittany and its fishing industry, the owner of *Maitenes II*, W.B. Luard, also joined the secret services. He started as an unpaid volunteer with the Operations Section of SIS which was responsible for mounting clandestine cross-channel operations in French fishing boats which had escaped to England after the Fall of France. Then in January 1941 he was appointed to an RAF Station in Cornwall as its liaison officer where

W.B. Luard who before the war owned *Maitenes II*. He also navigated *Trenchemer* for Walter Bell

he 'rendered outstanding service' in helping British intelligence. He also made valuable contributions to air-sea rescue operations by designing the K-dinghy sailing gear, an aircraft catamaran dinghy, and compiling RAF dinghy drift tables.

Brooks Richards (Sir Brooks from 1976), who joined the club in 1937, also used his design and sailing skills in irregular warfare. He began designing boats when, aged 16, he worked with Luard on the construction of several in Cornish yards. His first, *Natanis*, was built for Luard himself. The next, a 35ft LWL design called *Wyndfall*, he designed for his father. Then came *Windstar*, designed for Lt-Colonel Philip Ionides and later owned by Sir Philip Hunloke[1].

Photographs of Lt Brooks Richards RNVR dressed as a Breton fisherman aboard a sardine pinnace, P11, in September 1942. They were taken during a SIS clandestine operation to try to land in occupied France two of de Gaulle's most distinguished agents, Remy and Michel Pichard

courtesy Sir Brooks Richards

1 Hunloke took the club's present Patron sailing in *Windstar* but, as Richards commented, the young princess 'grew up to prefer horses'

Richards' next project, again for Luard, was called *Windstorm* and in 1939 he designed the Class I ocean racer, *Astrape*, for his father, one of the last boats launched by the Berthon Boat Company at Lymington before war broke out. In the summer of 1941, Richards, as a sub-lieutenant RNVR, transferred to SOE and was posted to a base on the Helford River, next door to Claud Worth's house. There he served as second-in-command to Gerry Holdsworth, a member from 1946, aboard a flotilla of early clandestine craft assembled by SOE to ferry its agents to and from occupied France. At different times, both Richards and another amateur designer, Nigel Warington Smyth, who joined the RORC in 1947, also designed and tested small surf boats and dories for taking agents and supplies ashore.

In 1942 F.B.R. Brown visited Helford, and he and Richards and Holdsworth, as an exercise, sailed round the Fastnet Rock in one of SOE's fishing boats 'to see whether it was still there', making Brown and Richards one of the few members to have visited the famous landmark during the war years.

However, they were not the only ones to do so as in 1943 several yachts belonging to the Irish Cruising Club held a race around the Rock. Peterson was a guest aboard the commodore's yacht, and several other RORC members also apparently took part. A right royal row developed about this when 'The Walrus' –alias Group Captain Haylock–criticised the ICC in his *Yachting World* column. 'That is the advantage of being neutral,' he wrote, 'and, without lifting a finger to fight against the common enemy, of being protected by the strong arm of the Royal Navy.'

Unfortunately for 'The Walrus', he had picked a quarrel with the wrong people as many ICC members were retired officers with distinguished records, one of whom was a famous commodore of convoys, and nearly all those taking part in the race had relatives fighting on the Allied side. Peterson wrote indignantly to *Yachting World* calling the comments 'ill timed and ill tempered', and Haylock was obliged to retract and apologise.

Another member who joined SOE, and who subsequently found his sailing skills very pertinent to his predicament, was Brian Passmore[1]. Before the war he had shared the 11-ton Laurent Giles designed sloop, *Prelude*, with three other members, all Army officers–Major Millis Jefferis, Captain Jim Gavin, and Captain W.A. Purser–who had built her themselves in an empty stable on the edge of Aldershot parade ground. She was the forerunner of the modern offshore racing light displacement boats and she won the club's Class III points championship in 1938, and went on winning races right through into the mid-1950s.

When war began Passmore joined the RNVR and in 1941 he volunteered to work for SOE's Far East arm based in Singapore. When Singapore fell in

1 after he died in 1985 his many sailing friends donated a perpetual trophy, the Passmore Bowl

courtesy Public Record Office

The 60ft prahau *Siderhana Johannis* in which Lt Brian Passmore RNVR escaped from Sumatra in 1942. He took the photograph himself

February 1942 he escaped by boat to Sumatra and on 9th March 1942 set sail from Padang with 17 others in a dilapidated 60ft prahau, ballasted with shingle, with the object of reaching Ceylon. During this epic 1,600-mile voyage the crew had to face the attentions of Japanese aircraft and monsoon conditions which the official report on the voyage said the famous tea clippers of the last century would not have braved.

The prahau could not have been easy to handle for she was ketch rigged with such an enormous main boom that the mainsail overlapped the mizzen. This obliged the crew to haul the boom over the mizzen whenever they wanted to go about, not an easy manoeuvre at the best of times. Water and food were in short supply and they had no luck fishing.

Eventually, after 36 days at sea, the prahau was spotted off the coast of Ceylon by a friendly cargo ship. This took the prahau's crew aboard, ending a voyage which the official report said 'must rank as pretty well unique in the annals of sailing.'

But perhaps the most remarkable voyage, or series of voyages, were the clandestine missions sailed by the commodore, Michael Mason. Mason wrote that people told him that he designed the whole war to suit his idea of fun. Hostilities certainly seemed to suit his temperament.

'I have been a big-game hunter for very many years,' he wrote, 'and the finest big-game animal I know is a capable enemy with a gun in his hand.'

Mason's war began earlier than most people's. In 1937 he took part in the club's Heligoland Race in *Latifa*, and then entered, and won, a German race round Heligoland, the only foreign boat to participate. After the race he and another member, Jock Bodilly, walked round the island taking detailed notes of all the fortifications which they sent to the Admiralty.

This act of espionage[1] started a series of events which led to Mason being asked by the Director of Naval Intelligence to sail *Latifa* around the southern and western coast of Ireland to chart likely places where German U-boats and their supply ships could safely take refuge. Mason started out in April 1939. Besides the paid hands he had aboard two other club members, Gerald Garrard and Cyril Holland-Martin, a cousin of George Martin. Starting at Queenstown and going as far as Loch Foyle, he explored every little indentation in the coast. His accomplishments as a polyglot included a smattering of Gaelic. This was useful in gaining the confidence of the local people who were sufficiently innocent of the outside world to think his White Ensign–Mason was an RYS member–was the Guinness house-flag.

The voyage took three months. At the end of it Mason sent a detailed report to the Admiralty and then took part in the last prewar Fastnet Race. After the race Mason was summoned to meet the C-in-C Western Approaches, Admiral Sir Martin Dunbar-Nasmith, who asked him to withdraw from the La Rochelle Race and return to the Irish coast.

This time Mason chose to go in a 350-ton fishing trawler as suitable camouflage for his activities of searching for U-boats and their mother ships. If he found any he was to report their presence by radio which was hidden in the fish-hold and manned by a naval signals rating. He enlisted the trawler's skipper and crew, and as his second-in-command took aboard Alfred Rosling, the club's vice commodore from 1935-38.

Shortly before they left war was declared and Mason and Rosling were commissioned by Dunbar-Nasmith as lieutenants RNVR. Mason was forever grateful to the admiral as it saved him from the usual medical examination which he would not have passed (he had a gammy leg).

Besides going aboard every merchantmen they came across to see if they were disguised U-boat supply ships, Mason and Rosling watched for U-boats at night, their loitering places including the turning point of the club's most famous race. 'Some places,' Mason wrote, 'especially off the mouth of Kenmare River and the Fastnet Rock, I felt were sort of focal points for shipping and that we might actually see submarines on the surface at night. We used to lie hove-to without a light showing; just watching.'

1 Maurice Hope, a regular Royal Artillery officer who crewed in the Heligoland Race in *Rose*, was also involved in some extra-curricular spying. He and Mason probably provided the first confirmation that Heligoland had been refortified following its disarmament in 1919

The Spyship *Latifa*

Latifa was surely the only club yacht ever to be employed as a spyship. In the spring of 1939 the Admiralty ordered Michael Mason, seen here at *Latifa*'s helm after the war, to investigate the inlets of Southern Ireland as likely boltholes for German U-boats and their supply ships. Behind Mason are Major Ian Major RM (left) and Lt-Cdr Ainsley Forsyth, both club members after the war

all photos courtesy David Mason

Some of the photographs Mason took to record the coastline he explored

During a subsequent voyage Mason was arrested at Wicklow as a spy—which he was, except that the Irish police had confused him with a German agent they were looking for. He languished for a week in Arbour Hill prison before being released.

This ended any further escapades for Mason in Ireland but he was then sent on a sabotage mission to try and block the Danube before spending the remainder of the war in more normal pursuits such as training Royal Marine instructors in unarmed combat and then commanding various landing-craft flotillas. When he died in 1982 his obituarist in *The Times* wrote of his 'combination of seamanship, linguistic ability, physical and mental stamina, and accuracy with his revolver.'

The 1945 edition of the club handbook lists 33 members of the club who had died on active service, a very high proportion of the total membership.

~

At a meeting on 23rd May 1945 the following resolution was proposed by the committee's chairman, Hugh Tetley, and carried unanimously: 'The Flag Officers and Committee of the Royal Ocean Racing Club record their deep regret and sense of great loss at the death on Friday, 27th April, of Commander E.G. Martin OBE RNVR, Admiral of the Club. He established ocean racing in this country on a firm basis, and the club will always remain grateful to him for the inestimable services rendered by him.'

Martin had been posted to Campbeltown in September 1940, but the climate did not agree with him and he was plagued by rheumatism and bronchitis, and in the autumn of 1943 he asked to be relieved. But the Admiralty obviously could not spare him and he was forced to soldier on. During the war years he kept up his correspondence with Herbert West. Some of his letters written in 1943 and 1944 have survived, and while much of what he wrote concerns the war and his health he does also hark back to the days of peace as well as pondering on the future of ocean racing.

In May 1943 he wrote to West that he had been giving a good deal of thought to the future of the club. 'We shall have to reorganise things, I think, and I am probably the one to start the ball rolling.' He thought the sport had become too expensive so that 'the men who could only race in a very modest way could not win any of the best prizes. This must be changed if I can bring it about.'

He wanted to start a small RORC class for yachts of about six tons which would be crewed over suitable courses without paid hands; and proposed that the most important prizes such as the Fastnet Cup should go to the winner in the division in which most boats crossed the finishing line. 'There will be an outcry from the rich men in the club, but I shall rather enjoy that.'

These ideas were contained in a *Yachting World* article he wrote in November 1943 which also discussed lowering the costs of sails by altering the YRA rule for sail measurement. He told West this might start a general stir, especially within the YRA. 'Some of the Council don't approve of me, as I resigned from it about fifteen years ago because I did not like its ways: tho' of course I didn't give that reason. But after resigning I devoted myself to the development of the RORC, which some of them tried to kill by ridicule in the Yachting Press–the secretary, B. Heckstall-Smith, Burton and one or two more. As you know, they failed and we succeeded, and this has not been forgotten. I am quite certain I am right in aiming at bringing o.racing within the reach of as many people, especially young men, as possible.' If the article did lead to change 'I shall feel that I have made my third and last real contribution to British yachting. Very few people know that it was I who got the dinghies made first into a YRA[1] National class–outlining the organisation when I was a member of the YRA Council–and this in turn became an "International 14-footer" and "National 12-footer class": there are now 800 or 900 boats in the two together!'

By 1944 Martin, troubled by the climate and an excessive work load, was having increasingly bad bouts of bronchitis. There is mention in his letters of his being allowed to come south but regrets, too, that he did not have a home to return to. Then, in the autumn, the Admiralty at last released him and he retired, almost certainly on medical grounds. One of his officers wrote: 'You will be sorely missed we know, and your successor will find your place difficult indeed to fill, as with the men who man the tugs, Campbeltown and Commander Martin were synonymous terms. We trust that your health will improve with retirement, and that you will spend many happy days with a different type of ship, your own *Griffin*.' It was not to be.

1 there is no mention of this in *Minute by Minute* by Gordon Fairley, the story of the RYA

Chapter Six

OCEAN RACING RESURRECTED

THE CLUB celebrated peace in Europe by electing Prince Bernhard of the Netherlands a life honorary member in July 1945. In August Peterson reported that the Dinard Yacht Club had agreed to the club holding the Dinard Race the following month. He also reported that the Cs-in-C Portsmouth and Plymouth were prepared to assist if it took place; and on 13th September 1945 eight yachts started from Cowes–five in the Large Class, three in the Small–all escorted by a destroyer to guide them through the *minefields, via a mark boat off Brixham, to their destination.

By the time they reached Brixham the wind had reached Force 7 and three of the entries, including Owen Aisher's *Yeoman*, the first of a very long line of distinguished racing yachts, retired. The others set off across the Channel, but two soon had to turn back. It must have been a tricky passage as all the French navigational lights had been destroyed.

Mary Bower–now owned by a non-member after her original owner, Colonel Bryson, had been killed in an air raid–won line honours and was also first on corrected time. 'Pete' Peterson and Iorys Hughes, sailing the Brooks Richards-designed yacht *Windstorm*, won the Coupe de Dinard for the Small Class despite having to spend an uncomfortable night hove-to off Alderney because the weather was so foul and the marks so uncertain. The crews received a warm welcome and receptions were held by the St Malo and Dinard Yacht Clubs.

In October 1945 Jim Smellie, who had been rear commodore since 1939, was elected vice commodore and 'Pete' Peterson rear commodore, and the composition of the committee was changed to include such stalwarts of postwar ocean racing as Owen Aisher and Myles Wyatt (Sir Myles from 1963). Colonel Evans, who had taken over from Maclean Buckley as treasurer in 1943, resigned and the former practice of combining this post with that of the secretary's

The Class III *Mindy*, 28ft, 3in. LWL, which F.B.R. Brown designed and co-owned with various members at different times. Launched in 1939, she won six flags out of seven starts that year and was awarded the Ortac Cup for gaining the largest number of points in the club's Small Class. In the immediate post-war period she maintained a phenomenal success record, winning the Forsyth Cup and Maas Cup twice, as she did the Ortac Cup in 1948 and 1950 for winning the class III championship

was again adopted. Mason remained the commodore and Heckstall-Smith the club's measurer, but it was decided not to nominate anyone as admiral 'as there was no one of sufficient eminence to fill it.'

At the same time a decision was made to stay at 20 St James's Place, if at all possible. An extension to the lease would be sought and a direct approach made to the current owners to see if it would be possible to buy the freehold.

By December 1945 Mason was back in the chair from his extraordinary war and in the New Year the first full programme of racing since 1939 was agreed. There were to be six fixtures, including a North Sea Race to the Hook of Holland which replaced the prewar Maas Race. The course for this race had to be referred to the Admiralty's Minesweeping Division and on its recommendation steel-hulled yachts were barred in case they attracted the attention of magnetic mines.

In March 1946 Peterson called a meeting of the club's flag officers 'to deal with a crisis which had arisen in its management' as no one had been found to replace him as secretary. Maclean Buckley wrote a minute on the subject which outlined clearly the difficulties of finding the right person.

'When the committee say that they want a secretary I imagine that the majority of them could not state with any exactness what they mean. They want somebody to run the club as somebody always has run the club from 1928 to 1946, but they have only a hazy idea of what is entailed and how the club has arrived from nowhere to where it is today...

'There has been only one take-over by a secretary–by Peterson in 1939–and then the Club was being put to bed, the clubhouse was tiny, and all racing had come to an end. It is true that the Club was made to sit up in bed and become extremely vigorous and launch out into all sorts of new directions, but that happened later [he must have been referring to moving into 20 St James's Place]. Today a take-over would have to be made at the most difficult time possible when the Club is setting out to re-open its racing activities and re-establish itself as the national authority on ocean racing.'

What was needed was a man of the calibre of a managing director who, though responsible to the committee, would have to guide it too, and would often have to make decisions without its aid. Was such a man available?

It seemed at first that Barraclough, who had recently returned from active duty in the Far East, would fill the post admirably, but then he was offered a civilian job with the Admiralty and had to withdraw his application. However, he was available until the autumn and was appointed hon. sailing secretary for the season to help Maclean Buckley who, rather reluctantly, had agreed to stand in as secretary until someone suitable could be found.

'I soon found that Dick Buckley was a very sick man,' *Barraclough wrote later, 'he was able to do the office work, and especially the organisation of the racing; a job at which he was very adept. But he was not fit enough to chase round the country starting and finishing races, so this job fell upon me.'

The management of *Griffin* which, along with £200 to fit her out, H.E. West[1] had generously given as a memorial to George Martin, was solved much more smoothly. The sub-committee appointed to deal with how she was to be

1 he was made a life honorary member in 1947 and died the following year

run received expert help from Brigadier Barry who had been involved in organising the Royal Artillery Yacht Club. He also undertook to keep an eye on *Griffin* at Cracknore where he had reserved a mooring for her, and at the next meeting offered to become the first Griffin secretary whose job it was to arrange the crews and see that competent members were put in charge of her.

From Sydney, where he was stationed, Illingworth had written to the club suggesting it should present a challenge trophy to the Cruising Yacht Club of Australia, which had become the organisers of the Sydney-Hobart Race, provided the event was held under RORC rules. Illingworth had been responsible for the first race in December 1945 and had won it in *Rani*, his 30ft LWL doubled-ended light displacement cutter. His suggestion was accepted and it was agreed to spend up to £30 on a bronze copy of the original seahorse carved by George Martin.

In May 1946 the technical sub-committee submitted its first postwar report which recommended some minor adjustments to the rule and that the bottom limit for the Channel Races and similar fixtures should be lowered to 23ft LWL. The measurement changes, to come into force in 1948, were approved but the decision about altering the LWL limits for races was held over until the autumn when it was agreed that from 1947 the classification of yachts taking part in RORC races should be by rating: Class I would be for yachts of 38ft and below 60ft rating, Class II for yachts of 27.5ft and below 38ft rating, and Class III for yachts of 19ft and below 27.5ft[1] rating. Minimum waterline lengths were abolished except for a lower limit of 24ft for Class III to avoid making an over-canvased dinghy or other freak eligible.

In July 1946 the committee was at last able to appoint a secretary when Ralph Swann, one of the war's first RNVR officers to reach the rank of Commander, accepted the post. Maclean Buckley remained treasurer as a temporary measure until Myles Wyatt took over from him in the autumn, and at the 1946 AGM he was elected the club's admiral. Mason remained commodore and Ted Gore-Lloyd became vice commodore as Smellie wished to retire. Money, as always, was a problem and subscriptions had to be raised to five guineas with a two-guinea entrance fee from 1st January 1947. However, the club could not afford a hall porter–who might have prevented the theft of overcoats during the New Year's Eve party–though the house committee did launch out in November 1946 and buy a Hoover.

Money was also a problem for many members, especially younger ones, and Peterson drew the attention of the committee to the expensive business of standing large rounds of drinks at the bar. The wartime *Rule of Four* must have still been in force as it was decided to display a notice in the bar drawing the attention of members to the rule.

1 From June 1949 a minimum LWL yacht was allowed to compete in the Fastnet provided she rated at 27.5ft

The weather was lousy in 1946. Before the start of the Plymouth-Dun Laoghaire Race Kees Bruynzeel's *Zeearend* was blown ashore in Plymouth Sound during a gale and badly damaged. Her crew were offered places among the other starters and Bruynzeel himself was given a berth on E.G. Greville's *Erivale*. The old adage about an ill wind certainly applied to *Erivale* that year for Nick Greville, who was racing aboard his father's boat, remembers that 'it was largely due to Bruynzeel's skill that we were able to win the race.'

Despite the poor weather, which caused an inordinate amount of windward work, there was an unexpectedly large turn-out of yachts for what was an ambitious programme of eight races. As an editorial in *Yachting World* commented, it showed 'the remarkable vigour with which ocean racing has been resumed.'

The inaugural North Sea Race proved particularly popular and drew seven entries for the Large Class and 12 for the Small. The course approved by the Admiralty took the yachts north to Smith's Knoll lightship, then south again to the Galloper lightship before crossing the North Sea to the Hook. It was made more complicated by a last-minute decision to substitute the Galloper for a nearby buoy designated GH2 'because of grandmotherly apprehensions,' by the Admiralty, 'about a hoard of sailing yachts careering about at the junction of two steamer lanes.'

Some of the entries took hours to find GH2 while others, including the winners of the two classes–*Maid of Malham*, now owned by Bridget Livingston, and G.D. Lock's *Brambling*–did not even bother to search for it, reporting afterwards that by their dead reckoning they had turned it correctly. After some anxious hours by those who had not sighted the buoy, the committee accepted their declarations because, as the race report stated, 'in any similar event, much depends on an implied and accepted element of sportsmanship', and then added that even the finishing times had been taken by the yachts themselves, as if to imply that this meant cheating was out of the question.

By the standards of what was to happen in later decades the report is a quaint, rather touchingly naive, document. But with eerie prescience it touches on many of the club's postwar problems–crowded shipping lanes, the non-sighting of a turning mark, the question of cheating, and boats taking their own finishing times–all these matters were later replayed in spades, though the minefields that lay ahead were only metaphorical ones.

As it happened the weather that year proved more dangerous than the minefields, for after the race Hugh Tetley's *Thalia* was engulfed in a fearsome thunderstorm while sailing down the Maas waterway. Among those aboard were Michael Mason, Alan Paul, and prospective member Gerry Holdsworth. While Mason was on deck 'a fat streak of blue electricity,' as Paul described it, 'flashed across the saloon', singeing Mason on the way. Mason survived, but the club apparently nearly lost its commodore for Paul wrote that after the thunderbolt had struck he was 'a gaunt, charred figure in his black oilskins.'

The North Sea Race was to become, for many years, one of the club's most popular fixtures, partly because it was always held over the Whitsun weekend, but mostly, one suspects, because of the generous hospitality of the Koninklijke Roei-En Zeilvereeniging 'De Maas', or Royal Maas Yacht Club as it was always known to members who raced there.

'Many Englishmen taste, for the first time, that strange drink beloved of the Dutch, Genever,' rhapsodised 'The Walrus' who joined the club in 1946, 'but a taste so easily acquired. Then there is the dinner in the clubhouse. What a dinner! A meeting of members of two great maritime nations. What an atmosphere of seamanlike sympathy!'

Much interest during the race had been focused on a 30sq. metre called *Tre Sang*. 'Perhaps the most interesting novelty for long distance racing,' the race report commented afterwards, calling her 'one of the two best 30s in this country. Her crew consisted of two only–Marine Commandos who took her round in fine style and she was amongst the earlier finishers.'

Tre Sang belonged to 'Blondie' Hasler who had bought her in the autumn of 1945 and had spent the winter converting her for ocean racing. The 30sq. metre class was a well-established one for racing around the buoys, but to have such a light displacement yacht take part in ocean races was something quite new, especially as her LWL measured only 27ft, 2in. With her long overhangs and low freeboard she rated very badly, but Uffa Fox, who had an eye for a boat if anyone did, had long extolled the sea-going qualities of the 30sq. metre and during 1946 Hasler proved him right. By the end of the season * *Tre Sang* had accumulated sufficient points to win the Small Class championship by a large margin and came a remarkable third, behind *Maid of Malham* and *Lara*, out of the whole fleet.

Early in 1946 Michael Mason had offered to lend *Latifa* to the club for that year's Bermuda Race. Enough money was raised, or so it was thought at the time. Iorys *Hughes was appointed her skipper, and he, Peterson, and a volunteer crew–the American press called them 'eight of England's most eligible bachelors'–sailed her across the Atlantic. Illingworth, who was still in Australia, agreed to join her as deckmaster. He hitched a lift in an American troop transport to San Francisco, and then flew to New York where *Latifa* had just arrived at Nevin's Yard on City Island for a badly needed refit. Nevin's did a good job on her but the bill, in Illingworth's words, was 'pretty horrifying', and Owen Aisher had to start an appeal to cover the deficit which amounted to £1,650 for the whole undertaking.

Latifa being loaded for her Transatlantic voyage to compete in the 1946 Bermuda Race

After her refit *Latifa* was floating down on her marks, so Illingworth stripped everything he could out of her. He even took out twelve crates of whisky and wine which he dispatched to Bermuda to await *Latifa's* arrival. Peterson never forgave him for going to such extremes as the crates never reached their destination. Despite all these preparations *Latifa*, which was scratch boat, only finished sixth in Class A on corrected time in a windward race which proved to be the slowest on record.

At home *Griffin* did well in her first season as the club's boat, coming first in Division A in the Solent-Brixham, second in Division A in the Dinard, and second in the Open Division and first in Division A in the Channel Race, but had to retire during the Solent-Plymouth. She also did some cruising. Altogether 27 members sailed in her and paid £1 a day for the privilege of doing so (upped to 25s. in 1947). They found her, in Barry's words, eminently suitable for her purpose, 'easy to handle, very seaworthy, and fast enough to stand a chance of a flag in every race.'

When Barry found he could not run both *Griffin* and the Gunner's yacht a replacement for him had to be found. In February 1947 John Bush, a member since 1936, was appointed to the post. 'It was pure chance that I became hon. Griffin secretary,' he wrote later. 'I was sitting in the club room one evening early in 1947 when there was a committee meeting in progress in the Fastnet Room. The subject of the future of *Griffin* was being discussed and Howson Devitt, a very old friend with whom I had sailed for many years, having seen me in the Club room had the idea that I might be a suitable candidate for the job.'

His brief for *Griffin* was to give provisional members the opportunity to qualify for membership, and for other young people to participate in ocean racing. She was to be entered for as many club races as possible. The skipper for each race had to be an experienced member with two other members acting as his mates, and the five remaining places were to be taken from the club's crew list. Later an honorary bosun was appointed.

Considerable work had to be done on *Griffin* to make her suitable for her task. The galley, which consisted of two primus stoves bolted to a bench in the fo'c'sle, was obviously inadequate as was the sleeping accommodation. Her engine had been ruined by frost during her wartime lay-up. It was never replaced and so all her lights, including her navigation lights, were oil lamps. In her first season under Bush she sailed 3,500 miles and 21 members, 18 provisional members, and 5 cadet members sailed aboard her with 12 of the provisional members qualifying for full membership. A later Griffin secretary, John Roome, said she proved ideal for training as she had no less than 20 halyards down her mast 'so you could keep everyone busy'.

Sailing matters apart, the committee found the domestic side of running the club in the postwar years somewhat onerous. Before the war the club had been part of a tight-knit society where everyone knew everyone else—or at least knew of them. The war had changed all that. Different *mores* prevailed; different standards were in force. In February alone two members presented cheques which 'bounced', a third behaved so badly in the club that he was asked to resign, and a fourth 'brought the two barmaids from the Goat Club into the clubhouse, with the result that they have lost their jobs.' Quite how one action led to the other was not recorded.

a photograph that captures the period perfectly: John Bush takes a sunsight aboard *Griffin* while in the background a coal-burning single-stack merchantman steams serenely by

courtesy John Bush

The trouble was that the club's popularity as a social centre, combined with the necessity of finding more members to finance it, must have begun to dilute the quality of the membership. In June 1947 the vice and rear commodores wrote a memo to the secretary which not only reveals their fears that this was happening but shows their thoughts on the club's standing.

'Our recent experience in the North Sea Race and the succeeding jollification at *Rotterdam, have made us think very deeply about our methods of scrutinising applications for membership. We have come to the conclusion that our present procedure is inadequate. The Royal Ocean Racing Club is the National Body organising off-shore racing. It enjoys a very high reputation all over the world. It may be compared with the Jockey Club or the MCC. When it acquired a clubhouse in 1936 it became, to some extent, socially conscious. It cannot be regarded as a mere association for the organisation of a sport, or a body like the Automobile Association. Without being exclusive in a snobbish sense we are of the opinion that it ought only to elect people who are likely to be a credit to the club.'

There was a tendency to feel, the minute continued, that once a yachtsman had completed a qualifying course to the satisfaction of the owner of the yacht in which the candidate had sailed then he could expect automatic election. This was quite wrong as the candidate should be capable of performing at least one aspect of ocean racing–including cooking–competently. But more than that the candidate, the minute implied, must be a reasonable individual. Both flag officers had 'met people in Holland who had successfully completed the course whom we have no desire to meet or associate with anywhere in any circumstances.' If such undesirables became members it was bound to do the club harm and would discourage the best type of yachtsmen from seeking membership.

However candidates had been chosen in the past 'we can, in our submission, now afford to be more particular.' This did not mean the club was interested in a person's ancestry or his education, but it should be concerned about his habits and his character. On the whole, the minute added, the RORC had succeeded in bringing together an extraordinarily nice crowd of people. 'Even our lunatics and even our drunks have their pleasant aspects.'

The committee agreed that the qualifications should be tightened and the rule relating to the election of members was altered so that every candidate had to be proposed or seconded by a committee member.

There were also problems about measurement which were aired at the same committee meeting. Ray Barrett, who, the previous autumn, had taken over as hon. measurer from *Heckstall-Smith, and as secretary of the technical sub-committee from Maclean Buckley, stressed that he had to have more co-operation from owners. More and more clubs and regatta committees were using the RORC rule for their ordinary handicap races and he was being inundated by requests to measure yachts whose owners had no intention of ever racing in an RORC event. He suggested local offices, and much stiffer fees, and 'emphasised that the success of the club was largely bound up with its rating rule and the technical side.'

The admiral, Maclean Buckley, said he thought the technical side had been declining for some years and stressed how important it was for the hon. measurer to have assistance but confessed he did not know how this could be done. Commander Swann said he agreed with Barrett as to the importance of the rule and suggested the answer was to get a secretary who could help with the measurement. He did not believe the club could afford a secretary who was not able to do this, which he could not, and that he was therefore resigning. He did so in September and Peterson took over again on a temporary basis.

In the autumn Aisher replaced Wyatt as hon. treasurer and as Mason did not wish to serve another term Illingworth was voted the new commodore as from 1st January 1948. At the same time Alan Paul, an amateur yacht designer of considerable flair, a member since 1935 when he qualified aboard *Rose*, and a committee member since 1937, was appointed secretary; and F.B.R. Brown became secretary of the technical sub-committee, so taking some of the weight off Barrett's increasingly bowed shoulders.

During the war Paul–popularly known as The Apostle or 'Possle' for short– had served in the Auxiliary Fire Service and as a runner crew. His appointment came at a critical moment in the RORC's development. 'At that time the club's position was decidedly precarious,' he wrote later. 'We had not many members [700], very little money and a dilapidated clubhouse from which the owner was trying to eject us.'

In January 1947 the owner's agents had reluctantly agreed to extend the lease until May 1948 at £500 per annum, but would, it seems, grant no further extension. Peterson was one of those who campaigned strongly to remain. 'We should do nothing to remove ourselves until we are given peremptory notice to quit by the landlords,' he wrote Paul on 1st March 1948. 'In other words, I think we should squat in 20 St. James's Place for as long as possible.' This the club did, until in March 1949 the owners, having had their appeal for a business licence rejected, at last decided to start negotiations with the club for a new lease.

With everything rationed and labour strictly controlled, Paul's first serious problem came when the assistant secretary, who had most of the records in her head, announced that she was going to leave to get married. Several possible applicants were barred from taking the job as the RORC was not considered essential to the country's economy, but from the spring of 1948 Paul was ably assisted by Hope Kirkpatrick, an ex-ATS officer and a one-time concert pianist, who, before she retired in 1974, was elected to the committee and is now a life honorary member.

'It was a case of the blind leading the blind,' Hope was to write later of her first years at the RORC. 'There was one small black book in which all ratings were noted, and I literally had, with his [Paul's] help, to build up a system for all facets of the club.' At first she didn't feel very welcome and after five months thought of leaving, but then a future vice commodore, 'Buster' de Guingand, and his wife, invited her out, and from that time on she felt at home. When she retired she looked back with some nostalgia 'on those early days when the Flag Officers used to come and discuss everything and the members used to help turn the handle of the roneo machine and assist in getting out the circulars. They were memorable days because we felt we were building up a marvellous club,' which indeed they were.

An important newcomer to the RORC in 1947 was Adlard Coles[1]. In his classic manual, *Heavy Weather Sailing*, he wrote that until then he had just taken an armchair interest in the sport

courtesy Erroll Bruce

Two of the club's most distinguished members to join in the immediate postwar period were Adlard Coles (right) and Erroll Bruce, seen here shaking hands at the end of the 1950 Transatlantic Race. Coles' *Cohoe* narrowly beat *Samuel Pepys,* skippered by Bruce

but that in 1946 he decided to have a shot at it himself. He bought the light displacement *Cohoe* which at just over 25ft LWL was large enough to compete in all the RORC events except the Fastnet. He spent the winter modifying her by increasing the size of her accommodation– which, nevertheless, was still described by Laurent Giles' partner, Humphrey Barton, as 'like living in a tunnel'–and fitting a lighter engine. His first race was the Southsea-Brixham. In rough weather that Adlard Coles thrived on–16 of the 28 starters retired for one reason or another–*Cohoe* was the only Class III yacht to finish and beat every Class II yacht on corrected time.

However, the 1947 season was dominated by Illingworth's return to British ocean racing. Before he had left Australia he had already decided to build a successor to *Maid of Malham* which he was going to call *Myth of Malham*. A Class II ocean racer, *Myth*, along with *Tre Sang* and *Cohoe*, showed that ocean racing for the immediate future was going to be dominated by cheaper, light displacement yachts. With postwar austerity making money in short supply, they

1 his autobiography, *Sailing Years,* was published in 1981

Illingworth: A Founding Father of Modern Ocean Racing

photo Beken of Cowes

photo Beken of Cowes

John Illingworth's contribution to ocean racing was immense. With *Maid of Malham* (above), seen here with the double spinnakers that the club allowed for two seasons only, he established his reputation as a topflight sailor; with *Myth of Malham* (right), in which he won the Fastnet Races of 1947 and 1949 and scored a string of other victories, he revealed his skills as a designer; and by the 1965 season, when

courtesy Sandy Illingworth

remained competitive to the end and during his last season, 1969, he campaigned his 38ft LWL Class I *Oryx* (below) as a member of the French Admiral's Cup team. He and Angus Primrose had originally designed *Oryx* for Francis Bouygues, before Illingworth became her co-owner with Robert Dégain. He died in 1980 aged 76

this photograph of him aboard *Monk of Malham* was taken during that year's Fastnet Race, he was a seasoned competitor who had co-designed a whole succession of successful yachts, including *Minx of Malham* and *Mouse of Malham*. He said he was at his best in 1949–the year the first edition of his classic book on ocean racing, *Offshore*, appeared–and that thereafter his powers were on the wane. This may be so but he

courtesy Sandy Illingworth

were the only practical proposition for the young and impecunious. The Labour government's hostility to yachting didn't help matters. The imposition of 33⅓% Purchase Tax on new sailing boats was narrowly avoided, but the government then banned licences to build them because of the shortage of timber.

These postwar restrictions did not stop Illingworth who, as a senior naval engineer officer, knew how to get what he wanted and where to get it from. With the experience of *Maid of Malham* and *Rani* behind him, he had already put a lot of thought into his new boat. By the time he had arrived in the United States to sail *Latifa* he had her worked out in detail in his notebook. When he reached England he rang Jack Laurent Giles who told Humphrey Barton: 'John is back and I have just been talking to him over the telephone. He wants a "flat out" for the Fastnet.'

'That's splendid news. What sort of boat will she be?'

'Oh, minimum as regards size. Rather light displacement. No sheer or bulwarks. No doghouse. Very short overhangs.'

Thus, as Phillips-Birt noted, were the lineaments outlined of a startling new conception in ocean racing design which proved to be 'about the heartiest slap in the face that conventional yacht architecture had ever received.'

Besides her unusual appearance *Myth*'s design reflected the new professionalism Illingworth brought to the sport. His concern for weight amounted to an obsession: it has been said that he even demanded that the handles of tooth-brushes be shortened before they were brought aboard[1]. He was also a fanatical sail trimmer. One member, Bernard Hayman–who worked as a draughtsman for Robert Clark for four years in the late 1940s and succeeded Haylock as editor of *Yachting World* in 1962–recalled that when he crewed aboard *Myth* in the 1950s he was 'determined not to make a mistake on The Master's Boat.' Early in the race he asked where Illingworth liked the sheets to be cleated only to be told by a regular crew member: 'Don't worry about that. We very rarely cleat anything on this boat. John is sail-trimming all the time.'

Perhaps *Myth*'s most unusual feature was a removable bow as both Illingworth and Giles suspected that her radical design would force a change in the RORC rule, and they wanted, when long overhangs were no longer penalised so severely, to be able to add a more graceful bow. This appendage brought a howl of outrage from one American commentator. 'Any body and any rules,' he wrote, perhaps slightly tongue in cheek, 'that produced such a dreadful looking monstrosity, with fake bows that zipper on and off to chisel on different rules, ought to be hove overboard before the sport is contaminated–especially since she turns out to be so fast.'

Myth's rig was as radical as her hull. At that time the RORC rule still rated the foretriangle at only 85% of its total area, and staysails could have a foot

1 he was also, in the words of a Polish naval officer whom Illingworth helped convert several feluccas for clandestine use in the Mediterranean during the war, 'a genius for making use of every cubic foot of space.'

Painting of *Yeoman III* by Montague Dawson depicted during the 1951 Fastnet Race which she won

photo Beken of Cowes

The 'terrible twins',
the one tonners
Clarionet and
Roundabout which
dominated the
1966 season

courtesy Paul Antrobus

Noryema V and
Ron Amey. *Noryema V*
was one of the British
team in the 1967
Admiral's Cup series

photo Beken of Cowes

Frigate, sailed by Robin Aisher, swept the board in 1973, winning the Somerset Memorial Trophy, the Alan Paul Trophy for consistently high performance, and the REYC Challenge Cup for winning the Class II championship

Rt. Hon. Edward Heath at the helm of the fifth *Morning Cloud* in 1978

Alastair Black

Bob Fisher

Don Street

The 17-ton (TM) *Iolaire* was owned 1929–31 by T.P. Rose Richards, the club's commodore, 1934–37, then by two other members, Lt-Colonel J.S. Alston and J.R. Edmonds. After the war Bobby Somerset, the club's commodore, 1951–52, bought her and raced her for several years. Don Street Jr., a member since 1955, has owned her since 1957. He changed her rig from cutter to yawl and has cruised far and wide in her

length of up to 150% of the base of foretriangle. This meant the foretriangle area was excessively cheap, rating-wise, compared to the mainsail area. Illingworth therefore drew a sail plan which exploited this, prompting a horrified Giles to remark that her mainsail was 'just a flag abaft the mast.'

Myth was built in Scotland and launched in July 1947. She immediately showed her close windedness during the Clyde Fortnight and then went on to win, in quick succession, a race from Roseneath to Portsmouth and then the Channel Race, and started the Fastnet Race as the boat to beat. But no one managed to and in a mainly light weather race she won the Fastnet Cup from the other 26 starters which included the 1939 winner, *Bloodhound*, now owned by Myles Wyatt, Ted Gore-Lloyd's *Benbow*, E.G. Greville's *Erivale*, and Bruynzeel's 1937 winner, *Zeearend*.

At the other end of the scale, and perhaps more representative of the Fastnet fleet in 1947, was *Thalassa* now owned by Alan Baker. *Thalassa* had first taken part in the Fastnet as far back as 1927 and was not a serious contender for a prize. But this did not mean those aboard her–Thalassians they called themselves–were not going to have a good time. This was summed up by the yacht's cook, 'Sandy' *Sandison, as follows: 'a) Race *Thalassa* as hard as possible on every possible occasion, and b) extract in the doing of this the maximum amount of fun and enjoyment', which included eating well, drinking deep, and refusing to take anything, or anyone, especially the owner, seriously. *Thalassa*'s log for the 1947 Fastnet included the ship's Articles in doggerel and it sums up the Thalassian philosophy well. Part of it reads:

> We ain't over anxious to labour,
> But realise the ship must be manned;
> So we'll put in our eight hours daily
> And for sixteen will quietly get canned.
> The Captain may eat at our table,
> He's a sociable sort of a chap,
> Provided he minds of his manners
> And keeps a tight hold of his trap.

At the same time as Illingworth had been elected the club's commodore he had also become commodore of the Royal Naval Sailing Association, and one of his first moves had been to introduce a new light displacement class, the RNSA 24s, which were 24ft LWL.

Illingworth's idea, which foreshadowed the popularity of level rating racing, was to create a class of small ocean racers, all with the same rating, which could also race inshore without handicap. Laurent Giles designed the hull and Illingworth the rig. To start the class Illingworth built *Minx of Malham*; and three other members, Major Dick Scholfield, Commander Bill King, and Norman

Jones, built *Blue Disa*, *Galway Blazer*, and *Ben's Choice*, and the RNSA built *Samuel Pepys*. The class had a remarkable record, particularly *Minx of Malham* which won the Class III championships in 1949.

Illingworth's victories in *Minx of Malham* that year included a notable one in the Dinard Race. While celebrating in the Dinard Yacht Club bar after it, his navigator, Mary Blewitt—whose father, Colonel Ralph Blewitt, a member since 1936, had founded the Royal Artillery Yacht Club in 1933—told him he was a bloody fool not to enter *Myth*[1] for that year's Fastnet. He replied that that was

Start of the 1948
Santander Race

all very well but the race was only three weeks away and where was he going to obtain his crew in such a short time. Mary responded to this challenge by promptly recruiting one from those in the bar–including Pam Ryan, who shortly afterwards married a future commodore, Peter Green (Sir Peter from 1982).

That year's Fastnet entries had a south-westerly gale hit them before they had passed the Lizard. Despite poor visibility, no depth sounder–not then permitted –and tacking into the teeth of a full gale, Illingworth put his faith in his primitive American direction finder, which was working well, and followed

Bloodhound between Land's End and the Scillies. He later said this gave him the edge over those still in the race, though Mary Blewitt believed it was because, except for about half-an-hour off the Lizard on the way out, *Myth* never hove to, while *Latifa*, for example, did so for about eight hours.

The rule had been revised to plug the gaps that Illingworth had so brilliantly exploited in the previous Fastnet. But *Myth* still won, and won convincingly by over eight hours on corrected time from the Class I winner, *Bloodhound*, one of the nine to finish that year out of 29 starters. Second in Class II was the Gunners' new *St. Barbara*, which was just beginning her long and distinguished ocean racing career–she participated in every Fastnet Race between 1949 and 1965 when she was replaced by *St. Barbara II*.

While Illingworth was winning the Fastnet in *Myth*, Commander Erroll Bruce[1] sailed *Minx* to victory for him in the inaugural Wolf Rock Race. The course for this was from Cowes to Cherbourg, round the Wolf Rock, with the finish at Plymouth, a distance of 310 miles, and had been instituted that year for Class III boats not then eligible for the Fastnet (it was also held in 1951, 1953, and 1954). After it Bruce became a member and soon proved himself one of the outstanding ocean racing yachtsmen of his generation.

In January 1950 the long-running saga of negotiating for the clubhouse came to a head. Peterson and Aisher who, with Wyatt, had been responsible for the negotiations, were at last able to tell the committee that an agreement had been made to buy the freehold for £17,500 with the vendors having no further liabiity in respect of renovation not covered by the War Damage Claim which was still outstanding. Then in May 1950 Peterson reported that contracts had been exchanged. Completion was to be delayed for a year, giving, it was hoped, the club sufficient time to find the purchase price. In the mean time, it had to be borrowed from the vendors.

The club's programme was now gaining momentum every year. Besides established fixtures such as the Fastnet, Dinard, North Sea and Channel events, the Scandinavian races were revived with ones to Kristiansand in 1947 (from Blythe), 1948 (Harwich), and 1950 (Dover). There were also regular fixtures to Ireland and in the Irish Sea; to Belle Ile and Santander in even-numbered years; and to La Rochelle in odd-numbered ones.

With the conclusion of the negotiations for the clubhouse and a steadily expanding programme, it can be said that the postwar era of re-establishing ocean racing had been successfully concluded. But what lay ahead was probably beyond the dreams of even the most imaginative member.

1 his autobiography *From Duck Pond to Deep Ocean* appeared in 1997

Chapter Seven

THE 'DREADFUL, SHAPELESS, ENDLESS BOXES' ARE BROUGHT TO HEEL

I N 1948 the Frers-designed Argentine sloop, *Joanne*, owned by René Salem, had been shipped to England to take part in the club's programme and had stayed to race in the Fastnet the following year. To reciprocate this gesture Dick Scholfield shipped his RNSA 24, *Blue Disa*, to Buenos Aires to enter the 1950 1,200-mile race to Rio de Janeiro which had been established in 1947 on a triennial basis. She finished ninth in her class.

A new CCA rule came into force in 1950 as the 1940 version was, one commentator noted, 'unintelligible to everyone except the Measurement Rule Committee, a few naval architects and God Almighty.' It now took light displacement yachts into account, a change that encouraged the RNSA's *Samuel Pepys*, skippered by Erroll Bruce, Bill King's *Galway Blazer*, and Adlard Coles' *Cohoe* to enter the 1950 Bermuda Race. Though officially too small to enter–the CCA imposed a minimum overall length of 35ft for the race–the RNSAs were given special dispensation. The CCA thought *Cohoe* was an RNSA 24, too, and when it discovered she was not, Coles' entry was refused, and he had to resort to adding a false bow to *Cohoe* before being allowed to compete. Other British entries that year included Jack Rawlings' new 43ft LWL *Gulvain*, a larger development of *Myth* and one of the first yachts to be built in aluminium, a type of construction which was to become *commonplace for top ocean racers during the 1970s.

Galway Blazer did best but only managed to finish fourth in Class C, with *Gulvain* gaining a respectable ninth place in Class A. With the exception of

the clubhouse under
repair in 1951 after
wartime bomb damage

Galway Blazer the British yachts then raced back across the Atlantic to Plymouth for prizes donated by the RORC and the Royal Bermuda Yacht Club. A distance of 2,780-miles, it proved to be, in the words of Phillips-Birt writing in the late 1950s, 'perhaps the most exacting and prolonged test of down-wind sailing that modern yachts at least have ever experienced', and was won by *Cohoe* in a corrected time of 14 days, 7hrs. 21min.

At the end of 1950 Somerset succeeded Illingworth as commodore, Myles Wyatt was appointed vice commodore and Dick Scholfield became rear commodore. At the first committee meeting in 1951 Illingworth, who the previous year had helped found the Junior Offshore Group (JOG) to cater for smaller yachts, proposed that one or two club races should be organised for those between 20 and 24ft LWL. His motion was defeated by nine votes to two, but this was just the first shot he fired in his long, and eventually successful, battle to get smaller boats accepted by the RORC.

In March there was an early indication of the advertising and sponsorship problems which dogged the 1980s. When the John Lewis Partnership notified the club it was forming a sailing club and building a new boat, which it would probably wish to enter for club races, the committee 'raised no objection to the use of the name of the firm in this connection'; but when Alan Paul reported a firm had approached him wanting to offer a prize in a club race to advertise its new line of toilet goods, the committee declined 'with a suitable expression of regret.'

In May 1951 an extraordinary general meeting was held at which the committee was authorised to raise money to pay for the purchase of the clubhouse.

It was agreed that any member lending the club one hundred guineas free of interest would have their subscription waived until the sum had been repaid to them. The very satisfactory sum of £12,725 was raised in this way, the balance of the purchase sum being met by a bank overdraft, and completion was able to take place in July.

The club's war damage claim was at last approved and a grant for the repair of damage (it eventually amounted to £7,511.0s.1d out of the £8,401.19s.7d claimed) was allowed by the War Damage Commission. Under the supervision of a member who was an architect, Colonel H.T. Barnard, work began in the summer on repairing the roof, making the top floor habitable, and restoring and redecorating the rest of the clubhouse which had to be closed for about six weeks. This was not before time as underfoot the first floor was far from safe and rain was inclined to fall on members standing around the bar.

courtesy Hope Kirkpatrick

While the clubhouse was shut Alan Paul and Hope Kirkpatrick shared an office on the second floor. No. 21 had been knocked down after it had been gutted by fire bombs and all Hope had between herself and Green Park was a tarpaulin. Phillips-Birt relates that 'in a morning of high drama' the contents of the office were lowered through a hole[1] in the ceiling of the Fastnet Room, though he doesn't elaborate on this unusual operation. Presumably it was through this hole that, as Phillips-Birt also relates, anyone standing in the kitchen basement was able to see through four storeys to the sky.

Despite this disruption 15 races were held during the 1951 season, the largest programme the club had so far ever organised. But as always in odd-numbered years, the main focus of interest was the Fastnet, though, so far as foul weather was concerned, the opening fixture, the Portsmouth-Harwich, ran it a close second. This 170-mile race began on 27th April. It was bitterly cold and blowing half a gale. One by one eight of the nine competitors gave up until only *Griffin* remained, and after she had finished, her skipper, John Bush, suggested that in future hot water bottles should be carried as part of the boat's medical equipment.

The Fastnet attracted 29 starters, the same number as in 1949, and was the most international race yet with seven nationalities competing. The pick of the English starters that year were Geoff Pattinson's Class I sloop, **Jocasta*, and Owen Aisher's Class II *Yeoman III*, while the Dutch fielded Kees Bruynzeel's 36ft LWL *Zeevalk*, chine built and displacing less than five tons. The Australians made their debut with Phil Davenport's Class II *Waltzing Matilda*, which had

Hope Kirkpatrick joined the club in 1948 as Alan Paul's assistant. She retired in 1974 and is now one of the club's few life honorary members

1 this could not have been caused by a bomb as some have supposed. Fire bombs were not designed to penetrate such a distance while a high explosive one would have wrecked the interior

sailed from 'Down Under' via the Straits of Magellan; and for the first time since 1937 the Americans were represented when Kennon Jewett's *Malabar XIII*, navigated by the indefatigable Alf Loomis, which arrived from Spain after winning the Havana-Santander Transatlantic Race.

But the yacht to beat that year was *Circe*. Owned by the Swede, Carl Hardeburg, and built by another Swede, Bengt Plym, she had the so-far unbeaten combination aboard of her designer, Olin Stephens, and his brother, Rod, who skippered her. Aisher wrote later of *Circe* that 'Every detail had been thought of, nothing superfluous. The boat looked naked; one had to put quite a lot of time into examining everything to see whether he [Rod Stephens] had really got enough halyards and pieces of string to take him anywhere. He had –just!'

The day of the race dawned wet and ugly with the wind gusting to 50mph. Alf Loomis wrote afterwards that he had never seen less propitious conditions. 'If it wasn't raining cats and dogs I don't know what it was raining.'

The day before it had been decided to send the fleet through the Needles Channel and to delay the start until 1600 to give it the benefit of an ebbing tide. But the wind was from the south-west and it kicked up a nasty sea. *Malabar XIII* was an early casualty when she was dismasted and driven over the Shingles, and eventually she had to be taken in tow by the Yarmouth lifeboat. *Jocasta* was luckier. After her steering gear broke, she was also driven over the Shingles. But she did not ground, the emergency tiller was shipped, and she kept sailing.

Retirements came thick and fast, and soon half-a-dozen entries were back at Cowes in various states of disarray. Even the newest and the best found it too hard going. C.F. Cartwright's *Tilly Twin* retired to Cherbourg with rigging problems, as Dick Scholfield's *Fandango* did to Brixham, and *Griffin* had to put into Plymouth with a leak and a split mainsail. An accident aboard *Bloodhound* forced Myles Wyatt to spend the rest of the race in his bunk and Michael Mason's *Latifa* had to return to Cowes for 'Pete' Peterson to receive medical treatment after being injured in the galley.

Only *Yeoman III* kept hammering to windward without reefing, so that at the Lizard Aisher was only 15 minutes astern of the much larger *Bloodhound*. By now the wind had dropped and it soon became variable. Some yachts were even becalmed as they approached the Rock and *Jocasta* hit it a glancing blow when she rounded third shortly after *Bloodhound* and *Circe*. *Yeoman III* also diced with danger when she saved ten minutes by passing between the lighthouse and the Short Rock about 400 feet to the north.

Bloodhound and *Circe* had a close tussle the whole way back to Plymouth arriving within ten minutes of each other. *Circe* took line honours but it was

the smaller *Yeoman III* which won by a convincing five and a half hours on corrected time.

'The Dutchman in *Zeevalk* was the real enemy,' Aisher wrote afterwards of Bruynzeel's yacht which someone had called the largest Sharpie ever built. 'How the hell he got along with his floating streamlined kitchen cabinet the night it was really blowing hard, I cannot imagine.'

However, *Zeevalk* did not perform as well as *Yeoman III* in the light airs which followed the blow, but still managed to finish just over five hours behind *Circe* to come second on corrected time.

Though *Griffin* was able to enter the last two events of the season—finishing second in her class in the Plymouth–La Rochelle Race—doubts were expressed in the autumn as to whether she could continue to race for much longer. A committee member, F.A. 'Sandy' Haworth, offered to sell his 21-ton cutter *Phryna*[1] to the club for substantially less than she would have fetched in the open

Owen Aisher at the helm of *Yeoman III* in which he won the 1951 Fastnet Race

1 designed by Malden Heckstall-Smith and William Meek, she had been built for member Bobby Bevan, an advertising executive who thought up the slogan 'Guinness is good for you'

market. Some felt his offer should be accepted, but after the hon. treasurer, Owen Aisher, had cautioned that the club could not really afford to run a club boat at all–*Griffin* was being quite heavily subsidised from the club's funds–it was decided to decline Haworth's offer and to continue using *Griffin* for a further season at least.

In the New Year Bush managed to alleviate *Griffin*'s financial situation by running a sweepstake on the Grand National which raised over £450 so that she ended the 1952 season with only a slight deficit. So successful was this form of fundraising that it became an annual event. However, 1952 was not a good year for the club boat on the water as she was run down by a naval tug during the Channel Race and was out of commission for some time. The collision aggravated a weakness in the scarf between keel and stem, and though she was repaired in time to take part in the Dinard Race she took a good deal of water as well as carrying away her forestay rigging screw.

She was still leaking during the Southsea-Brixham Race when the new rigging screw broke, and it must have been obvious to those who raced in her that her days as an ocean racer were numbered. It was not a particularly successful season for the club either with a sharper drop in entries than had been expected even in a non-Fastnet year.

Pressure continued to grow for the committee to allow smaller yachts to enter the Fastnet and in November 1952 Erroll Bruce, who had won that year's Transatlantic Race in *Samuel Pepys*, made a formal request to the committee to this effect. Pressure was also applied from across the Atlantic, for the same month Rod Stephens wrote asking that *Loki*, which his brother had designed for G.B. Pinchot, be made eligible for the 1953 Fastnet. But as she rated less than the minimum rating allowed, his request was refused.

The Americans did not allow the matter to rest there and the following month Alf Loomis wrote with typical panache to the commodore, Robert Somerset. 'My friend Giff Pinchot called me up on another matter this morning and then said that it looks as if the RORC will not allow his *Loki* to sail in the Fastnet Race next summer because of her small size. (She is 38ft overall and 26ft on the water line). He said he is inquiring into what he must do to raise her rating–and that's the first time I ever heard of any owner who wanted to raise his rating–and I said: "What the hell, the CCA made an exception from its rules to permit the RNSA 24s to enter the Bermuda Race, and if the RORC won't make an exception in favor of *Loki* where is this wonderful international reciprocity that I've been boasting about all these years?"

'Well, where indeed is it? In the 1950 Bermuda Race *Loki* won in her class, and not only beat *Samuel* [*Pepys*] by 13 hours on elapsed time and 9 hours corrected, but saved her time on all but six boats in the class above her. It may therefore be accepted that if *Loki* were permitted to take part in the Fastnet she would get to Plymouth in ample time to be received by the committee before the committee shoved off for La Rochelle.

'Incidentally, I am making a request similar to this to the Race Committee of the Transpacific Yacht Club whose rules deem *Galway Blazer* to be too small for the Honolulu Race. Wouldn't the RORC feel embarrassed if it denied *Loki* and then learned that the TYC, whose race is nearly four times the length of the Fastnet, had lowered the bars for *Blazer*?

'In all seriousness I think that if *Loki* sails for England this summer she should be permitted to enter the Fastnet–if for no other reason than that no American boat has completed the course since 1937.'

When Wyatt, who in January 1953 succeeded Somerset as commodore, replied pointing out the difficulties, Loomis admitted that the problem is 'indeed a poser, but it is one which might have been foreseen when in 1950 the request was made to the CCA to permit the RNSA 24s to enter the Bermuda Race.'

He then went on to say that only the previous evening, at the CCA's winter dinner, someone had said to him, in effect: "What's the matter with your friends the British? We let them sail their small boats in our most important race and then they take the stand that their Wolf Rock Race is good enough for our small boats." Others, Loomis added, had expressed themselves in similar vein 'and I gained the distinct impression that here was a chance for *le beau geste* which the RORC would be unwise to miss.'

1952 Race Programme

This deftly applied pressure had its effect and at a committee meeting on 10th February 1953 Wyatt requested that eligibility for the Fastnet be reconsidered in the light of Loomis' correspondence. He himself was not able to be present and the meeting was chaired by the new vice commodore, John Bush, who had recently been relieved as Griffin secretary by C.T.H. Cowen. Bearing in mind the sudden decline in race entry fees in 1952, and the obvious fact that the average size of yachts was decreasing, the admiral, Maclean Buckley, strongly expressed the view it was vital to the club's future that smaller yachts should not be discouraged. Dick Scholfield and Adlard Coles presented counter-arguments but eventually Buckley's proposal that Class III should be eligible for the Fastnet was accepted.

The numbers for the Fastnet in 1953 rose to 40–the largest ever–and for the first time the *fleet was large enough to be started by class. Allowing Class III yachts to take part had little to do with this increase as only nine of them started. But in an exceptionally light-weather race it was the smallest yachts which cleaned up. Sir Michael Newton's *Favona* won the Fastnet Cup and another Class III yacht, *Lothian*, came second on corrected time. In third place overall was the Class II winner, Selwyn Slater's *Uomie*, with *Loki* fourth. In fifth place, and second in Class II, was another American entry, *Carina*, skippered by Dick Nye, two names which were to dominate the Fastnet for some years to come.

When Class III owners were polled that autumn as to whether they wished the Class to be eligible for future Fastnets, 22 owners replied in the affirmative and only five were against.

Nineteen Fifty-Three was the year that one of the most remarkable yachtsmen of modern times joined the club. 'If I was going to sail, I must learn to do it properly,' Francis Chichester (Sir Francis from 1967) wrote in his autobiography, *The Lonely Sea and the Sky*. 'I thought that the Royal Ocean Racing Club sailors would be the ones to learn from, because they raced in all weathers.'

He qualified as a member aboard *Griffin* in the 1953 Dinard Race, but as no one seemed interested in having aboard an air navigator whose knowledge of the sea was at that time very limited, he bought a 24ft LWL day sailer, *Florence Edith*, and spent the rest of the season learning to handle her amongst the sandbanks off Brightlingsea, bouncing off several of them.

Chichester records that when his wife, Sheila, arrived for her first sail in *Florence Edith* neither he nor his boat were anywhere to be seen. Eventually she found an old fisherman who had seen them. 'Oh, you mean that there yellow boat? She be lying on Buxey Sands, and it's lucky 'tis fine weather, otherwise she'd be sunk when t'sea rises. What's more, there be thick fog coming up, and if she do get off the sands, it'll be a long time before you see her in Brightlingsea.'

Sheila was immediately advised by the friend she was staying with to obtain a divorce, but Chichester turned up eventually and the following spring, having converted *Florence Edith* for ocean racing and renamed her *Gipsy Moth II*, took part in the North Sea Race. At that time he had only been in one other race, his qualifying one, and his crew had never been in any, so it is not surprising that they finished last (last but two on corrected time). However, this did not deter Chichester and by the end of the season he had sailed *Gipsy Moth II* over 2,500 miles. 'Our racing record was one of the worst in the club,' he wrote, 'but I was learning.'

He was indeed for the following year (1954) he won the Southsea-Harwich Race. Altogether *Gipsy Moth* took part in sixteen RORC races during the next four years before Chichester became diverted into a new kind of ocean racing by a notice 'Blondie' Hasler had pinned up in the clubhouse. It had been there for at least two years during which time, according to Hasler, Alan Paul had been kept busy rubbing out members' 'unsolicited, usually adverse, comments.'

During the 1950s Hasler had tried to interest the club in experimental yachts–his efforts to do so are covered in the next chapter–and the notice was about recruiting competitors for a Single-Handed Transatlantic Race. The first of these took place in 1960 and eventually led to Chichester's spectacular solo circumnavigation in 1966-7.

It might be thought that by 1953, with its extensive racing programme and recently renovated clubhouse, the RORC was so firmly established, and was so successful, that the worst of its financial problems were behind it, especially as prosperity was at last beginning to return to the country after years of postwar austerity. However, in October 1953 there was an extensive discussion by the committee about the cost of running the newly renovated clubhouse and it was only when it was put to the vote that it was unanimously decided to retain it. A motion to increase the subscription for members over 25 to six guineas was defeated, but it was raised from four guineas to five and it was agreed that race entry fees and measurement fees should also be increased.

Race entry fees were increased by transferring the main financial burden to the crews of participating yachts. A yacht's entry fee was reduced to £1, which was retained if it failed to start, and a crewing fee of £8 for Class I, £6 for Class II, and £4 for Class III, was now payable, though only if the yacht started. The owner was responsible for the payment of both fees 'but crews are expected to reimburse the owner when they take part in the race.' As a result income from entry fees nearly doubled, from £652 in 1953 to £1,235 in 1954, and very few complaints were received.

It was also decided that the club's finances must be put on a more secure and permanent basis, and at an Extraordinary General Meeting in the spring of 1954 it was agreed that one thousand unsecured, non-interest bearing Notes should be issued at £25 each. A member could subscribe to up to six Notes, each of which would exempt him annually from payment of one guinea of his subscription. As the highest rate of income tax at that time was 97.5%, the

courtesy Erroll Bruce

'No fancy heavy weather gear to wear in those days' is the caption under this photograph of *Griffin* during the 1953 Fastnet Race. The helmsman, D.E. French, looks pretty relaxed. H.S. 'Uncle' Rouse is second on the left

Notes proved highly popular and allowed the club to return the money lent by members to purchase the clubhouse and clear a number of other debts related to its refurbishment.

Not for the first time the question of carrying inflatable dinghies during a race was raised in March 1954, by the Royal Norwegian Yacht Club among others, but the committee decided to retain the Special Regulation which required an ordinary dinghy to be shipped. While of limited value in emergencies, it was thought an essential part of any yacht's equipment 'not only to carry crew and stores between ship and shore, but also for such normal evolutions as laying out ground tackle in the event of running ashore, or for taking mooring warps when entering harbour.'

It was therefore resolved that 'While the RORC fully recognise the value of a raft or inflatable dinghy as a safety measure when carried in addition to a serviceable dinghy, they cannot recommend that dinghies not be carried and, as a further point, would emphasise that there are other items of normal cruising equipment, such as cooking stoves, water tanks, anchors and chains and spare gear which, it could be argued, might be left ashore for certain races. This is a policy to which the RORC would not wish to give support.'

In January 1954 the committee decided to form a new technical sub-committee with the object of advising the main committee whether the present rule should be amended or replaced. Traditionally, this sub-committee had comprised members who were experts in their field. In 1939 it had been composed of such illustrious names as Clark, Charles E. Nicholson, Fife, Mylne, and Laurent Giles. By contrast, the new sub-committee had seven non-technical members–though it did include a Senior Wrangler–and its function now was to examine the evidence of the experts before giving its recommendations.It

Bonzo VII and Special Regulations

During the 1950s the club's Special Regulations made it compulsory to carry a rigid dinghy on deck. So Norwegian RORC member, Biørn Pedersen, fitted his into the cockpit of his yacht, *Bonzo VII*, a frequent competitor in the Skaw and Round Gotland Races. It weighed only 40lb. and was, in his words, 'well protected against seas, away from deck or cabin top where it causes trouble and windage. Note the compass in a drawer under the dinghy's thwart and how the hinged seats, low down, make the cockpit safe and comfortable. The cockpit is self-bailing, so is also the dinghy'

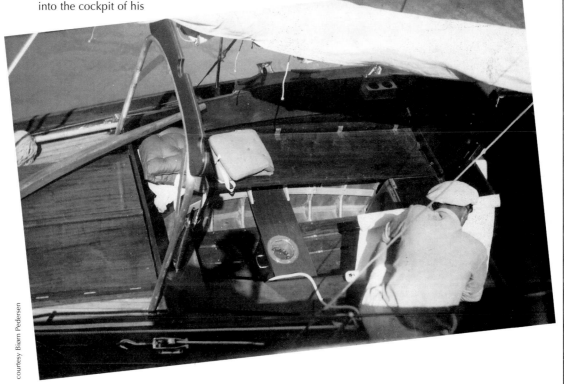

courtesy Biørn Pedersen

first met in June 1954 to consider the exploitation of the rule by the latest breed of yachts, as exemplified by *Myth of Malham*, *Fandango*, and *Gulvain*. These designs, which the hon. measurer, Ray Barrett, called a 'dreadful crop of shapeless, endless boxes', had exploited a loophole in the rating formula which had been only partially plugged by changes introduced at the beginning of 1949.

Phillips-Birt, for one, believed these changes to be very unsatisfactory. In particular, he thought the application of the clause intended to catch the light displacement rule cheaters was so vague that in certain yachts it produced a lower rating instead of a higher one! The sub-committee's view was that there was a general tendency for long ends to be too heavily taxed, that beam conferred too great a bonus, and that flotation in light and moderately light displacements yachts was overstressed. It therefore proposed changes relating to the length and depth measurements when it reported to the general committee in January 1955.

These did not prove popular with Barrett who had been working on a new rule for some years. He believed the sub-committee had not given his rule fair consideration–a forewarning of gales to come–and he now gave the sub-committee's recommendations a thorough mauling. He said some of its contents were 'so pregnant with danger as to be really frightening', and wrote: 'Oh dear! Oh dear! Oh dear! Are we out for a new rating or mathematical gymnastics?'

*Memoranda flew here and there and, like acquiring the clubhouse, threatened to be come another saga that would run and run, and while it ran the vast majority of members did what they had always done which was to grumble about their ratings, and to keep racing and enjoying it.

The new technical sub-committee was headed by one of the current rear com-modores, 'Sandy' Haworth, the idea of two rear commodores serving simultaneously having been sanctioned by the 1952 AGM. A

photo Beken of Cowes

Ray Barrett coming ashore with the 'tools of his trade' after measuring a yacht. The date is 1951

marine Lloyd's insurance broker by profession Haworth, who had joined in 1936, had campaigned his own yachts, *Glance* and *Phryna*, after the war and in 1951 had, with Kenneth Poland and a small band of enthusiasts, founded Lloyd's Yacht Club. It had taken just a day to collect the necessary funds to build the club's first yacht, the Class I *Lutine*, which was to do so well in many club events and was to prove an ideal recruiting centre for new RORC members.

The other rear commodore at that time was the Hon. Ray Pitt-Rivers, the owner of *Foxhound* and the club's first female flag officer. The daughter of Lord Forster–a one-time governor-general of Australia and a keen yachtsman–she was an actress by profession, using the name Mary Hinton. She made an impressive first appearance on the ocean racing scene when her converted 8-metre, *Christina*, which rated badly, only failed to win the 1950 Dinard Race by

15 minutes on corrected time, coming second to *Bloodhound*. It was the first of many friendly contests she had with Wyatt's yacht for she then bought *Bloodhound*'s near sister ship, *Foxhound*. In her she won two Dinard Races (1952 and 1953) and various other RORC events, and finished second to *Lutine* in

Class I in the 1955 Fastnet Race. The next year she entered the Bermuda Race, the first female skipper ever to do so, but sold *Foxhound* the following year.

The 1955 season attracted 281 entries. Though a new race, Dartmouth-Gibraltar, produced only three starters, and the Irish Sea Race only five, the Fastnet posted another record with 47 entries. *Lutine* won her class in the Fastnet for the second consecutive time, and came top of it in the individual points cham-

courtesy David Lawman

Ray Pitt-Rivers, the club's first female flag officer, aboard *Foxhound*

pionship. *Uomie* was the Class II champion, and Class III was won by *Mouse of Malham*, co-owned by Illingworth and Peter and Pam Green.

Mouse was designed by Illingworth, who was soon to be a full-time yacht designer in partnership with Angus Primrose. A remarkable boat which on a 24ft LWL displaced a mere 2¼ tons, Illingworth wrote that she crept through every tiny loophole in the rule, 'but she was completely seaworthy, which is the final criterion.' He had researched the RORC records with his usual thoroughness and had discovered that what really stood out amongst the winning yachts was their ability to reach well. He therefore took a lot of trouble with her yawl rig: 'two headsails forward, a tiny mainsail and eventually an enormous mizzen staysail, the latter nearly 30% larger than the mainsail.' Irreverently called *Bat of Balham* by those who had not sailed in her, or, more feelingly, *Baby Belsen* by those who had, *Mouse* was a precursor of the modern ocean racer, for Illingworth had designed her with a separate skeg and rudder and a short fin keel. Curiously, this configuration, which was to become all the

photo Beken of Cowes

Max Aitken, seen here aboard *Lumberjack*, was one of the club's strongest supporters

rage in the following decade, was not accepted by the ocean racing fraternity at the time and Illingworth dropped it from later designs.

But the yacht which attracted the most attention that year was Dick Nye's Class II *Carina II*, one of the first ocean racers to use synthetic sails. Slightly beamier and longer than his earlier yacht, she went like greased lightning in a mainly light-weather Fastnet, not only leading her own class by miles but rarely out of sight of Class I. The Spanish owned *Mare Nostrum* took line honours, but *Carina II* won by a convincing 3hrs, 20min. on corrected time from *Lutine*.

At the end of the 1955 season another famous post-war ocean racing name, the Hon. Max Aitken, joined the club having qualified in that year's Fastnet Race in his 47ft LWL staysail schooner, *Lumberjack*. In those early postwar years, when many believed Britain to be bankrupt and exhausted, Aitken was a flag-bearer for his nation, particularly in American waters. A strong believer in the larger yacht–'never race offshore on less than 40ft waterline'–he built a series of ocean racers, some of them brilliant, others not so good. For the 1957 season he built the 58ft LWL shoal-draught centreboarder, *Drumbeat*, which looked superb but proved an expensive flop.

At a meeting in October 1955 Ray Barrett said that, for a long time, the committee's treatment of him had been unsatisfactory and he would resign if relations were not improved. He pointed out that the rule he had been working on had been given no consideration by the technical sub-committee, nor any reason why it had been rejected. He then went on to list other instances of what he considered slights against his position as hon. measurer before leaving the meeting—no doubt to stunned silence.

The committee agreed that the commodore, Myles Wyatt, should write to Barrett, pointing out that the club was most grateful for his long years of service, that no slight had ever been intended, but that the committee must reserve the right to require all club officials to work within the limits defined by them. A suggestion that Barrett be invited to become a member of the sub-committee was rejected after Wyatt pointed out that the whole objective was to keep experts off it.

The letter was no doubt written but the following month Barrett resigned, both as hon. measurer and as a member, and told the yachting press he had done so, and why. His many friends urged him to think again and in the end he wrote the committee requesting that his resignation as a member be rescinded. The committee agreed, but thought he had behaved incorrectly by informing the press of what was after all a private matter. The commodore wrote to him stating this, and adding that the committee would be only too glad to welcome him back but that he must not discuss the new draft rule, either in England or in America where he was soon to lecture.

The implication that he might divulge such confidential information was too much for Barrett who replied that he knew the commodore's letter had been written with the most friendly intentions possible which was the only reason he had not sent it straight to his solicitors. Under the circumstances, he added, there was nothing he could do but do what he had done originally: resign from the club.

Barrett, an engineer by profession 'with a mathematical bent', had been one of the club's linchpins since the earliest days and was so highly regarded that in 1950 he had been made a life honorary member. Though, on his own admission, he had known nothing about the complexities of yacht ratings and measurement in 1925, by 1932 he had learned enough to be appointed one of the club's official measurers, and by the time he took over from Heckstall-Smith in the autumn of 1946 he had become one of the foremost authorities on the subject and had contributed enormously to the new rule then being drawn up.

Even more valuable had been his ability and enthusiasm to rebuild a system of measuring yachts which before the war had, in any case, existed in only a rudimentary form. The surviving records in 1946 had been sparse and largely inaccurate and there had been very few measurers to help him. He had worked frantically hard in his unpaid post measuring yachts, calculating ratings, training new measurers, and giving lectures both in Britain and Europe 'to spread the gospel.'

'A tape, generally of the calico variety, a few pieces of string and a folding rule was considered adequate measuring equipment,' he had told his audience during one of these lectures, 'nor did the odd foot or two of error or "help" in the final rating disturb anyone unduly.' Then a new generation of designers and yacht owners appeared and 'we really had to start learning how to measure. In 1947, a designer who shall be nameless, insisted on my re-measuring one of his yachts because he said the LBG was 2½ inches too long. By that time I had made myself a set of tools which really would give the right answer.'

So successful was he, and those who supported him, that by 1960 the yachting organisations of 16 other countries were using the RORC rule for rating purposes and several had measurers trained by the club. These countries issued their own certificates, though they did not constitute official RORC ratings and foreign yachts entering RORC events always had their ratings recalculated. Also, when asked, the club supplied at cost, worksheets and logsheets; measurers' notebooks; sample rating certificates; a treatise on the preparation and checking of worksheets; and details of the RORC measuring kit which could be provided or made up by the country requesting it. By 1962–from which time all foreign yachts entering an RORC event had to have a valid RORC certificate–there were an estimated 2000 yachts in Britain which had been measured and given a rating, 700 in Scandinavia, 80 in Germany, 700 in Holland, and 500 in France. All this showed the immense value of Barrett's contribution. But the disagreement with him, which no one was able to patch up, did not delay the new rating rule being introduced for the 1957 season shortly after he died.

It was decided not to appoint another measurer but instead to employ a full-time rating secretary, a post admirably filled by Brigadier L.R.E. Fayle who had been helping out with the measuring for some years. He had been a member since 1933 and had been largely instrumental in developing the club's 1935 scantling allowance. A regular officer in the Royal Engineers, he had often crewed in *Ilex* before the war, and it was on his initiative that the REYC's highly successful *Right Royal* was built in 1951. He had also helped to extract from Germany a number of German racing yachts as war booty. Aptly known as *'Windfalls', they were subsequently distributed to Service yacht clubs.

Fayle's first task on being appointed rating secretary was to organise the remeasurement of the entire fleet, a daunting task which was nevertheless accomplished without too many problems. But it proved expensive with the club's balance sheet going into a £200 deficit by the end of 1958 because of it.

Chapter Eight

WHO REALLY WON
THE ADMIRAL'S CUP?

I N MAY 1956 the committee was informed that there might be an opportunity to buy the lease of the house next door to the clubhouse, No. 19 St James's Place. Despite its rather dubious reputation for being *haunted, Owen Aisher, the hon. treasurer, was quick to see the advantages of acquiring it, though the extra space was not at that time needed. On this occasion its purchase eluded the committee, but the new lease was a short one and the opportunity, it was thought, would eventually come to purchase the property.

The 1956 season was ruined by atrocious weather. The severe conditions encountered during the Cowes-Plymouth Race, in which only three yachts finished out of 21 starters, drove some to seek shelter in Cherbourg; and it was blowing almost as hard at the start of the Plymouth-Belle Ile. But it was in the Channel Race that boats met the most severe weather conditions.

The race started in gentle breezes on the evening of Friday 27th July, but the wind increased steadily throughout Saturday and by midnight south-west gales for Portland and Plymouth were forecast, veering north-west. Gusts of up to 86 knots were experienced in places and winds reached Force 11 at the Lizard, though the worst of the storm seems to have been confined to a narrow band of water close to the English coastline.

The depression was slow moving and the storm lasted for nearly four days. *Lutine* was first home and missed the worst of the weather when she finished at 1100 on the Sunday, though she had to sail through 50-knot squalls before arriving under the lee of the Isle of Wight. But *Bloodhound*, only ten miles astern of her, was hit by the full force of the storm east of the Nab Tower.

Because of the spray and rain, visibility was only 50 yards to leeward; to windward it was nil. The mizzen had to be handed when the track on the boom began to lift, which left *Bloodhound* under staysail only. She was then lying seven points off the wind and making hardly any headway, and at 1100 the staysail

split. It was replaced by the storm jib, but half-an-hour later the luff hanks of this broke and the yacht began drifting towards the Owers Rocks. As a last resort her crew let go the 120lb anchor. This brought her up short of the breakers off Selsey Bill, but as she was in great danger of being driven ashore the crew were taken off by Selsey lifeboat which returned the following morning to take her in tow. The anchor must have become jammed amongst some rocks for both flukes had been broken off and it was a miracle that it had held.

Selwyn Slater's Class II cutter *Uomie* also had to be abandoned after her forestay fitting pulled out of the deck, and then a rigging screw parted while she was under bare pole. So great was the turbulence caused by the storm that mud and pebbles were flung aboard her by the mountainous seas as she drifted to leeward of the Owers; and as there was a grave danger that she would be driven ashore a frigate that was standing by took off her crew. Luckily, she drifted clear of Selsey Bill and was eventually picked up by a French fishing vessel which took her into Dieppe.

The remains of *Bloodhound*'s anchor which saved one of the most famous ocean racing yachts of all time from almost certain destruction during the 1956 Channel Race

The REYC's Class II *Right Royal* was dismasted close to the Le Havre buoy in the early hours of Sunday morning. Her crew were not able to fashion a jury rig and as the weather worsened so did her predicament. However, a staysail lashed to the pulpit created just enough windage to control her as all Sunday she ran before the rising wind at about four knots while her crew attempted to prevent her being pooped. The cockpit was filled several times but the crew managed to keep her on a course which took her through the Straits of Dover. After a run of 130 miles she reached the Dyck light vessel, and was able to make fast to it before being taken in tow by the Dunkirk lifeboat.

Less fortunate–though she survived the experience–was the 10-ton light displacement cutter, *Tilly Twin*, owned by Fred *Cartwright. When Cartwright received the gale warning on Saturday evening he decided to retire as he had to be back on Monday morning. By the time the yacht reached a position some 7 or 8 miles south-east of St Catherine's she was under staysail only. But the wind suddenly veered and increased to Force 10, so the staysail was lowered and she ran under bare pole.

Tilly Twin meets Bognor Beach

both photos courtesy Peter Cartwright

ABOVE: *Tilly Twin* ended up on Bognor beach when she was hit by the storm in the 1956 Channel Race

LEFT: her crew were all rescued and were taken to the local fire station. Fred Cartwright is left foreground

As the staysail was being gathered in by the two foredeck hands, a huge wave hit her amidships even though she was running before the storm. One of the deckhands was swept overboard and sustained a broken wrist, but managed to retain hold of the staysail sheet and was hauled aboard by the other. But the dinghy, two lifebelts and the electric flare were lost overboard, the doghouse framing was cracked, one of the stanchions snapped, and water poured in through the ventilators. Another crew member who was in the cockpit was thrown over the stowed boom which was five feet above the cockpit floor, and two others with him were submerged in a torrent of water, but luckily their lifelines held.

By now the barometer had fallen to the lowest ever recorded in that area and *Tilly Twin* was in deep trouble. A 5,000-ton tanker passed her but was in difficulties itself and could do nothing to help. The yacht continued to run before the storm with the crew streaming out everything they could find, including her CQR anchor which was towed on 30 fathoms of nylon. She was driven over Selsey Shoals and eventually, with the visibility slightly improved, the beach at Bognor Regis could be seen ahead.

It seemed inevitable that she would be driven ashore but some 200 yards off the beach the anchor caught on some rocks. With her stern firmly held her cockpit was quickly swamped, and it looked as if she must fill and sink. Adding to the skipper's predicament was his realisation that the crew member with the broken wrist was very badly hurt and had to be got to hospital. He therefore decided to risk surfing his yacht up on to the beach.

The anchor line was cut and *Tilly Twin*, though she received a severe jarring, reached the shore intact, her deep keel acting as an effective drag as she touched down broadside on. Miraculously, her crew were able to walk ashore, and a crowd soon gathered. 'A man tried to make a rope fast to the stern,' Cartwright noted later. 'He wanted to claim salvage. I told a policeman also up to his shoulders to tell him to take it off.'

The injured crewman was rushed to hospital, and the rest of the crew were taken to the fire station where they were dressed in women's clothes supplied by the Women's Institute. *Tilly Twin*[1] was later lifted on to a transporter by a crane. Remarkably, when she was refloated she did not leak a drop and only one outer plank of the double diagonal hull had to be replaced. Out of 23 starters in the race only *Lutine* in Class I, *See Hexe*, *Theta* and *Joliette* in Class II, and *Rondinella* in Class III managed to finish.

A special sub-committee, headed by 'Buster' de Guingand, examined 19 reports submitted by owners of their experiences during the race. Its conclusion was that the basic lesson to be learned was a very old one, 'namely, that in severe conditions such as were experienced it is far better to be out at sea in open

1 to emphasise how lucky Cartwright and his crew had been a ten-ton yacht foundered off St Catherine's in the same storm and three of the crew of four were lost

water away from land influences, where, provided the vessel is well found and not hampered by the human element, she has the best chance of coming through without serious trouble. In general the reports show the remarkable qualities of the modern sailing yacht in being able to look after herself subject to and in spite of human error.'

In April 1954 Bush had been reappointed Griffin secretary. When John Roome took over from him in September 1955 the future of the club yacht had again come under consideration. The sweepstake, now an annual affair, had usually covered her costs, but in 1955 she had to have a new mainsail and had ended the season in deficit which the club had to cover.

On the plus side she was still popular with members and there had been no difficulty in finding either crews or–unlike some previous years–experienced members to skipper her. She had also become well known and was now something of a tradition, and keeping her going somehow would mean that no large capital outlay would have to be expended on a replacement–that is if the committee thought she should be replaced.

On the down side she could, in Bush's words, 'hardly be considered representative of modern ocean racing'. Also, she was not a popular cruising charter as she had no engine, her old fashioned rig frightened off young prospective skippers, her gear was expensive to maintain, and her performance did not encourage younger members to get crews together to win a particular race.

A sub-committee had been formed to consider what was to be done. This had recommended that the club should continue to run a yacht but that *Griffin* should be replaced, though no one quite knew how or what with. The crunch had come when she 'fell off' a particularly large *wave in the 1956 Channel Race storm. This removed so much of her caulking that the crew had to pump continually until she reached the shelter of Newhaven. She was recaulked but it was obvious that her racing days were over.

Then in March 1957, after Wyatt had replaced Maclean *Buckley as admiral and the vice commodore, Vernon Sainsbury, had become commodore, the matter was resolved to everyone's satisfaction when the hon. treasurer, Owen Aisher, and two other members, Sir Giles Guthrie and Charles Gardner, gave *Yeoman III* to the club and she was renamed *Griffin II*.

Aisher, of course, had been her original owner when she had won the 1951 Fastnet but he had then sold her to Guthrie who changed her name to *Alitia*, and he in turn had sold her to Gardner. They presented her fitted out and ready to race, but asked that a fund be raised of not less than £5,000 for her maintenance and a future replacement, and this fund received a useful addition when the first *Griffin* was sold for £1,750. At the end of the following year Roome was able to report that she had been fully booked for the races and had also had several charters.

Sir Myles Wyatt (left) aboard *Bloodhound* with Lady Wyatt (third right)

1 Tim Jeffery's official history, *The Champagne Mumm Admiral's Cup*, which covers the series from 1957 to 1993 in greater detail than is possible in this book, throws more light on the Cup's origins

Discussions about how to encourage the Americans to race in British waters had apparently been going on for some years[1], and eventually Wyatt and Peter Green had come up with the idea of some sort of team competition between the two countries. According to one version, Green had put the idea to G.W. Blunt White, a former CCA commodore, while racing aboard Blunt White's boat, *White Mist*, during the 1956 Bermuda Race. Blunt White had endorsed it enthusiastically as several CCA boats, including *White Mist*, were already planning to participate in a Transatlantic Race in 1957.

Green, Wyatt, Illingworth, Pattinson and Selwyn Slater then clubbed together to buy a cup for the proposed races and a nineteenth century racehorse trophy was found by Slater which was bought and reinscribed for £300.

The club's archives do not reveal the exact story, but from an early undated draft of the rules it would appear that the trophy—now known, of course, as the Admiral's Cup after Wyatt's position as the club's admiral—was at first called 'The 1957 Gold Cup[1]', for though solid silver it was gold-gilted. This early draft included stipulations that the cup was to be contested for between owner members of the RORC and the CCA; that two of the races were to be over RORC qualifying courses, one of which was not to be less than 400 miles (the Fastnet was not mentioned); and that the cup was to be 'the sole property of the 1957 winners' who would be the sole deciders as to where, when and on what terms it would next be offered for challenge.

At some point it was decided that the two RORC events were to be the Fastnet and Channel Races, but otherwise all the rules in the early draft presumably remained in force. For though the Deed of Trust, which was signed in 1958, appears to have been drawn up prior to the first series it did not govern it; and when Green told the committee in May 1957 that the new series was to be a purely private affair the committee agreed that it 'should be kept on a private level for the time being'.

Originally the two teams were to field five boats each but two Americans had had to withdraw and could not be replaced. As *Bloodhound*, one of the British team, was larger than the other competitors Wyatt offered to step down. The fifth British yacht had not been chosen, so this left Geoff Pattinson's *Jocasta*, *Myth of Malham* in which Illingworth and Green were now partners, and Selwyn Slater's *Uomie*. Opposing them was the American team of *White Mist*, Bill Snaith's *Figaro*, and Dick Nye's *Carina II*.

Besides the Fastnet and Channel fixtures, the series included the Britannia Cup and the New York Yacht Club Cup Races, both held during Cowes Week. Points were awarded in each race according to placing, with the Channel Race counting double points and the Fastnet triple.

The English team won that historic first series by the narrowest of margins, 70 points to 68. At a committee meeting held at the Royal Western Yacht Club after the Fastnet Green announced the winners, outlined the rules governing future series, explained that from then on a challenge for the cup could be entered on behalf of a team from any country, and that arrangements for the races would be organised by a *management committee appointed by the vice commodore, 'Buster' de Guingand, and John Bush who were to be the Cup's trustees. Perhaps this is when the club assumed control of the series, but there is no record of this.

A shadow remains over this first series which seems not to have been made public at the time—or since. At a committee meeting in September Peter Green was asked to explain why *Myth of Malham*, the highest point scoring yacht in

1 after the series both *The Times* and *The Field* reported it as being for the 'Admiral's Gold Cup'

Dick Nye's *Carina II* was a member of the first Americans' Admiral's Cup team. One of the crew was Norris Hoyt, who took these photographs during the 1957 Fastnet Race, the culmination of the first Admiral's Cup series
ABOVE: the cook, 'Sandy' Sandison, slaving in his galley
ABOVE RIGHT: skipper Dick Nye takes a well earned nap
RIGHT: Nye at the helm in rough weather

Dick Nye's *Carina II*

the competition, had taken part in the Fastnet Race without anchors, an infringement of Special Regulations.

Green explained that the day before the Fastnet the yard at Cowes, while attempting to slip her, had removed all the yacht's heavy gear and had failed to replace her anchors. This error had not been discovered until Illingworth found the anchors missing during the La Rochelle Race and had immediately reported their absence to the secretary.

Green then left the meeting.

The committee agreed that there had been no intention of evading Special Regulations, and that the infringement had been reported immediately it had been discovered. De Guingand said the committee was entitled to use its discretion and by 16 votes to two it was resolved that *Myth* should not be disqualified. Max Aitken then asked if the Americans should be told of the infringement. The commodore replied that he would discuss this with the admiral and that a private letter might be sent. Dick Scholfield suggested this might be a mistake, as it might give the impression that the committee's action was not completely justified, and at a meeting in October Sainsbury announced that the admiral had advised that the Americans need not be informed of *Myth*'s infringement.

The absence of anchors in such a light displacement yacht as *Myth* would certainly have affected her performance for the better, though whether it could have accounted for the 2hrs,3min.,37secs in corrected time which separated her from the next American competitor, *White Mist*, seems most unlikely.

But imagine the fuss today if a top Admiral's cupper was found to have infringed Special Regulations, even accidentally! She would very likely be immediately disqualified or, at best, heavily penalised. Either way, *Myth* would have been out of the running, and, with the ownership clause in operation, the Cup could have gone the way of the America's Cup in 1851 and not be seen outside the United States for over a century...

The Admiral's Cup aside, the 1957 season will be remembered for another classic Fastnet, and for the epic duels during it between two Class III competitors, *Elseli IV* and *Cohoe III*, and between two Class II ones, *Figaro III* and the club's *Griffin II*. The weather was comparable to the 1927, 1930, and 1949 races, for when the 41 entries came to the line it was blowing at least Force 7–some competitors including Illingworth thought it Force 9–from the west-south-west. Apart from the Americans the foreign competition comprised two French starters, three Dutch, three Germans and two Swedes.

One of the Swedes was Gustav Plym. A member since 1954, he had entered the race in a boat of his own design, *Elseli IV*. When he asked Vernon Sainsbury if there were any last minute orders because of the weather, the commodore replied cheerfully: 'None whatsoever. There is a gale warning, but there is no real vice in it. Good luck.'

This proved somewhat sanguine as once out of the Medina River Plym found enough wind to put six rolls in his mainsail, and just before the start he set a storm jib. However, this soon proved inadequate against such a quality opponent as Adlard Coles' *Cohoe III* and he soon changed up to a working jib. *Elseli IV* kept hammering down-Channel in the teeth of an adverse tide and a rising Force 9 gale, though afterwards Plym wrote in his book *Yacht and Sea* that if he had been more sensible–and more experienced–he would have done what Coles did which was to put into Dartmouth and rest his crew, and wait for the tide to change in his favour.

It was *Griffin II*'s first Fastnet as the club boat. Though she was admirably suited to the conditions she was not, according to one member, Johnnie *Coote, in first class nick as she had a few dodgy winches and a limited sail inventory which included *Mary Bower*'s old cotton mainsail. 'This more or less filled the measured area but set like an unfrapped awning in a breeze' and by the time the Rock had been reached every batten in it had broken and had ripped out their pockets. With a strong north-westerly blowing on the run back the mainsail was dropped for repairs and the genoa and jib set wing-and-wing. The genoa had to be sheeted to the end of the main boom as the spinnaker boom had come adrift, and had 'speared clean through the deck' and almost prevented 'a sleeping peer of the realm from later breeding three splendid children.'

Soon after Bishop Rock *Griffin II* began racing neck and neck with *Figaro III*, owned by the American, Bill Snaith, with only a few hundred yards separating the two boats. 'There was much activity on board,' Coote wrote later, 'led by a lively ringmaster with a jaunty baseball cap and a large cigar. Mizzen staysails were hoisted and lowered. The mizzen itself went up and down like a yo-yo. Headsails were frequently changed. But the relative positions of the two boats did not vary. For our part in *Griffin II* we only had two usable sails left. They were the ones already hoisted, so we had little option but to sit and watch and listen.'

Figaro III won the battle by just over three minutes, beating the club boat into fourth place in Class II by over an hour on corrected time. Only three others in their class finished.

By the time *Elseli IV* approached the Rock the weather had improved. But then the wind began to increase again and the morale of the Swedes dropped when they were beaten round the famous turning mark by an unidentified competitor. They thought it was the Class III *Galloper*, another of F.B.R. Brown's successful designs, and their only objective now was to overtake her.

At times on the way back *Elseli IV* was surfing at 11 knots, but when they were pooped Plym knew he had to reduce sail. Just as they were all considering how to do this the problem was solved for them as the genoa split for the second time. The Eddystone was passed at midnight and just over two hours later *Elseli* crossed the finishing line after nearly six days and nights at sea. Then out of the darkness a sail was seen to leeward. It was obviously the boat they had been attempting to beat.

'Good morning. Who are you?' one of *Elseli IV*'s crew shouted.

'*Cohoe III*. Good morning. And who are you?'

'*Elseli IV*.'

'Well done, *Elseli IV*.'

'Well done, *Cohoe III*.'

The congratulations were deserved for only 12 yachts finished the race and *Cohoe* and *Elseli IV* were the only two yachts to do so in Class III. Adlard Coles, who had beaten Plym to the finish by half an hour, beat the Swede by over four hours on corrected time to win Class III. Coles also thought the race a memorable one, writing that it was said to have been one of the roughest in the history of the event. For their fiercely fought battle in such adverse circumstances Plym was made 'yachtsman of the year' in Sweden, and Coles was awarded the same honour in Britain.

Illingworth won Class II in the veteran *Myth of Malham*, but the overall winner was Dick Nye in *Carina II*, now rerated as Class I. This was a remarkable performance by the American for he had now won the Fastnet twice in succession. And he had done it the second time in a yacht which had been structurally damaged, as early in the race the yawl fell off a wave and cracked a frame. She leaked the entire time and the crew had to pump her every hour throughout the race.

'Is every man a tiger?' Nye would roar to encourage them.

'Gr...gr...gr...gr,' the crew yelled back.

Two club members, 'Buster' de Guingand and 'Sandy' Sandison, were crewing in *Carina II*, and when the boat crossed the finishing line de Guingand recorded that *Nye shouted his now famous remark: 'All right boys, we're over now, let her sink.'

At the annual dinner that year, the record number of members present (412) were told it had been one of the club's most successful seasons. There had been 324 starts in the programme of 13 races which had included a new event to open the season, the 225-mile Lyme Bay Race. But the commodore, Vernon Sainsbury, admitted that the Fastnet had 'put us back on our heels'. He then announced that the committee intended to exercise its right to inspect all entries to ensure they followed the club's Special Regulations, for it was determined to make quite sure that boats carried all the safety equipment listed in Special Regulations, as well as ascertaining that their hull, gear, and sails were sound.

The decision to tighten up Special Regulations, which were now completely revised, must have been prompted by the problem of *Myth*'s anchors, though the severe conditions during the 1956 Channel Race and the 1957 Fastnet had shown up equipment deficiencies in some of the entries. Echo sounders were, at last, allowed as their cost had dropped, but the committee continued to insist that rigid dinghies be carried even though inflatables were by then in common use. For reasons of expense, it was reluctant to make inflatables compulsory, but it was criticised in the yachting press for not even including them in the list of recommended equipment. They were made optional in 1961, in place of a rigid dinghy, and compulsory in 1964.

~

In the spring of 1947 Hasler had sold *Tre Sang* to another member, Commander Bill King, and had spent that season sailing with Illingworth who had asked him to help work up *Myth of Malham* for the 1948 Bermuda Race. Shortly before the race he retired from the Royal Marines on medical grounds and after it devoted his time to cruising, writing his classic pilot guide, *Harbours and Anchorages of the North Brittany Coast*, and to designing a 'radical cruising boat'. In 1953 he had built a 5-ton folkboat called **Jester*, which incorporated many of his ideas for single-handed sailing such as self-steering gear—he invented the first commercially viable one—and a lapwing rig (modified Ljungstrom rig). She was listed as a club yacht and in May 1953 he had asked that she be given a rating in order to compete in certain local handicap races, but nothing seems to have come of this.

Then in October 1957 Hasler and another retired Royal Marines officer, Ian Major, who was also a member, decided, in Hasler's words, 'to have a go at the Committee of the Royal Ocean Racing Club in an attempt to make them admit experimental boats to ordinary offshore races.' They put forward a proposal under the rubric 'The Development of Yacht Design Under the RORC Rule.' In it they quoted one of the stated objects of the club: to 'study and encourage the design, building, navigation and sailing of sailing vessels in which speed and seaworthiness are combined, by any means including scientific research and practical demonstration.' This, they reasoned, must mean 'amongst other things, the encouragement of development and experiment aimed at improving the breed. Specifically, it implies that any unconventional boat which is a bona fide attempt to solve the problems of offshore yacht design should be encouraged to take part in RORC events, so that she can be properly tested against the best of the existing breed.'

However, they went on, in practice any proposal to admit or measure an unconventional vessel was looked upon unfavourably by RORC members because the club believed that a) it would not be possible to measure such a craft accurately; b) if and when she was measured and rated there was a risk she might defeat the rule by obtaining an unfairly low rating; and c) she might be unseaworthy.

The authors therefore proposed an addendum to the rule which would state that 'It is not intended that any part of this Rule of Measurement should discourage or prevent bona fide experiment or development work aimed at improving the breed of offshore racing boats. Any owner wishing to experiment with a boat that would be either prohibited, or impossible to measure, under the strict letter of the Rule, may apply for his boat to be rated as an "experimental design".'

The applicant would have to establish to the satisfaction of the committee that the experimental features of his vessel were aimed at improvement and not merely to obtain a favourable rating, and that the boat was in fact seaworthy. If the committee was satisfied on these points then the boat would be given an arbitrary rating so that it could race with the fleet, and that this rating would be deliberately high 'in order not to upset the balance of existing ratings...so that the experimental boat will have little chance of winning on corrected time, at any rate during her first season. It will be subject to review annually, at the end of the season, provided that the boat has finished at least two races during that season.'

When this proposal was discussed in committee, Haworth and Fayle objected to the principle of giving ratings without measurement, and it was pointed out that some experimental yachts embodied features specifically prohibited by the rule. The committee referred the matter to the technical sub-committee who were asked to examine the rule with a view to replacing prohibitions with suitable factors for the assessment of prohibited features. If this could be done, then experimental yachts could be rated.

In March 1958 Fayle explained to the committee the technical sub-committee's recommendations for replacing prohibitions, along with other minor amendments to the rule of measurement, and these were sent to Hasler. However, the penalties that an unorthodox yacht was likely to incur were so heavy that they virtually amounted to a prohibition in themselves, and though letters continued to be exchanged until 1962 there the matter rested.

The 1958 season proved somewhat disappointing as the number of starters for the club's extensive–over-extensive, some committee members suggested

–programme of 14 races was much lower than the previous year's and even lower than 1956. *Griffin II* came in for some criticism as well with Selwyn Slater stating that she was badly found. When he had taken her on a race the steering gear had broken, the sheets and halyards had been in an appalling condition, and the eggs had been bad.

Other committee members thought this was 'overcooking' it a bit, but Slater was such a splendid character that his criticisms were probably taken in good part. 'He could have passed for Alfred Doolittle in Covent Garden, from baggy trews to knotted kerchief, calloused hands and weatherbeaten features,' a friend wrote when Slater died in 1978, and added that he had 'left an indelible mark on the post-war ocean-racing scene.' He had quickly grasped the significance of John Illingworth's *Myth of Malham* and had commissioned Arthur Robb to design him *Uomie* and then *Ramrod* in which 'he and his rollicking crews won countless races and both Class Championships.'

Apparently he drove to work–though no one knew for sure what he did–in an Aston Martin once owned by the comedian Tony Hancock and which he 'nurtured like a Stradivarius'. On one occasion, when he was taken to dine at the Royal Yacht Squadron, he turned up in his seaboots, though after much persuasion he agreed to borrow the Steward's shoes. As one of the original donors of the Admiral's Cup he always insisted it had been bought in the Portobello Road as it would have been quite contrary to his style to admit it had come from Garrards.

In November 1958 Sainsbury announced that the club had been offered the freehold of No. 19 St James's Place provided negotiations could be completed by 25th December. This left little time and the negotiations were obviously fraught, but in January 'Buster' de Guingand announced that the club's offer of £18,050 had been accepted, and that the current tenant had been granted a ten-year lease. It was to prove another piece of forward thinking which has subsequently paid dividends.

In January 1958 the Duke of Edinburgh had been made a life honorary member and that December was the guest of honour at the club's annual dinner and prize giving. At it the club's admiral, Myles Wyatt, made the oft quoted remark that 'ocean racing is the wettest, slowest, most expensive and most uncomfortable way of getting nowhere that the wit of man has ever devised.'

This went down well and in his speech the Duke of Edinburgh took much the same line. 'I have just enough knowledge of sailing and the sea,' he remarked, 'to have an unbounded admiration for anybody who belongs to this club, but if I had any more knowledge I would probably think that you were all nuts.'

After the dinner the Duke enquired how the new rule worked exactly and was sent, via his aide de camp, chapter and verse by the secretary.

'The system of handicapping winners of RORC Trophies,' Paul explained, 'is by Drinking Time Allowance (D.T.A.) based upon Trophy Tunnage Rating (T.T.R.) which is calculated as follows in the case of, say, the Britannia Cup:

B = Greatest diameter of Trophy

Aa = Alc Area

D = Quarter Beam Depth

d = Dent Correction Factor

F = Phroth Factor

$Aa = \dfrac{B^2}{4} \times \pi = 0.785B^2$

$T.T.R. = 0.785B^2 (D{-}F) - d$

F.G.S. = Forward Girth Station of the personal winner of the trophy

F.I.G.S. = Forward Inner Girth Station of the above

G.S.D.f. = Horizontal distance between F.G.S. and F.I.G.S.

therefore $D.T.A. = \dfrac{T.T.R.}{G.S.D.f.}$

The Aralus Plate requires an additional formula:

Ap = Area of Aralus Plate

Bg = Diameter of champagne glass

$\dfrac{Ap}{Bg}_2$ = Champagne Glass Load Factor (C.G.L.F.)

Champagne glasses are then measured and the Champagne Glass Tunnage Rating is worked out as above and multiplied by the C.G.L.F. to give the T.T.R.

It is all quite simple really.'

In January 1959, when the membership had reached 1,800, the question of an international rule again arose some 30 years after it had first been mooted. Sainsbury, who had been corresponding with Olin Stephens on the subject, asked the committee's view as to whether the CCA should be encouraged to adopt a form of the RORC rule as it appeared dissatisfied with its own. If such a proposal were adopted, and the rule became an international one, the RORC would be bound to lose control.

After a discussion and a vote it was decided that it would be much better for the RORC to continue to operate its own rule, but that Sainsbury should continue the discussions to try and bring the two rules closer together, particularly in the matter of sail area measurement where it was thought that British yachts were at a disadvantage when racing in American waters.

Perhaps the Americans thought they were at a disadvantage racing in British waters, for a team did not challenge for the Admiral's Cup in 1959, though Dick Nye came over again in *Carina II*. On the instigation of member Jean-Claude Menu, France became the first nation to challenge for the Admiral's

Capt. John Illingworth

Adlard K. Coles

Peter Green

Vernon Sainsbury

E.P. de Guingand

F.B.R. Brown

C.H. Van Dam

Alan H. Paul

David W. Baddeley

Owen Aisher

Derek J. Boyer

Selwyn Slater

Cartoonist Fred May captures some of the more colourful characters
at the 1959 RORC dinner for the readers of *Yachting World*

Cup after it had been thrown open to world wide competition, entering his *Marie-Christine III*, Fernand Hervé's *Eloise II*, and Georges Craipeau's *St François*. The Dutch also sent a team in 1959, and though the French did not do well the Dutch proved to be every bit as tough as the Americans.

Yachting World

A.W. Goudriaan aboard *Olivier van Noort* during the 1961 Admiral's Cup

The British team picked to defend the Cup were Illingworth and Green, again in *Myth of Malham*, Selwyn Slater in his new yacht *Ramrod*, and *Griffin II*, skippered by Gerald Potter with a picked crew of members. *Ramrod* won the Channel Race with *Griffin II* winning her class, but the Dutch fought back, winning the Britannia Cup with W. van der Vorm's *Zwerver*, and after the New York Yacht Club Cup Race the British team were just three points ahead of the Dutch. It all depended, once more, on the Fastnet and its triple points, which notched another record that year with 59 entries.

It was a mixed race weatherwise: calms early on, then fog, followed by gales which resulted in all three French Admiral's Cup boats retiring with broken gear. Two of the Dutch boats, A.W. Goudriaan's *Olivier van Noort,* and *Zwerver*, sailed by Otto van der Vorm, did well, the former finishing second in Class I and the latter fourth, with the Dutch team's third boat, Bruynzeel's *Zeevalk*, finishing ninth. But the Dutch were pipped at the post by the British team, which retained the Cup by 135 points to 123, mainly because *Griffin II* was second overall as well as in her class.

However, the overall winner of the race, the S & S designed Class II yawl, *Anitra*, came not from France, Holland, Britain or the United States, but from Sweden. Owned by Sven Hansen and navigated by Mike Richey, *Anitra* sailed a near perfect race. But close to the finish a tricky decision had to be made. Faced with a lee shore and no visibility, and where a difference in 400 yards in Richey's dead reckoning could have spelled disaster, Richey turned to Hansen and said: 'If my navigation is correct, we shall make Plymouth breakwater [the finishing line] and win the race, but if it isn't we shall pile up on the rocks outside. It's your yacht, you decide.'

Hansen told him to go ahead and *Anitra* beat the second boat, *Griffin II*, by just over three minutes on corrected time. The gales hit those behind and the last yacht, *Rummer*, took eight days to finish.

Chapter Nine

NO BEARDY WEIRDIES, PLEASE

THE RORC has always found other yacht clubs helpful and co-operative in the running of its offshore races, and nowadays its relationship with them is usually both smooth and professional. But at the start of 1960 there was a spat with the Royal Southern and Royal Southampton Yacht Clubs when they protested to what was by then the Royal Yachting Association (RYA) about the club starting races in the Solent during Cowes Week.

'It is felt that Cowes Week should be sacrosanct to yacht racing in the Solent,' the Royal Southern argued. 'The Royal Ocean Racing Club, a Club younger by 100 years, is taking advantage of the traditional gathering of yachtsmen at Cowes and in the Solent during the first week in August...

'Many members of the Royal Southern Yacht Club are also members of the Royal Ocean Racing Club, and applaud that Club's great achievement in long distance yacht races, but they stress that these efforts should not clash with the traditional dates during Cowes Week for "in-shore" racing.'

The Royal Southampton Yacht Club agreed and thought that 'to have a clash of major events between the senior clubs is surely a tragedy for the sport and contrary to the yachting spirit which Cowes Week has so successfully portrayed for a hundred years or more.'

The RORC commodore, Vernon Sainsbury, did not agree: 'Far from detracting from the success of the handicap classes in Cowes Week, we believe that the RORC has materially contributed to their popularity, both by virtue of its Rating Rule and by attracting foreign entrants, particularly in Fastnet years.'

He pointed out that most RORC races were run in amicable association with other clubs, and that the club's programme had been agreed at the Solent Clubs Racing Association's fixtures meeting without dissent. Regrettably there was bound to be some overlapping in August, but the RORC's programme had to fit in with the racing fixtures of four or five other countries.

The RYA, the pig-in-the-middle of this disagreement which had been bubbling for some years, told the aggrieved clubs that such collisions of interest were inevitable. Some 1,500 fixtures had to be squeezed into a comparatively short summer and that 'the rapid development of yachting' made it essential for give and take on all sides, and there the matter rested.

With the prime minister of the day announcing that the country had never had it so good, the reason for the rapid development the RYA mentioned was doubtless due to the fact that economic revival, and its accompanying affluence, was reflected in the increased number of starters in club events. After the disappointment of 1958, the 378 starters for the 1960 programme was not far behind the 430 for 1959, and was way up on the 262 in 1958. Then in 1961 there was a quantum leap with 590 starters competing in the 14 fixtures, approaching double the 324 for 1957.

There was also growing evidence of the club's influence internationally. At the end of 1960 there was a request from Sweden asking for the RORC to sponsor a 340-mile race from Gotland to Helsinki in July 1961; the same month a letter from the President of the Société des Régates Rochelaises expressed his distress that the club would not be visiting La Rochelle the following year; and in March 1961 there was a request from the Royal Bermuda Yacht Club for the RORC to present a trophy for their new ocean race.

All this boded well for the future but, so far as Illingworth was concerned, the club's growing influence and popularity was attracting yachtsmen who had no right to be members. At the December 1960 AGM he and Angus *Primrose, the naval architect who had formed a yacht design firm with Illingworth, and a third member, put forward a formal resolution that a candidate had to have either completed a Fastnet Race or two other qualifying races. Illingworth argued that originally the Fastnet had been the qualification for membership and that this rule had been watered down to enable the club to expand more quickly. Now, with nearly 2,000 members, it was time to make the qualification more difficult in order to get 'a better type of member'.

Sainsbury, somewhat tartly one suspects, asked Illingworth if he thought the club was getting the wrong type of member to which Illingworth answered that a number had been elected on the strength of one Dinard Race sailed in light weather. Sainsbury thought very few people did one race, and of those who did very many were noteworthy overseas members, such as the commodores of the Royal Bermuda Yacht Club and the Cruising Yacht Club of Australia, yachtsmen who might otherwise not have joined because they were too busy to take part in more than one event. He added that during the year a

Quiver III and her
owner, Ren Clarke.
Clarke was a member
of the British Admiral's
Cup in 1961, with
Quiver III, and in 1965
with Quiver IV

photo Beken of Cowes

Yachting World

new certificate of competency had been introduced which asked searching questions about the prospective candidate from the owner of the boat in which the candidate had sailed. This, and the comment from the hon. treasurer that more stringent membership qualifications would almost certainly adversely affect the club financially, resulted in the motion being soundly defeated.

The AGM also agreed that the classes for 1961 should be altered as follows: Class I 30ft to under 70ft rating; Class II 24ft to under 30ft rating; Class III 19ft to under 24ft rating.

The 1961 season opened with the Lyme Bay Race, sailed in light weather and mostly poor visibility. One of the smallest entries, *Sea Lancer*, finished first, not only on corrected time but overall. This caused such amazement that the navigator's charts and logs were examined but it was found that she had indeed covered the course properly.

There was an exhilarating ride for the entries in the next race, the Southsea-Harwich. The winners in each class were decided in the last 30 miles which was sailed to windward in half a gale amongst the East Coast shoals. Outstanding were the two smallest entries, both Illingworth and Primrose designs. Illingworth skippered the winner, *Maica*[1], which beat *Alcina*, with Angus Primrose aboard, into second place. The wind rose to Force 7 on the beat from the Outer Gabbard to the Sunk and the Gunners' yacht *St Barbara* was dismasted. Another service yacht, *Petasus*, owned by the Royal Signals Yacht Club, was driven aground on the Sunk Sand, and both had had to be towed in by the lifeboat.

The third fixture, the North Sea Race, produced a record 81 starters. It began in light winds, but that night the sheer size of the fleet caused problems at one of the course's turning marks, the West Hinder. By then the wind had freshened to a good Force 4 and 50 yachts or more, all bunched together, were running towards it. Some chose to tack as they rounded the mark and to beat back through the fleet which increased the confusion. At least a third of those involved in the mêlée were carrying illegal masthead lights and some also had their crosstree lights on which blinded their helmsmen.

As one commentator wrote 'The air seemed full of lights and flogging canvas', and there were several near misses. In one incident a Class III yacht was nearly run down by a Class I competitor which was 'lit up like a Christmas tree' so that her helmsman had no night vision. Spinnakers became entangled round the jibstays of many yachts which led to three yachts being dismasted. No less than 34 others had to retire for one reason or another before the race was won by the Dutch-owned *Hestia*.

The confusion of the North Sea Race was soon overshadowed by a tragedy in the ever-popular Dinard event, won that year by Mike Vernon, the club's current

1 owned by Henri Rouault, *Maica* won the Class III Championships in 1962, the first French boat to do so

vice commodore, in his new Robert Clark-designed Class II steel sloop, *Assegai*. It started in high winds which reduced the 110 entries to 80 starters, but the storm which developed was quite unexpected. At its height *Ramrod* was riding out the night almost hove-to. 'Steve' Stephenson, a part owner of *Ramrod*, was on watch with a crew member, Richard Fell. David Maufe, one of the mates, recalls that he was about to go on deck to relieve Stephenson who was at the helm. He could see from below that Fell, was 'sitting with his arms behind him and he must have been cold and tired, and a bit seasick, and he didn't have a lifeline on. I heard the spray go across the cockpit but it wasn't solid water or anything, but it pitched Dick across the cockpit where he was sitting on the weather side and into the sea.

'We threw a lifebuoy and we heard him shouting "help" in the water but we couldn't see him. It was difficult to hear him above the noise of the gale and thrashing of the sails which we lowered as we started the engine. We never saw him and the shouts gradually became fainter.'

This was the club's first loss of life during a race since Colonel Hudson had been swept overboard from *Maitenes II* during the 1931 Fastnet. It provoked another member of the club to ask the RYA to identify the individuals responsible for what occurred 'by allowing these races to start under such conditions, the outcome of which, from what I have heard, has shocked the public as well as many sailing enthusiasts.' He also suggested that the RYA issue a ruling to the RORC that races should either be postponed or cancelled should gales be imminent and/or if the wind at the start exceeded Force 6 or 7.

The letter was discussed at a RYA Council Meeting when the Duke of Edinburgh was in the chair. The RYA's reply to it appeared to condone what was considered by the club to be an unorthodox approach to the RYA. Alan Paul promptly wrote to the member reminding him that the *responsibility for starting always lay with the owners taking part. He added that the RORC committee 'took great exception to his action in going directly to the RYA without expressing his views to the officers of his own club, whose policy and actions he criticised so strongly.'

The member was invited twice to attend committee meetings to explain his actions and give his views, but he did not do so and subsequently resigned.

The same month two other members, Dr. J. Kempton and P. Tilbury, were lost in a Force 10 storm in the Bay of Biscay while cruising. The sole survivor of this tragedy, David Logan, a cadet member of the club, steered the yacht for 25 hours until rescued by a fishing trawler.

The 1961 Admiral's Cup attracted four overseas teams–the United States, France, Holland, and Sweden–to try and wrest the cup from Britain. Although it was only the third series, competition amongst British contenders was fierce, and for the first time several yachts were specially constructed to gain a place in the team. However, the only new yacht to be selected was Ren Clarke's *Quiver III*, designed by Charles A. Nicholson, which had won her first two offshore races, come second in the Dinard Race, and second in her class in the Round-The-Island Race. The choice of *Myth of Malham and Griffin II*, now rated as Class I, to be the other two members of the team did not pass without comment. 'The Establishment was hard to break' was how a member, Paul Antrobus, put it later in *Ocean Racing Around the World* which he co-authored.

Popularity always has its downside and in 1961 the crowded starts to the three classes in the Fastnet, which attracted 95 starters, inevitably increased the danger of collision. Just before the gun for Class III *Capreolus* collided with *Faem*. The latter was so seriously damaged that she had to retire immediately and *Capreolus* retired later in the race.

It was a heavy weather race and the eventual winner, Otto van der Vorm's 39ft cutter, *Zwerver*, was knocked down twice 30 miles from the Rock, and was forced to heave to for five hours before continuing. In all 30 yachts retired, while others lost much ground by running before the storm. The increasing power and size of the modern ocean racing yacht was evident that year with Kees Bruynzeel's super ketch, *Stormvogel*, taking line honours.

Following his success with smaller light displacement, plywood-built yachts Bruynzeel, who was then living in South Africa, wanted to try the same technique on the largest yacht allowed under RORC rules. He decided on a glued-up hull of four layers for *Stormvogel*. The inner and outer ones were of 9.5mm mahogany laid lengthways, while the two middle ones were 4.76mm laid diagonally. This made the hull so rigid that only light frames were necessary. Van de Stadt drew him a preliminary plan which included Bruynzeel's idea of having a free-hanging rudder placed far aft at the waterline.

When Bruynzeel showed this to Olin Stephens, who had designed *Zeearend* for him, the American designer commented that a free hanging rudder would have an adverse effect on the yacht's speed as it interfered with the waterflow from the keel. Bruynzeel's argument that it would help keep the boat on course in bad weather and heavy seas did not convince Stephens at the time, though he later used the idea, even on 12 metres.

Bruynzeel then took *Stormvogel's* plan to Laurent Giles, who was enthusiastic, and the yacht's rigging was designed by Illingworth. As no yard in 1960 had any experience of building such a yacht, Bruynzeel decided to construct her in a shed at his lumbermill in Stellenbosch and she was launched, after some difficulty in getting her there, at Cape Town.

The Admiral's Cup results in 1961 showed British yachtsmen that a more modern, hard-nosed approach had to be made, for the Americans won

all photos Yachting World

ABOVE LEFT: Otto van der Vorm skippered the Dutch yacht *Zwerver* in the 1961 Admiral's Cup
ABOVE RIGHT: J-C Menu skippered the French yacht *Marie Christine III* in the 1961 Admiral's Cup
BELOW LEFT: Sven Hansen skippered *Anitra* for the 1961 Swedish Admiral's Cup team
BELOW RIGHT: Peter Green, the club's commodore at the time, skippered *Myth of Malham* for the British Admiral's Cup team in 1961 which came second

convincingly after accumulating a big lead in the Channel Race which they never lost during the rest of the series.

At the 1961 AGM Primrose and Illingworth, and others, again proposed more stringent qualifications for membership. Those backing it thought that with 2,000 members the personal touch was being lost. With one short race being the only qualifying requirement, it was thought the club was ignoring the original concept on which it had been founded. The proposers of the motion wanted a candidate to have sailed, and completed, qualifying races which totalled at least 500 miles.

The new commodore Peter Green—who had taken over from Vernon Sainsbury at the beginning of the year and at 37 was the youngest ever to be appointed—had already written a circular to all members opposing the amendment: 'The whole matter boils down to the question, what sort of club do we want. There seems to me to be three alternatives. 1) We continue much as we are at present. Though the membership is growing, due to deaths and resignations the rate of growth is slowing down and this is likely to continue for the future. 2) A much smaller club composed of a collection of "nautical beardy weirdies". 3) A much more select and smaller type of yacht club.'

He believed either of the last two alternatives would mean a much diminished membership which would result in a huge increase in subscriptions if the present clubhouse was to be retained. 'The "beardy weirdies" probably could not afford it and the third category who could afford it probably would not be interested in ocean racing.'

A higher standard of qualification might raise the status of the club and make yachtsmen more anxious to join, but it would also make it more difficult for young people to qualify, especially those in the services. Probably Illingworth's proposal would, the commodore concluded, 'exclude far more worthy members than undesirables. The club is big enough and strong enough to wear a few of the latter.'

The amendment was defeated by 38 votes to 9.

Before the 1962 season began the club's Patron and the Duke of Edinburgh bought *Bloodhound from Wyatt and then lent her to the club for the Dinard Race which she only just failed to win. A columnist in one daily newspaper later accused her crew of ignoring the plight of another entry which had been dismasted, though the race analysis later proved that Bloodhound was a long way ahead of the stricken yacht at the time. Legal action was instigated by the crew, and the matter was settled when a three-figure sum was paid into the Griffin fund and a paragraph regretting the original statement was published by the newspaper.

That year the Southsea-Harwich Race was the coldest ever, but there is no mention in the race reports of hot-water bottles being employed and only three of the 29 starters retired. The North Sea Race had a record 90 starters and 250 competitors attended the dinner afterwards at the Royal Maas Yacht Club. The crews entering the Cowes-San Sebastian Race, in which 31 yachts took part, were lavishly entertained at the finish, with a free official dinner and tickets to the local bull fight. Altogether, the season attracted 563 starters, a huge increase over the previous non-Fastnet year of 378.

The popularity of the Admiral's Cup had further intensified the competition to make the team and though it was still chosen on the opinion of the selection committee, not on a points system, five regular RORC events, and two other races round the buoys, were now named for the 1963 contenders to race in. After these had taken place the selectors–Myles Wyatt, Mike Vernon, and Alan Paul–chose Clarion of Wight, owned by Derek Boyer and Dennis Miller,

photo Beken of Cowes

Ron Amey's *Noryema III*, and Max Aitken's *Outlaw*, with *Quiver III* as reserve yacht. Peter Green was appointed team captain.

The series attracted teams from six countries including, for the first time, Germany. It also saw the debut of Boyer and Miller who became one of the most successful partnerships in ocean racing history. Stanley Malone, who had crewed for Boyer on his previous yacht, introduced the two of them.

'When I started ocean racing in the early 1950s,' Malone recalled, 'it wasn't so easy to find a berth. If you had experience owners would take you; if you didn't they wouldn't. Typical catch 22 situation. But I managed to get one or two races under my belt in a yacht owned by a naval dentist called Hunter. There were no winches on her, everything was done by tackle! In those days–the early 1950s–ocean racing was unbelievably casual. At night the watch sang rugby songs and made cocoa, no one thought of trimming the sails, much less hanging off the weather side.'

Bruynzeel's magnificent *Stormvogel* in 1962

In 1957 Malone had met Derek Boyer quite by chance, as the yacht he was aboard moored alongside Boyer's *Mystery of Meon*. As one did in those days both crews had had a drink together and looked over each other's boats, and when Boyer discovered that Malone had ocean raced he recruited him for the 1958 season in his new boat, *Pym*, which won Class III that year.

'We were short of a navigator for the last-but-one race of the season, from Brixham to Belle Ile, and I suggested Dennis Miller who I occasionally sailed with from Lymington. He came and brought with him the first Brookes and Gatehouse hand-held Homer Heron that we had seen, as in those days all one had by way of a navigational aid were those BEME loops, great grey boxes with a loop on the top. It was an infinitely better piece of gear. Anyway, we won the race and Dennis went down very well.

'They were quite different characters. Derek, very organised, Dennis very casual and a bit of a hell raiser.'

Miller raced with Boyer for three more seasons and then built his own yacht and asked his girl friend, who was blessed with a sense of humour, to perform the launching ceremony at Lallow's. Instead of intoning the time-honoured phrase for launching a boat she cracked the champagne bottle smartly over the bows and said: 'I name this yacht *Damian* and God help all who sail in her'.

Neither Miller nor Boyer had done very well in the 1961 Fastnet and in the post mortem that followed they decided to team up and build a yacht specifically to win a place in the Admiral's Cup team and to win the Fastnet. But they couldn't agree who should design it until one day Boyer said quite casually that he had met Olin Stephens who might be willing to design something for them. As Stephens was the one designer that one or other of them did not dislike he was commissioned to design *Clarion of Wight* for them, and she proved to be the first really successful postwar British S & S design to be built to the RORC rule.

The Admiral's Cup competition in 1963 was another closely fought encounter amongst the six nations vying for the trophy. Sweden did exceptionally well in the Channel Race; the British team exceptionally badly. Sweden retained her lead after the Britannia Cup which one of her team, *Staika III*, won. But the New York Yacht Club Cup was dominated by the British team and after it they trailed the Swedes by only four points with the Cup holders, the Americans, one point behind the British. So, as was to happen so often, the outcome rested on the Fastnet.

The start was in typical Fastnet weather, Force 6 on the nose, and was marred by a collision between *Clarion of Wight* and *Primevere*, skippered by John Illingworth though he was not at the helm at the time. One of *Clarion*'s spinnaker poles was broken and her deck was holed. She was able to continue but there were rather too many accidents that year. Bill Snaith's *Figaro* got into a

Painting by Laurence Bagley of the rescue of the crew of *Griffin VI*
by the French yacht *Lorelei* during the 1979 Fastnet

Peter Nicholson at the helm of one of his designs

Chris Dunning (left) has so far owned eleven yachts named *Marionette*. The seventh one, photographed here by Barry Pickthall, was a member of the winning British Admiral's Cup team in 1977

Jonathan Bradbeer, the club's commodore, 1988–1990

Eddie Warden Owen during the 1989 Admiral's Cup series

Mary Pera (née Blewitt) joined the club in 1947. A Life Honorary Member, she received the British Nautical Award for Lifetime Achievement in 1999

Ted Turner steering G. de Guardiola's *Locura*, one of the American team in the 1983 Admiral's Cup series. He was one of the club's rear commodores, 1976–78

Graham Walker,
1997 Fastnet Race

Graham Walker's fourth
Indulgence which helped
return the Admiral's Cup
to Britain in 1989

The Farr-designed
50-footer, *Jamarella*,
a member of the
winning British
team, during the
1989 Admiral's Cup
series in which she
was top boat.
Owner Alan Gray is
nearest the camera
on windward side

terrible tangle when her liferaft was blown overboard and promptly inflated, though this did not stop her from winning Class I; *Outlaw*'s gooseneck sheered before the start and she had to cross the line under headsails only; *Assegai* lost her mast off Bolt Head; *Corabia* lost hers off the Longships; a tanker ran down *Micronette* near the Eddystone, forcing her to retire; and *Quiver III*'s forestay bottlescrew snapped, though by some miracle her mast did not go overboard.

There was also some damage amongst the crews. Those aboard *Marabu* succumbed, almost to a man, to seasickness, and the skipper of *Belmore II* had to be put ashore with concussion. However, this did not stop *Belmore II* sailing an exceptional race, coming third in her class and fourth overall. Afterwards a crew member answered the question in the race analysis sheet as to what had affected the boat's performance: 'Get rid of your skipper, somehow.'

Two of the US team, *Figaro* and *Carina II*, did brilliantly but the third, *Windrose*, could only manage 22nd place in Class II. This let in the British for *Clarion* won the race convincingly, though her crew had an agonising wait while Illingworth's protest over the collision at the start was sorted out. If it had been upheld the Americans would have kept the Admiral's Cup for another two years. But it was not and Britain won the Cup back by 250 points to the Americans' 237.

All 13 events of the club's programme in 1963 had a record number of starters, 830 in total. However, as Alan Paul put it, an impression had 'been gaining ground in recent years that all is not well with the RORC time scale and one often hears the comment that a big boat can only win if she gets a lucky break'.

A suggestion that the club change over to Time-on-Distance system, as was the practice in Sweden and the Mediterranean, was not accepted, but it was recognised that the weakness of the club's Time-on-Time TCF system was that, whenever the wind fell light, or there was a period of calm, the small boats built up their time allowances at the expense of the larger ones. If these conditions prevailed for any length of time the boat with the lowest rating almost always won. What's more, ocean racers had improved in efficiency out of all recognition since Barrett's time scale had been first introduced in 1936, and the smaller yachts could now keep going in strong winds and rough seas, conditions in which only the larger yachts had previously thrived.

During the 1950s any advantage the TCF system may have given to smaller yachts had not mattered much as relatively few large ones had taken part in RORC events. But the arrival in 1963 of such super-yachts as *Bolero*, *Capricia*, and *Stormvogel* now made it necessary to alter the time scale to give better results, and an alteration was accepted by the committee for use in 1964 on a trial basis.

Clarion of Wight, which won the 1963 Fastnet Race and was top boat
in that year's Admiral's Cup series

photo Beken of Cowes

courtesy Derek Boyer

Growing dissatisfaction with the Interclub Points Championship was also discussed in committee. Up to the 1950s the contribution of certain clubs, such as the REYC and the West Mersea, to the development of the RORC and its races, could undoubtedly be traced to the keen rivalry promoted by the inter-club contest. But during the early 1960s the disparity between local clubs and the national associations and service yacht clubs, which were also allowed to compete for the shield, became more marked. The RORC's French equivalent, the Union Nationale des Croiseurs (UNC), for example, had come third in 1961, second in 1962 and had won in 1963.

The commodore thought a restriction might be put on yachts racing for Service clubs whose owners had never belonged to that particular service. He also thought that UNC should not inveigle practically every eligible French yacht to race for that club.

Mike Vernon, who had just finished his stint as vice commodore and was to succeed Peter Green as commodore at the start of 1965, believed that the inter-club competition was no longer a very inspiring contest. Ordinary yacht clubs had little chance of winning the shield which gave them little incentive to encourage their members to go ocean racing and try hard to win it. It was, Vernon concluded, 'one of the prime duties of the RORC to do everything possible to stimulate such interest in ocean racing and I believe that only by positive effort will we be able to maintain the upward trend of entries.'

Derek Boyer with his aircraft. 'Only fools and birds fly' says the caption on the back of this photograph. But his help in flying RORC race organisers to their destination was of enormous help to the club in recent years

A sub-committee was formed to look into the matter. It came up with the solution that a club should be awarded the points gained in the best four races of four yachts racing for a particular club, not more than two of which were to be in the same class. This seemed to work satisfactorily and in 1964 West Mersea Yacht Club accumulated 15,329 points to win the championship from the Royal Naval Sailing Association whose best four boats were credited with 10,596 points.

The strain on office accommodation was also another topic for discussion. It had been necessary to expand, so some of the sleeping cubicles had been converted to storage and office space, and this now brought the availability of No.19 St James's Place into focus. As a first move the current tenant, who regularly broke his lease by sub-letting without the club's permission, was given his marching orders.

The hon. treasurer was already putting something aside for the development of No.19 St James's Place and a sub-committee was formed to consider how this could best be done. In February 1964 expert outside advice was sought which

Rod Stephens at the helm of Sven Hansen's *Capricia* which won line honours in the 1963 Fastnet Race

preferred several alternatives for the committee to consider: the premises could be leased again at a higher rent, or part of it could be converted for the club's use, with the rest being let; or it could be demolished and rebuilt; or both properties could be demolished and rebuilt.

In May 1964 first mention of the One Ton Cup appears in the minutes when the committee received a letter from Jean Peytel, of the Cercle de la Voile de Paris, saying that in 1965 his club wished to organise a series of races for representative offshore yachts from different countries. The ultimate object was to create an Olympic Class, so all yachts were to race at the same rating, a new and exciting concept for the ocean racing community.

The Lyme Bay Race in June, won by Frank King's *Excalibur*, saw fibreglass boats competing in an RORC event for the first time with five Class III Nicholson 32s taking part. Fibreglass, or Glass Reinforced Plastic (GRP) as it was called, had been in common use in the United States for building boats of all sorts for years, but it had been slow to catch on in Britain.

It was the start of a new age in yacht design and a forum of designers, Kim Holman, Angus Primrose and the designer of the Nicholson 32s, Peter Nicholson, brought together by *Yachting World* in October 1964, were all agreed that there was an impetus towards new designs, influenced by an ever-more competitive Admiral's Cup. Primrose made the point that 'The RORC rule is the only one at the moment which allows us to compete on level terms with the new materials that are coming in. And this is absolutely essential; if these things are going to be proven, there is nothing better to prove them in than the RORC classes. By and large the RORC rule is jolly good at the moment. It allows boats to be built in cold moulded wood or glass fibre–it even allows you to build in cement.'

The 1964 Dinard Race set a record for any RORC event when it notched up 129 starters, and there was again a record number of entries for an even numbered year, 652 yachts taking part in 12 events. However, the season was marred by several tragedies. A crewman aboard *Striana*, a French entry in the Lyme Bay Race, was injured and later died in hospital. Then, during the Santander-La Trinité Race in August, the fleet of 45 yachts was struck by a particularly severe gale. One French yacht, *Marie Galante II*, sank with the loss of three lives; another, *Aloa*, lost its skipper overboard after suffering a particularly severe knockdown; and a third was driven ashore, though no lives were lost. Letters flew to and fro in the yachting press, some blaming the club for starting the race, others supporting it for doing so, and once again the club had to emphasise that the responsibility for starting in a race lay solely with the skippers taking part.

The popularity of offshore racing was now putting those running the club under great pressure, as well as an extra strain on the finances. The large racing fleets that RORC races were attracting meant having more assistants at the finishes and the cost of chartering vessels to provide a mark boat also had to be covered.

These problems needed to be addressed. Decisions had to be made if the club was to go forward, but they had to be carefully considered. The workload on the committee was such that the commodore, Peter Green, circulated a note to its members in the autumn of 1964: 'You will have received the Agenda for the meeting on Wednesday 16th September and, like me, are probably appalled at the length of it.'

Most items were routine but some–the loss of life in the La Trinité Race, 19 St James's Place which was being vacated by the tenant the following spring, and an increase in the annual subscription–were going to create lengthy discussion and needed consideration by committee members before the committee met.

Owen Aisher wanted No. 19 St James's Place pulled down and rebuilt, but a preservation order had been slapped on it with the stipulation it had to be used for residential purposes. A construction firm whose managing director, Maurice Laing (Sir Maurice from 1965), was a member, supplied an architect who gave an estimate to join it to No.20, and to convert it into an additional five bedrooms for the club and a self-contained maisonette which could be let. This was accepted and work began in December 1965. By then 'Buster' de Guingand, in his role as the club's solicitor–a role John Roome took over when de Guingand died in 1973–had levered out the tenant some months before his lease expired.

Laing went personally to the chief architect of Westminster Council to put the case for the building to be given a licence for professional purposes, but this was refused. It was decided not to lodge an appeal, and work to join it to No 20 was not started.

The maisonette would bring in some income–it was let on a five-year lease in October 1966–but additional revenue would be needed to run the building and furnish it so there was a second issue of debentures to help defray these costs. Also, for the first time in ten years, there was a subscription increase to ten guineas with an entrance fee of £6 for those over 25.

The yachting press felt this increase was justified. 'Young men are queueing up to get in,' wrote one journalist. 'Some of the earlier members are now pretty long in the tooth, but the RORC is to a large extent a young man's club, and, as such, it is a tremendous asset to the young generation of yachtsmen. It is possible to get a three-course lunch for under 10s [50p], bed and breakfast costs 25s, and a double room with breakfast for only double that sum.'

Where else, he asked, was it possible to find such good value in the heart of London's West End? Members and candidates seemed to agree with him for, after a slight drop in 1965, membership continued to climb so that by the end of 1967 it had reached 2,447.

Chapter Ten

ENTER THE ONE TONNERS

IN FEBRUARY 1965 there was another tragedy at sea when 66-year-old Robert Somerset was drowned after his boat, *Trenchemer*, hit a rock while attempting to enter Mandraki harbour at Rhodes in heavy weather. Somerset, who was the heir to the Duke of Beaufort, was returning from Singapore to Majorca where he had lived for some years. As *Trenchemer* was foundering *Somerset attempted to rescue two women who were below, but all three went down with the ship, though a friend and the crew of three Spaniards were rescued.

A Somerset Memorial Fund was started, which was generously supported, particularly by American members. Paul Hammond donated the Somerset Memorial Trophy which is awarded annually to the yacht of the year; and when the Greeks organised a race in their waters in 1966, which took place under RORC rules, one of the trophies was a Somerset Memorial Cup.

In February 1964 John Roome had relinquished his post as Griffin secretary and his replacement, Commander K.N. Hoare, reported that, in view of the number of new boats being launched, and the fact that a club boat must charge fees, it was going to be very difficult indeed to obtain new skippers and mates among the younger members for the 1965 season. It was decided not to fit her out as a contender for the 1965 Admiral's Cup team; and the member who had put her on the Shingles Bank during the 1964 Round-the-Island Race was given a wigging.

Immediately after their success in the 1963 Fastnet Miller and Boyer, having done what they set out to do, went their separate ways. Boyer kept *Clarion* for

courtesy John Roome

John Roome

another season before selling her to Maurice Laing, while Miller returned to Olin Stephens for a new yacht which he aptly called *Firebrand*.

At that point British ocean racing was still in the era where it was, as Tim Jeffery put it in his official history of the Admiral's Cup, 'trying to throw off the last of cruising mentality, though cockpits were still snug, saloons had tables and crews had their cook. British yachts also had Lloyd's Register of Shipping, a classification society whose 100 AI certification was deeply ingrained in the British psyche as being an absolute prerequisite for a yacht to be considered a yacht.'

Rod Stephens commented that the British yachts at that time 'were all right in a blow, just slogging through that short chop you get in the Channel, when finesse didn't matter too much. You only had to look at the fittings. They were heavy, inefficient, like something off one of the old "J" Class.'

An Australian yachtsman was even blunter, saying that if an ocean racer didn't in some way resemble a square rigger the British didn't regard it as a proper yacht!

This was an era which had started to come to an end with *Clarion of Wight* and in the two succeeding summers was polished off by Peter *Nicholson's *Rocquette* and Miller's *Firebrand*.

Rocquette, launched for the 1964 season, was Nicholson's answer to *Clarion*. He built her as light as possible and her construction was in a different league to what had gone before: a plywood deck and laminated frames in light mahogany with two skins of planking, an inner one of spruce and an outer one of mahogany. She was the first British ocean racer to have a flush deck, with a small doghouse set well aft. From *Rocquette*, which he owned and raced, Nicholson developed two other flyers which successfully defended the Admiral's Cup in 1965: Ren *Clarke's *Quiver IV* and Amey's *Noryema IV*.

Firebrand was equally revolutionary. This was partly because her underbody was redrawn to take in data from tank testing the hull of the new America's Cup 12-metre *Constellation*, but more critical to her performance was her new rod rigging and Hood sails which were the first in Britain. However, the most important factor was her crew who set new standards in the sport. Miller described them as 'a determined bunch of ruffians who would give up all else for a season's racing.' On the water they were brilliant; off it they were sometimes a problem. After several incidents during the 1965 season, their conduct brought down the wrath of the committee on Miller's head and he was warned that if there was any trouble in future he would be banned from the club's races.

Rod Stephens saw *Firebrand* as a pivotal turning point for ocean racing in Britain and she, too, made the Admiral's Cup team which that year faced fierce competition from a newcomer: Australia. All the Australian team did well but the 13-year-old *Caprice of Huon* in particular was sailed quite brilliantly, winning the Britannia Cup, the New York Yacht Club Cup, and Class II in the Channel Race. This outstanding performance put Australia only 14 points behind the British who led the series going into the Fastnet.

Except for the tailenders, who had to endure an unpleasant slog home in an easterly which gusted to force 7 at times, the 1965 race took place in unusually clement weather, enabling the huge *Gitana IV*, owned by Baron de Rothschild, to smash the record which had been held by *Nordwind* since 1939. She completed the course in an elapsed time of 3 days, 9 hrs, 40 min., averaged 7.3 knots round the whole course and 8 knots from the Fastnet Rock.

Nevertheless, it was a small boat race and was won by the 24ft LWL *Rabbit*, designed and raced by the American Dick Carter. Built with a spade rudder about three feet aft of her fin keel and with a trim tab on the keel itself, she was similar to the split configuration Illingworth had used on *Mouse of Malham*. She was equally radical above the waterline with her halyards running inside her metal mast.

'Even the 12 metres don't do it like this,' commented Ted Hood, who constructed the mast to Carter's design. Considering the development money that was poured into the America's Cup, this showed just how far ahead of her time *Rabbit* was and she was only the second Class III yacht ever to win the Fastnet. Unfortunately for the Americans, *Rabbit* was not one of their team and they finished fourth behind the British, the Australians and the Dutch.

One of the qualifying events for the British Admiral's Cup contenders was the Lyme Bay Race and in 1965 it had the sailing committee in a tizz. After the trouble in the first North Sea Race in 1946 a RORC rule had been introduced that a mark had to be sighted and identified, or that a qualified declaration had to be made. Also, the committee were governed by an IYRU rule which stipulated that 'when races are sailed in fog or at night, dead reckoning alone should not necessarily be accepted as evidence that a mark has been rounded or passed', so any qualified declaration now always had to be examined on its merits.

Normally, there was no problem over the interpretation of this rule as only a handful of yachts were ever affected by it, but the conditions for the Lyme Bay Race in 1965 were so murky that of the 72 yachts which started only 17 positively identified one of the turning marks, the Lyme Bay buoy, a unique situation for the committee as 33 skippers made qualified declarations. Of the remainder five did not do so—though it was plain from their data sheets that they had not seen the buoy—while others submitted track charts or provided data from their logs to show they had made every effort to ensure that they had rounded it. A few even lowered their racing flags when they failed to sight it.

Caprice of Huon passing the Royal Yacht *Britannia*. She turned in an outstanding performance to help Australia win the 1965 Admiral's Cup series

Yachting World

The committee asked to see the track charts and reports from all owners taking the first six places in each class who had not seen the buoy. But in the end it accepted all the qualified declarations, for it was not possible to examine everyone's log book, just as it would have been grossly unfair to disqualify anyone who had not positively identified the buoy.

However, as it was one of the selection races for the upcoming One Ton Cup as well as the Admiral's Cup, it was an important event, and those who decided to keep to what appeared to be the letter of the law ended up at a disadvantage. For example, *Cohoe III*, a contender for the One Ton Cup team, lost any chance of winning Class III when her crew spent over 14 hours looking for the buoy. When at last they spotted it they hit the sherry bottle, though it was only breakfast time.

'There is a strong feeling in the minds of the majority of competitors,' a participant wrote afterwards, 'and certainly in the minds of those in the fifty-odd boats who never saw the buoy at all, that this farcical and sadistic course should be omitted from the future RORC race circuit and that this year's race should be excluded from the qualifiers for a really serious defence of the Admiral's Cup. A few of the very lucky ones claim to have taken photographs of this wretched buoy. If the RORC don't look out they might find heavy bidding around April of next year for the negatives. Although my owner is honest you can never tell about the crew—I'm one of them and no masochist.'

On corrected time *Cohoe III* came last in the Lyme Bay Race but was selected anyway for the One Ton Cup team on her later results, her fellow members being *Golden Samphire* and the REYC's *Ilex II*. Belgium, France, Holland, Denmark, Sweden and the United States were also represented, though not all fielded three yachts, the maximum allowed, but this did not matter as it was not a team event.

The maximum rating for the One Ton Cup, which was held at Le Havre was 22ft under the RORC rule with all entries racing boat-for-boat without handicap, quite unheard of in offshore racing at that time. Rather like the early competitions for the Admiral's Cup, not many of the yachts for this first series, in which the RORC were represented on the sailing committee and the panel of measurers, had been designed for it. But if the boats weren't tailor-made for the event the crews were the best available. 'The trend of RORC Class III,' wrote one commentator, 'is to carry a demon dinghy helmsman aboard, and at Le Havre this was accentuated.'

Three races were sailed, two of 30 and one of 240 miles in length. None of the RORC entries distinguished themselves that year–the Cup was won by the Danish *Diana III*–but the yachting press made it plain that this was an event to watch and club members such as Owen Aisher, Derek Boyer, and Max Aitken and his sailing partner, Bobby Lowein, began building yachts for the Cup races which were to be held at Copenhagen in 1966.

The 1965 season was a record one with 965 starters in the club's races. However, during the previous four years Class I had declined not only as a proportion of the total fleet but also in numbers, and during the past two years only two new British yachts had joined it. In the same period Class II had remained almost static, though it had attracted more new yachts than Class I. The largest increase had taken place in Class III for which many of the new yachts had been built.

These statistics meant that the sizes of the classes, and consequently the chances of winning a prize, were now quite out of kilter. For example, 83 Class III and 47 Class II yachts had taken part in the Dinard Race while only 18 Class I boats had entered. Illingworth's solution was to have six classes. Instead, Classes II and III were sub-divided; and in any race where there were fewer than ten starters in a sub-division, the two would be amalgamated. The ratings were now:

Class I 29ft to 70ft rating
Class II(a) 25ft to under 29ft rating
Class II(b) 22.5ft to under 25ft rating
Class III(a) 21ft to under 22.5ft rating
Class III(b) 19ft to under 21ft rating

For the 1966 One Ton Cup Aisher went to Peter Nicholson for *Yeoman XIV* –Nicholson also sailed her in the races–while Boyer and Aitken both commissioned designs from S & S. There was little to choose between Boyer's *Clarionet* and Aitken's *Roundabout*, and both dominated the 1966 season to such an extent that they became known as the 'terrible twins', though Geoff Pattinson's *Fanfare* –designed by Kim Holman and built in 1964 as a contender for the 1965 Admiral's Cup team–also had a remarkable season. She came first in the individual points championship with victories in the North Sea, Dinard and Channel Races, and won the Somerset Memorial Trophy. She was then offered to the club at below-market price to replace the now ageing *Griffin II*, and the offer was accepted.

Both *Clarionet* and *Roundabout* were revolutionary designs in that they had short keels and a skeg right aft on which the rudder was hung, an underwater *configuration that was initially tried by S & S on *Firebrand* when, with *Noryema IV* and Commodore Mike Vernon's *Assegai II*, she went to the United States to represent Britain in the 1966 Onion Patch series. This series had been started in 1964 and was modelled on the Admiral's Cup with the Bermuda Race as its climax. Though *Noryema*, which came fifth overall, was the highest placed British team yacht in the Bermuda Race, the British won the series, but at Copenhagen the British team were again well down the One Ton Cup league table.

For the 1966 domestic season the RORC introduced two new courses, Harwich-Copenhagen and West Mersea-Breskens. But the hazards of racing in the North Sea, now crowded with commercial shipping, were emphasised that year when, just before the Southsea-Harwich Race, 2000 telegraph poles were jettisoned by a Finnish ship in the English Channel near Dungeness. There was just time to alter the course and only one yacht reported seeing the poles, near the Sandettie, but they were still around in the vicinity of the Hook of Holland when the North Sea Race started. This was a hard, windy race in uncomfortable conditions and of the 83 starters, 18 retired, though no one hit the poles. The Skaw, which had been added to the club's programme in 1953, was even rougher, forcing the retirement of 70 of the 107 starters; and the 26 starters in the Yarmouth-Lequeitio Race also faced rough and unpleasant conditions at first, though the crews were compensated by the warm welcome they received on reaching Spain.

The continuing popularity of the One Ton Cup encouraged the committee in 1967 'to find out if there is really a great demand for boat-for-boat racing' by instituting a 22 Rater Division to race in three of the club's shorter fixtures, but the focal point of the season was naturally the Admiral's Cup series.

That year nine countries competed, Finland and Spain for the first time, with the Australians and the Americans being the principal challengers to the British team of Arthur Slater's *Prospect of Whitby*, *Noryema V*, and *Firebrand*. The Australians, having so nearly won the trophy two years previously, were especially strong, their team consisting of *Balandra*, a sistership of *Quiver IV*, owned by Robert Crichton-Brown (Sir Robert from 1972); *Caprice of Huon*, this time skippered by Gordon Reynolds who had been her mate the previous series; and Ted Kaufman's *Mercedes III*.

This time round the Americans were wise enough to pick Dick Carter and his *Rabbit II* and their other two members were the much fancied *Figaro IV*, sailed by Bill *Snaith, and Vincent Learson's Cal-40, *Thunderbird*. *Rabbit II* performed well, winning the New York Yacht Club Cup, but *Thunderbird* rated badly under the RORC rule and the Americans failed to shine as a team.

It was the Australians who started the Fastnet 19 points in the lead from the British, and though Eric Tabarly deservedly won the race in his innovative *Pen Duick III*, *Mercedes III* was placed third out of the Cup yachts, *Balandra* was fourth and *Caprice of Huon* seventh, a consistency which easily won the Australians the trophy. 'We were new,' said Kaufman afterwards when commenting on the team's attitude, 'and we did things that according to tradition we had no right to do.'

That year the Falmouth-Douarnenez Race was held in such bad weather that most of the crew of the new club yacht, *Griffin III*, succumbed to seasickness and she had been forced to heave to. When, 24 hours after the last of the competitors had arrived, she had still not made an appearance a search was started, but she eventually turned up safely.

Griffin III was popular with members, but despite entering 10 races she had an undistinguished–though financially viable–season and at a 'wash-up' meeting that autumn the committee was critical of the lack of tuning up before a race. The Griffin secretary admitted this but added that she was also a more difficult yacht to sail than *Griffin II*. The following year she more than made up for her indifferent start. Under 20 different skippers she logged 7,400 miles, took part in nine races, came a respectable fourth in Class I, and was in use every week-end except one. Over 200 crewed aboard her in 1968 including 24 youngsters each of whom also had a week's training cruise aboard her.

Yachting World

Bill Snaith and crew members aboard *Figaro IV* during the 1967 Admiral's Cup series

At the same 'wash-up' meeting Vernon stated he had received a letter from the previous commodore of the Cruising Yacht Club of Australia informing him that a contest for a team of three yachts, on the lines of the Admiral's Cup, would be run at at the end of 1967, and he hoped a team[1] from Britain would be able to sail in what was to become known as the Southern Cross Series.

Vernon then went on to ask the committee's views on sponsorship now that so many sporting events were supported by commercial firms–for example, the 1967 Australian Admiral's Cup team had accepted sponsorship. A lengthy discussion ensued, at the end of which it was agreed that there was a distinction between the club's domestic programme and challenges for international events overseas; and that, provided sponsorship was given 'quietly and discreetly' for international series, there would be no objection.

For the 1968 season the fleet was divided into Alpha and Beta Divisions. Alpha Division contained yachts built and launched after 1st January 1965, and any yachts which had won first or second open prize in the 1965 Fastnet, or more than two Open first prizes in other RORC races in 1965 and 1966. All other yachts sailed in Beta Division and any yacht built before 1963 had an allowance of 1% deducted from her Time Correction Factor.

In April 1968 the club suffered a blow when its admiral, Myles *Wyatt, died, and he was succeeded at the end of the year by Owen Aisher whose appointment as hon. treasurer then passed to Peter Green. A member, G.C.G. Chaplin, sent a donation of £100 in Wyatt's memory to be used as the club saw fit. The committee bought a cup and called it the Myles Wyatt Trophy, and awarded it to the highest scoring yacht in the Admiral's Cup series.

At that time the admiral did not serve for any specified period, but before he died Wyatt had expressed the view that this should be altered so that the admiral should have a fixed term in office which could only be extended after an enforced interval. His son, Jeremy, a committee member, said that his father had known he was getting out of touch with the racing fraternity, but that he had been reluctant to resign when pressed to continue for another term of office. The rule was subsequently altered so that the admiral served for a five-year term, and, along with the other flag officers, was not eligible for re-election without a one-year break.

The same month arrangements were made to ship Miller's *Firebrand* and Arthur *Slater's *Prospect of Whitby* to the United States for the 1968 Onion Patch series. The third yacht was Ron Amey's *Noryema VI* and Dennis *Miller was the team captain. *Firebrand* and *Prospect* finished second and third in their respective class in the Bermuda Race but *Noryema VI* rated badly, and though the British team put up a good fight to finish second out of five teams, the Americans won the series.

1 three members–Amey, Boyer, and Miller–were prepared to go but a dock strike prevented their yachts being shipped

The 1968 domestic season began with the Lyme Bay Race, resurrected after being replaced in 1966 by a new race, the Bassurelle. But Lyme Bay seems to have been jinxed. Unlike 1965, the visibility was good, but this time the buoy's light failed–it was removed later and so was the course from the club's programme–and Maurice Laing's *Clarion of Wight* was an hour or more trying to find it with Derek Boyer's *Clarionet* taking almost as long.

Victory that year, and line honours, went to Geoff Pattinson's new Class I *Phantom*, being campaigned that year by her designer, Peter Nicholson. In an equally impressive performance *Phantom* also won the Southsea-Harwich by a margin of three hours, took the *Morgan Cup, and then won her class in the North Sea Race and the Cowes-St Malo (not to be confused with the traditional Dinard Race), making her the obvious recipient of not only the Trenchemer Cup (winner of Class I) but the Somerset Memorial Trophy.

Ever since he had helped found JOG, *Illingworth among others had been lobbying for lowering the waterline length for some RORC events. This pressure had been stoutly resisted but the new commodore, David Edwards, who had succeeded Vernon at the start of 1969 after serving as vice commodore for a year, was not averse to the idea. The lower limit had not changed since 1953 and over the years 'there has been,' he said, 'a steady decline in the size of yachts and also an appreciable increase both in speed of boats for their size and in sea-keeping ability.'

The committee agreed and two of the events in the 1969 programme, the 220-mile North Sea Race and the 210-mile Owers/Shambles/CH1 Race, were thrown open to boats too small to be eligible for Class III(b). Their designed waterline length had to be at least 22ft LWL with a minimum rating of 17.5ft, and they were to be grouped together as Class III(c).

In January 1969 the committee was asked to treat the 604-mile Middle Sea Race–inaugurated the previous year by a RORC member, E. Alan Green, who had trained in England in 1967 to become the club's measurer in Malta–in the same way as the Scandinavian fixtures and recognise it as a qualifying race for members. This was agreed to, provided the club had a part in controlling the event.

The Southsea-Harwich Race was started that year from Ryde because The Queen was reviewing the NATO fleet. In the Cherbourg-Eddystone-Solent Race *Griffin III* ended up on the Eddystone Rocks. No serious damage was done but the Griffin secretary subsequently remarked that he thought the rocks a dangerous mark and that the East Rutts buoy would be much better, a suggestion that was taken up for the course the following year.

A ban by the club on all but the most basic electronic equipment followed the appearance of the first on-board computer equipment at the 1969 Boat Show. It had always been the committee's view that the more exotic electronic

Griffin III (ex-Fanfare)

photo Beken of Cowes

aids should not be allowed until their costs became more reasonable, as had been the case with depth sounders.

However, it was not the high costs involved which led the committee to react so promptly on this occasion. Its opinion, expressed by the commodore, David Edwards, was that though 'anything that improved safety must be encouraged...devices such as a miniature computer and the linking together of electronic aids tend to reduce the human element which is an important part of the sport', an attitude which only began to change when Mary Pera (née Mary Blewitt), who argued against their ban in a letter to *Yachting World* in 1969, became a committee member in 1970.

Phantom's performance in 1968 made her a front runner to make the next Admiral's Cup team. Pattinson and his crew must have known their chances were good and started a regime to ensure their selection. In January her crew started an intensive course of physical training and by Easter they were on the water, as Paul Antrobus wrote in *Ocean Racing Around The World*, 'practising manoeuvres against the clock. Sometimes they did dry practice in *Phantom*'s marina berth at Camper & Nicholson's in Gosport, all to get timing right and save those odd seconds which can be the difference between winning and losing.'

There were 18 contenders for the team in 1969, eight of which had been built specially for the series. This was another huge leap. It showed how popular the series had become and the amount of professionalism that was now being invested in it. By the final weekend of inshore trials the contenders had been boiled down to 12. The commodore said it had been very difficult to choose the three yachts as the standard had been very high, though Ron Amey added that several owners had entered the selection races for a 'Jolly', and that this was 'not a good thing.'

Chosen from the final contenders were *Phantom*, built traditionally in wood, and two S & S designs, Arthur Slater's steel-hulled *Prospect of Whitby*, and *Casse Tete III* owned by Dave Johnson and Mike Hurrell. *Casse Tete* showed the direction in which boat building was moving–and moving fast. A GRP Swan 43, she was the first production boat to race in a British Admiral's Cup team.

Another innovation was that a team manager was appointed to give the backing the team needed ashore. Such back-up cost money and the introduction of commercial sponsorship, however 'discreet', was inevitable if the series was to be run professionally. Significantly, the tobacco company, Dunhill's, was allowed to provide such essentials as a results board and water transport for crews and VIPs and it, along with Qantas and Grants Whisky, also contributed substantial sums to ship the boats and crews of the British team (Arthur Slater's *Prospect of Whitby*, Max Aitken's *Crusade*, and Rodney Hill's *Morning After*), taking part in that year's Southern Cross series.

Nineteen sixty-nine was the year of the centreboard with Ron Amey's seventh *Noryema* and Dick Carter's *Red Rooster* having a different variation of it. Both yachts had been designed by Carter, though the design of *Noryema*'s drop keel had a good deal of input from Amey for it was retracted by hydraulic rams similar to those used for shifting stone ballast in his quarry business. The design was ingenious, with the vertical movement of the keel being controlled by spring-loaded rubber rollers. If *Noryema* ran aground there was an eight-inch 'give' in the keel which set the hydraulic rams automatically into action, a system Amey called his 'crunch' factor. He regarded the design as experimental which was why *Noryema* was given the suffix *VGX* (variable geometry experiment) and not *VII*. She did not make the team, but was made reserve boat.

Unlike *Noryema*, where the whole keel was retracted, *Red Rooster* had a simpler swinging centreboard. Its vertical movement was similar to that of a dinghy centreplate, though Carter had devised a system which prevented water sluicing in and out of the centreboard casing which would have caused drag. She was selected on Carter's reputation as the Americans did not hold trials, and anyway *Red Rooster* had only just been launched from the yard of her Dutch builder. Despite having little time to be tuned up *Red Rooster* performed magnificently in the Admiral's Cup series enabling the Americans to snatch the trophy from the Australians who had gone into the Fastnet with a healthy lead. The British team could manage only third place.

courtesy Simon Slater

Arthur Slater and his crew aboard the first *Prospect of Whitby* built in 1967. Altogether he had five built. Slater is sitting on a specially constructed seat which enabled him, despite having only one leg, to steer his yachts to some impressive victories. In some of his later yachts he steered from a specially installed bucket seat

For the first time Class III started first in the Fastnet, which was sailed mostly in light airs. It ended in controversy when the chronometer aboard Max Aitken's *Crusade* showed the yacht's finishing time to be over three minutes better than that recorded by the timekeeper on the breakwater. If *Crusade's* chronometer was correct *Crusade* had beaten the declared winner, *Red Rooster*, but officially *Red Rooster* had beaten *Crusade* by 68 seconds.

Aitken protested and at a committee meeting aboard HMS *Tyne* at Devonport on 15th August it was decided to appoint a protest committee, chaired by the Australian yachtsman, Gordon Reynolds. This took great pains to study all the evidence and did not come to a decision until an hour after the prize-giving had started, but it ruled that the official time should stand.

However, this was not the end of the matter for when *Crusade* was measured that autumn prior to being shipped to Australia it was found that a layer of fibre glass had been added to her plywood deck after she had been initially measured in her building shed. This addition altered her scantling measurement which meant she had been racing for the entire season with too high a rating.

When this became known the yachting correspondent of Aitken's *Daily Express* wrote to the yachting press and other daily papers asking for support to present a plaque to the proprietor as, due to the RORC making an error in his rating, Aitken had not won the Fastnet! The club was besieged by telephone calls and *The Times* reported that Alan Paul had apologised to Aitken because *Crusade's* rating was incorrect. Paul had done no such thing and the journalist in question admitted his error when promptly tackled by David Edwards. Edwards subsequently said in committee that it remained a mystery how the mistake had occurred. He had written to *Aitken saying he was very sorry about the whole business. Enquiries had shown it had certainly not been the fault of the measurer who earlier in the year had complained that owners took far too casual an approach to the measuring of their yachts.

Starters for the club's 1969 programme of 14 events numbered 824, a slight drop from the previous Fastnet year and a considerable one from 1965 when 962 yachts had participated in the same number of races. One event, the Skagen-Solent, had even been cancelled through lack of support. Non-Fastnet years had also shown a decline in entries. It looked as if a plateau had been reached. If the sport—and the club—was to continue to expand during the 1970s something new was going to have to happen.

It did. With the arrival on the ocean racing scene of a new international rule and of the Rt. Hon. Edward Heath (Sir Edward from 1992), the leader of the opposition Conservative Party, offshore racing took yet another quantum leap in popularity.

Chapter Eleven

THE IOR RULES, OK

THE INITIAL impetus for a common international rule came not from the RORC or the CCA, but from a group of Continental yachtsmen. The Germans, especially, felt 'somewhat unhappy' at having to measure their yachts in accordance with four different formulae depending on where they raced: KR in German races, SHR in Swedish events, RORC in British fixtures, and the CCA Rule in the Bermuda and some Transatlantic Races.

To try and standardise the four rules and, ideally, to find a universal one, an informal international conference was convened in June 1961 at the Park Hotel in Bremen at the instigation of a German yachtsman, Rolf Schmidt. Alan Paul and Olin Stephens were among those invited and at later conferences as many as nine nations were usually represented.

The Bremen committee, as it was first called, met again in October 1962 at 20 St James's Place which became its permanent base until 1998. It changed its name to the Offshore Rules Coordinating Committee (ORCC), and today is called the Offshore Racing Council (ORC). For several years the ORCC laboured in obscurity, and without much encouragement, until in 1966 the IYRU provided a catalyst: it approached the International Olympic Committee (IOC) with a request for ocean racing yachts to be given a class in the 1972 Olympic *Regatta and strongly urged the rule makers involved in the sport to develop an international rule by November 1968. This pressured those involved into serious negotiations.

The turning point came in 1967 when Fred Adams, the CCA commodore, wrote to Alan Paul suggesting that each club should give up its own rule for a new international one. A mailing in favour of this idea was organised worldwide by Olin Stephens and Dick Carter, two of the new rule's most active supporters, and was followed by a meeting in the club's Fastnet Room.

'That room was packed,' said Carter, who had joined the ORCC in 1966 and the RORC in 1967, 'and loaded with tension. Buster de Guingand was chairing the two sides and heard RORC commodore, Mike Vernon, reiterate that the RORC rule *was* international. Then the Norwegian delegate said: "Let's agree to agree!" and the whole meeting took off'.

Ironically, the IOC rejected the IYRU's proposal, but the impetus for change, once begun, was hard to withstand. It was a long, hard slog for the International Technical Committee which had been formed under Olin Stephens to draw up the new rule, but at an extraordinary general meeting on 28th January 1969 the RORC's commodore, David Edwards, was able to announce that the International Offshore Rule (IOR), as it was to be called, would be ready in its final form in the spring.

Olin Stephens (right) with RORC club secretary Alan Paul. They both attended the Bremen Conference in 1962 which ultimately led to the International Offshore Rule

The meeting hotly debated whether to accept the new rule. Robert Clark thought it too complex and questioned the values of length and sail area, and suggested that its use should be postponed for a year so that it could be tidied up and analysed. There were other adverse comments, too. In fact *Yachting World* reported that 'the wording was criticised, the cost of the new measurement was criticised, the geometry of the new inclining experiment was criticised, and the timing was criticised.'

Nevertheless, when a member proposed an amendment 'that this meeting supports the concept of an International Offshore Rule but will not adopt the rule until it is in its final form' it was defeated by 44 votes to 21 and the committee's resolution to adopt the new rule was approved by 49 votes to nil.

Despite the immense strain it put on all the measurers, IOR Mk II (Mk I was never used) was introduced in 1970 for all RORC races. Mark III came into force in 1973 and Mark III(a), an age allowance for yachts built four or more years before the season in which they were racing, from April 1976. By 1979 80% of the world's IOR fleet were racing under Mark III(a) ratings.

~

The introduction of IOR was an opportune time to regroup the RORC fleet for the 1970 season and it was now divided into five classes:

    Class I   33ft to 70ft rating
    Class II   29ft to under 33ft rating
    Class III   25.5ft to under 29ft rating

In March 1967 the RORC held its first press conference at the club to discuss, among other matters, the future of the RORC rule. From left to right: Brigadier Fayle (rating secretary), David Edwards (vice commodore), Mike Vernon (commodore), Alan Paul (secretary), and Philip Woolley (committee member)

Class IV 23ft to under 25.5ft rating
Class V 21ft to under 23ft rating

Alpha Division now contained boats built and launched after 1st January 1966, and older ones which had won first or second open prizes in the 1969 Fastnet, or more than two open first prizes in other RORC races during the previous two years. The rest sailed in Beta Division.

Other changes were in the air as those managing the club's affairs realised its performance needed sharpening. The unfortunate disagreement about *Crusade's* finishing time in the 1969 Fastnet–and the extraordinary result in the 1969 Dinard Race when, for the first time in the club's history, there was a tie[1] for the best corrected time–highlighted, among other matters, the urgent need to calculate a yacht's finishing time more accurately. In June 1970 Ron *Amey, one of the current rear commodores, suggested trying to find an electronic device that would time in yachts automatically; and when E. Alan Green joined in August 1970 as assistant secretary (racing), having been recruited by Edwards during a visit to Malta, he came to the same conclusion.

After studying the different systems used by horse racing, car racing, athletics, and other sports Green recommended the purchase of a Seiko electronic crystal chronometer–about the size of a modern laptop computer–as part of a new system of timing finishes which he intended to use. Its cost, £200, made the treasurer Peter Green 'gulp a bit' as it was a lot of money in those days.

Other equipment included a specially-modified gunsight telescope for observing yachts crossing the finishing line during the day; and for those crossing

1 between *Esprit de Rueil*, part owned by André Viant, in Class III(a) and Rodney Hill's *Morning After* in Class III(b)

at night a powerful image-intensifying 'telescope', nicknamed 'Twiggy', was used. Both these devices–the latter hot off the secrets list and accompanied by its minder, a retired Army officer–were lent by Rank Electronic Instruments. For foggy conditions, and to investigate its use as a timing aid, Seavista were persuaded to lend a radar. And to make gunnery simple Green introduced 'theatrical maroons' (electric cannon) which were fired–and still are–to tell a competitor crossing the line that he had finished.

The new equipment was assembled on Horse Sand Fort in the Solent, already being used as a finishing line for the club's races in the English Channel. It was also deployed for the Fastnet finish and later at Gilkicker fort near Gosport when the line was moved there. The Ministry of Defence, the owners of Horse Sand Fort, permitted RORC volunteers to work during the winter of 1970-71 to make an old gunnery-direction post on it into a habitable finishing platform. Telephone communications were installed as were generators for the floodlights, loudhailer, aldis lamp and other electrical equipment. Every item–which also included furniture, an Elsan lavatory, and twelve panes of glass for the lookout cabin and other windows–had to be shipped from Portsmouth. Both the Royal Navy, which transported the heavier items, and Trinity House's launches, which ferried personnel, gave invaluable help.

The club's racing secretariat has always relied on volunteers to help run its races. At Horse Sand Fort the principal timekeeper was Maurice Hope, 'an irascible brigadier, incredibly spritely, who was still running up and down the fort's ladders in his 80s'. Ideally, a team of seven manned the line, including the race director or his deputy, and this was split into two watches of three plus a cook. Nowadays the team at a Solent finish usually occupy an anchored committee boat. Elsewhere they can often just consist of two dedicated people, one of whom, typically, is hunched up against the rain at the end of a break-water while the other is huddled in a car nearby.

Ren Clarke is just one example of a member who gave tremendous help during the 1970s by turning out in *Quiver VII* so that she could be used as a committee vessel, a role now taken over by *Zulu*, owned by Brian Stewart, a member since 1950. Two more were Harold Rapp and then Derek Boyer who for many years gave invaluable assistance in ferrying finishing teams to their destinations in their private aircraft. Without their generosity, and that of many others too numerous to mention here, the club could not continue in its principal function of organising offshore races.

Several fixtures in 1970 were beset by weather problems: the new 200-mile Seine Bay Race took place in light airs; the Southsea-Harwich was hit by fog; there was fog *and* hardly a whisper of wind in the Dinard; and the Channel Race was also a horribly slow affair. However, the Cowes-Cork Race, jointly

Race Organisation 1970s' Style

Besides renovating the derelict gunnery direction post on top of Horse Sand Fort (right and below), a blue caravan, which had started life as a mobile Barclays Bank, was purchased to help those organising club races. With the help of Sir Maurice Laing and

Ron Amey, it was converted into a mobile race office where competitors handed in their crew lists and received Sailing Instructions. The caravan was moved, as required, between Camper & Nicholson's Gosport yard (centre) and Groves & Guttridge marina at Cowes, and it was also trailed to Plymouth for the finish of the Fastnet (left)

organised by the RORC and the Island Sailing Club to celebrate the 250th anniversary of the Royal Cork Yacht Club–which has strong claims to be the world's oldest yacht club–made up for these early frustrations with the fleet having a Force 6/7 full and by up the Irish Sea.

In December 1970 Westminster City Council, after being intensively lobbied by one of the rear commodores, Maurice Laing, and the vice commodore, Ken *Wylie, relented and gave permission for No.19 St James's Place to be used for club purposes. This was a major achievement as the only likely alternative would have been to sell both properties and find a new location.

For some years the RORC had rented an office at Cowes during Cowes Week. But in 1971, under a sponsorship deal with Dunhill's, a temporary clubhouse was erected at Groves & Guttridge's yard at Cowes. It had a clubroom and bar–administered by Douglas, the club's long-serving barman–as well as press, information, and administrative offices. This improved the facilities enormously, particularly for the foreign Admiral's Cup teams. These had previously been looked after by a host provided by the RORC but, apart from a cocktail party or two, precious little else had been done to make them feel part of the scene.

It was just as well that proper press arrangements were in place for never before had there been such intense interest in the Admiral's Cup series in general and in Edward Heath–whose Conservative Party had been swept to power the previous June–in particular. When he had become prime minister it had been suggested to him that he might give up ocean racing because of the security problems involved. He had flatly refused to do so and when attempts were made to put plain clothes policemen aboard his boat for a race he was equally adamant. 'Are you crazy?' German yachtsman Hans-Otto Schumann, and long-standing club member, recalls him saying. 'We did not work day and night to save a pound of weight here and there to end up with two big bobbies with size 48 shoes.'

After sailing for some years in dinghies, Heath had first tasted offshore racing when Maurice Laing had taken him on a Dinard Race in *Clarion of Wight*, and his meticulous planning and single-minded approach when he bought the first of his five yachts called *Morning Cloud* immediately propelled him into the top league. He went on to win many more events in an ocean racing career which spanned over a decade and included captaincy of the British Admiral's Cup team in 1971 and 1979, and the British team for the 1980 Sardinia Cup.

With the exception of Max Aitken's *Daily Express*, offshore racing had been regarded by the daily press as a minority sport before Heath had come on the scene, and had largely ignored it. Over the years the club had been constantly struggling for more publicity and in November 1969, on the prompting of David Edwards, it had published the first issue of *Seahorse*, as a forum for members and to try and stimulate media interest. Now, quite suddenly, offshore racing became a sport everyone was interested in and which even television began to cover in some depth.

When the RORC committee had sent a telegram to Edward Heath in June 1970 congratulating him on his political victory he had replied that he hoped to be able to ocean race whenever there was not a strike. He must have thought there would be no industrial action in the summer of 1971 for that spring he replaced his first *Morning Cloud* with an S & S 42-footer.

The second *Morning Cloud* performed well in the trials, in which 27 yachts competed, and was selected for the British Admiral's Cup team, along with *Prospect of Whitby* and Bob Watson's *Cervantes IV*. The reserve boat was Don Parr's *Quailo III*, a production Nicholson 55. With Peter Nicholson at the helm, she caused some embarrassment to the selectors for she showed a clean pair of heels to the chosen three in the Class I Points Championship, which she won, and in that year's Fastnet where she finished second overall.

Heath was chosen to captain the three yachts, the only time a British prime minister has led a British team in an international sporting event. The main foreign contenders were again Australia and the USA. Altogether 17 nations sent teams, a huge increase over the previous series which, for the first time, was governed by the IOR. Because Admiral's Cup crews were beginning to grumble about having to compete in crowded conditions with other yachtsmen, who did not take their racing seriously, the two inshore Admiral's Cup races –the Britannia and New York Yacht Club cups–were replaced by two new events, each 30 miles long, which were held the same week as the Cowes regatta, but were not part of it.

Competition was intense and lapel buttons became all the rage. The crew of two of the British team wore 'Ted's Ahead' and 'Slater is greater' while those aboard *Cervantes* had 'Cervantes has Panties' to show that Bob Watson's daughter was one of their number. However, it was felt they had gone a bit too far when, to show their superiority over one of the Australian boats, they also wanted to wear one which read 'Up your flue, Koomooloo.'

After one of the most testing Fastnets for some years, Britain regained the Admiral's Cup and the same team was chosen for that year's Southern Cross series in which they finished second to New Zealand. But the Fastnet itself went to Syd Fischer's 36ft LWL *Ragamuffin* and it was only appropriate that her crew, with true Australian subtlety, produced possibly the most apt button of the series. It read 'Rago's Arse Beats Class', and indeed she did. Her run back to the Bishop Rock remains, as member Bob Fisher wrote in his book, *The Admiral's*

Cup, one of the legends of this great event. With the north to north-east wind blowing up to 40 knots, the Australian yacht surfed the waves at 14 knots with her bow wave shooting seven feet up the mast. Though she took some minutes to recover from being knocked flat after a gybe broach, she averaged more than 9 knots during that 106-mile leg, more than enough to win her the race by over two hours on corrected time.

At the 1971 AGM the commodore reported that it had been a record year in every way and that in September the work to incorporate No.19 with No.20 St James's Place had been completed at the cost of about £22,000. The secretariat was now concentrated on the ground floor, all the club rooms on the first floor, and the upper floors became entirely dedicated to accommodation. Nevertheless, running the clubhouse remained an uphill struggle. In November the committee was told that the housekeeper was unfit, the head barman was in hospital, the steward was off sick, the cleaner had had to return to Spain, and the evening waitress had quit.

An otherwise successful season was marred by the loss of the Dutch yacht *Merlijn* while taking part in the North Sea Race. Though it was a clear fine night the boat was run down by a ship and there were no survivors from the crew of six. Commercial traffic in the English Channel was now so heavy that there was always the danger of another fatal accident and the course for the West Mersea-Zeebrugge, due to be raced in July, was immediately altered. Mike Richey, then the executive secretary of the Royal Institute of Navigation, wrote to the club warning of proposed legislation that would prohibit British ships from travelling against the flow of traffic in a separation scheme, and that this might possibly affect offshore racing. The response of the vice commodore, Ken Wylie, was that the club continue racing, and to do so sensibly, recognising that the risk was now higher than before; that the club welcomed lane discipline and that whenever lanes were crossed this would be done, so far as was possible, at right angles; and that the club had decided to abandon racing in the English Channel to the east of the Royal Sovereign Tower and in the southern North Sea.

Such a move entailed a complete rerouting of some of the club's traditional events and the Southsea-Harwich Race was dropped altogether. Later, the club stopped[1] using courses to the east of the Greenwich meridian, which marked the start of the traffic separation lanes, and more rerouting followed. But when the Department of Trade wanted alterations to the Fastnet course, Green argued the club's case with a senior official, and persuaded him otherwise.

On 1st May 1972 Mary Pera succeeded Alan Paul who had reached retiring age after serving as secretary for 25 years. *Paul was appointed rear commodore, and made a life honorary member. Much deserved praise was heaped on him for the great services to ocean racing he had performed, for which in 1966 he

1 there were exceptions during the 1990s, but as a general rule the club maintains this policy

Photo Beken of Cowes

Inset, Yachting World

Quailo III with (inset) Don Parr addressing a press conference
before the 1979 Admiral's Cup series

had been recognised with the award of the OBE. Perhaps his most outstanding contribution to the sport was, in Pera's words, to help European countries, staggering to their feet after the war, to start sailing again.

The club also lost another important member of the team when the rating secretary, Brigadier Fayle, died suddenly in February 1972. He was replaced by W.R. Matthews, who had sailed with Maurice Laing for a number of years. It was Matthews who instituted the Measurers' Convention which gave RORC measurers the opportunity to meet each other and to discuss ways of improving the service they offered. By 1977 there were over 30 measurers in the UK, Hong Kong and Malta who came directly under the club's rating office which in May 1968 had been set up in Bournemouth. The first International Measurers' Convention was held in London in 1975.

For some time the club had been holding an annual foreign members' meeting to sound out the feelings of foreign members about all aspects of the RORC. This was taken a step further at the end of 1972 when Pera's idea of appointing two additional rear commodores from the foreign membership was accepted. André Viant from France and Otto van der Vorm from Holland were the first to be elected to the new posts and later holders included the flamboyant American multi-millionaire Ted Turner–whose ex-12 metre, *American Eagle*, established a new Fastnet record of 79hrs,11min.,48secs in 1971 and who won the race in *Tenacious* in 1979–and Jean Louis Fabry who has done so much to cement Anglo-French sailing relations since he joined in 1973.

On the financial side 1972 was a sticky year, for expenditure had been high. The prospects for 1973 seemed no better. Overheads were rising alarmingly and would continue to do so–inflation and the introduction of VAT in April 1973 would both play their part there–while membership numbers, which now totalled 2,667, had increased by only 2% in two years. Income from entry fees had also dropped substantially as exceptionally long periods of strong winds, especially early in the summer, had disrupted the programme.

Edwards commented that one of the financial difficulties facing the RORC was that it had become a sort of National Authority[1]. Though a source of pride amongst earlier members this had now become quite a chore, for other clubs increasingly sought, amongst other matters, the RORC's help over the introduction of IOR, and this had proved expensive and time consuming. He might have also said that, as ocean racing expanded and began being used more and more as a sponsorship vehicle, so the club's organisational ability and know-how was also increasingly in demand, not just in Europe but all over the world. For example, by 1972 it was already supporting the organisation of the Middle Sea Race in the Mediterranean and the China Sea Race in the waters off Hong Kong; and was soon organising such global events as the Financial Times

1 the RYA had delegated to the RORC the responsibility for selecting British ocean racing teams

Clipper Race (1975) and the Parmelia Race (1979), as well as being involved in what has now become one of world's foremost sailing events, the Whitbread (now Volvo) Round-the-World Race which was first held in 1973.

Edwards wanted to raise subscriptions immediately, but his motion was defeated. However, when the new commodore, Maurice Laing, was elected in January 1973 rating fees were increased substantially–by then 55 yachts a week were being rated–and, for the first time, those taking part in the Admiral's Cup selection races were charged an entry fee.

Laing was as concerned about the club's standing as he was about its finances. 'At the moment we are at the peak of our achievement and are the most preeminent ocean racing club in the world.' The difficulty was to stay there. The RORC must not become known simply as the Admiral's Cup club, yet it no longer owned the rule which had given it such prestige in the past. 'We must look to our laurels if we are not to lose our position.' It was vital to find more members. Large numbers of younger people, he pointed out, were racing without joining the club, indeed 70% of those taking part in some races were not members and many of them saw no point in seeking election.

As one antidote to all the problems that were besetting the club, Laing, encouraged by Mary Pera, put forward the proposal that the RORC should announce immediately that it planned to involve itself in level rating racing. This proved a wise move for the Ton Cup classes were establishing themselves to the extent that such an experienced commentator on the sailing scene as club member Sir Peter Johnson Bt. was able to state in his *Yachting World* column that the One Ton Cup was the 'event which marked the turning point in the modern yachting scene...The award of this cup to ocean racing yachts was, too, the accolade which showed them as the inheritors of the mantle of classic yacht racing.'

So popular had level rating racing become that one participant even likened it to sex: 'You don't have to wait until afterwards to know how you are getting on, position is everything, and, most important, everybody who does it thinks it's great fun.'

The yacht of the 1973 season was undoubtedly *Frigate*. Designed by Dick Carter for Tony Boyden and Robin Aisher, the younger son of the club's admiral and a future club commodore, she won the Yacht of the Year Trophy, the Alan Paul Trophy for the most consistent performer of the year, the Admiral's Cup trials, the Class II Championship, and came third in the Admiral's Cup individual points.

In several ways *Frigate* showed the way ahead: at a time when the idea of a dual-purpose racer/cruiser still lingered on, she was an all-out racing machine and everything but everything was planned with the sole purpose of making her go faster. But it was not so much her design as Aisher's method of campaigning which proved that ocean racing was moving up another gear. For example, when beating to windward the crew sleeping below were shifted to the windward bunks while those on deck sat in a row with their feet dangling over the side, although, to remain in a legal position, they kept their torsos inside the lifelines. This perfectly legitimate tactic was later to become a matter of some contention.

Life was hard for *Frigate's* crew and before long they had invented a simple song to sing to keep themselves awake on the weather rail:

> When the Fastnet Race is over
> Oh how happy we shall be
> No more gybes or genny changes
> No more spinnaker peels for me
>
> No more sitting out to windward
> All the shouting will be past
> You can tell old Robin Aisher
> To stick his Frigate up to Groves and Guttridge[1]

The selectors for the British Admiral's Cup team chose *Frigate* and the third *Morning Cloud*, and did not repeat their 1971 mistake of omitting *Quailo III*. Heath was too busy to captain the team again and his place was taken by Robin Aisher. Although the team failed to retain the trophy, which went to Germany, the 1973 season was another incredibly successful one for the club with the number of entries in RORC events rising to a new record of 1,382 starts by 458 yachts.

The time was now approaching for the admiral, Owen Aisher, to step down. In October 1973 a sub-committee appointed to study the question of a successor submitted a list of the following desirable qualifications:

1. He should be a man of prestige and dignity who is well known in yachting circles and preferably also in the community. He should bring prestige to the club.

2. He should be worldly wise and able to give the club advice not only on yachting matters, but on all matters, and to see that we are on the right lines.

3. He should be able to 'open doors' generally, as well as in yachting circles.

4. He should be an active yachtsman who appears regularly on the yachting scene, although it is not necessary for him to any longer be actively engaged in our races.

5. He need not necessarily be British.

1 from *To Win the Admiral's Cup* by Dick Kenny which describes the 1973 series in detail

Superstar being loaded aboard the P & O cargo liner, *Westmorland*, for the voyage to Australia to take part in the 1973 Southern Cross series. *Prospect of Whitby* has already been lashed down and *Quailo III* was loaded later

courtesy Roger Motson

These stringent criteria reduced a long list of possible candidates to two but after a lengthy discussion neither was nominated. Instead, it was decided to alter the rules so that Aisher could continue for a further two years, which he agreed to do.

The club had another exceptionally good year on the water in 1974. For the first time a proper selection committee was convened to choose teams for the 1973 Southern Cross and 1974 Onion Patch series. They chose well and Arthur Slater's latest *Prospect of Whitby*, Don Parr's *Quailo III*, and Alan Graham and Dave Johnson's *Superstar* swept all before them in the Southern Cross series to win the trophy for the first time.

The British Onion Patch boats, Amey's *Noryema IX*, Chris Dunning's *Marionette*, and *Oyster*, owned by David Powell and Richard Martin, looked at first as if they would do the same, but the team, in the lead at the start of the Bermuda Race, was foiled by the vagaries of the Gulf Stream and finished the series second behind the Americans. The Onion Patch was followed by the first RORC-organised Transatlantic Race for many years. The British team all took part but the race, from Bermuda to Plymouth, a distance of 2870 miles, was won by Eric Tabarly's *Pen Duick VI* whose use of spent uranium as ballast caused something of a furore.

The outstanding domestic event that year was the One Ton Cup which the club organised at Torquay. During the middle distance race distress flares were seen and *Gumboots*, raced by boatbuilder Jeremy Rogers and his brother, Dr Jonathan Rogers, both club members, diverted from their course, as did three other competitors. The flares came from a burning yacht, which later exploded and sank. *Gumboots* rescued three adults and four children from it, but after continuing the race for several hours had to retire to Torquay to land one of the children who was sick.

This posed a tricky problem for the international jury as there was no precedent for compensating a boat that had not gone on to finish. Eventually it decided to award each competitor involved in the rescue what its crew requested. One got time, another their place at the last mark, and so on. *Gumboots* was awarded fourth place which put her in a strong position in the series which she subsequently won. It was the first British victory in any Ton Cup event, and Jeremy Rogers was later also awarded the Yachtsman of the Year Trophy.

This series proved typical of the unforeseen problems that can arise when organising offshore racing. A naval minesweeper was being used as the starting line, and Green and his team were told not to bring signal flags aboard as the minesweeper had its own set—in fact two sets one on either side of the bridge. However, when Green requested the flag 'S' be hoisted to indicate a shortened course one flag was lost overboard and the other could not be found. In the best traditions of the Royal Navy, which prides itself on never being presented with a problem it couldn't solve, the captain promptly summoned the bosun with a pot of paint, a blue square was painted on to a white flag which was hoisted in the nick of time.

In September 1974 a tragedy overwhelmed the third *Morning Cloud*. During a delivery trip without her owner aboard the boat encountered a storm at night in the English Channel. While about ten miles east of the Owers, and with the wind gusting to 60 knots, she was knocked down twice by rogue waves. Two of her crew of seven were lost and the survivors, three of whom were quite badly injured, had to take to a liferaft which was swept ashore the next morning. There were 11 other people drowned in the Channel that weekend.

~

One Monday morning in the autumn of 1973 Mary Pera had opened the clubhouse to find wide cracks in the walls, doors stuck open or jammed shut, ceilings falling down and hot water from a club next door flowing through the basement. A structural engineer sent round post haste by Maurice Laing assured Pera that as the cracks were not big enough to put her fist into the building would probably not fall down. It didn't, but it took Christopher Carter Jonas, the club's hon. surveyor, over a year of negotiations with the culprit–London Transport which was boring a new underground line–before restoration work could begin. It was not finished in time for the Patron's visit during the club's 50th anniversary year in 1975 to meet skippers and/or owners of that year's Admiral Cup, and Pera had to hide the patches of bare brick with flowers.

The club's 50th anniversary was also celebrated in a number of other ways. A ball was held in the Painted Hall at the Royal Naval College, Greenwich; the Jubilee Fastnet included such old timers as *Iolaire* and *Latifa*; a commemorative mug and plate were commissioned from the well known naval architect, Colin Mudie, a long-time member of the club; and there was a special Jubilee dinner at Grosvenor House attended by a thousand members and their guests who were entertained by the band of the Royal Artillery.

In 1975 JOG classes VI–VIII raced for the first

courtesy Janet Grosvenor

H.M. the Queen and Prince Philip receiving a commemorative mug and plate from the club's admiral, Owen Aisher, during their visit to the club-house on 21 July 1975 to celebrate the RORC's 50th anniversary

time with the RORC's class I–V, the smaller classes (V–VIII) having shorter courses where appropriate. A working party formed by the new commodore, John Roome, in the spring of 1976 recommended that this should continue in certain events where the lower rating limit was the IOR minimum. In practice this meant that the long-held RORC tenet of a minimum size was to be quietly dropped and some RORC events would be organised in co-operation with JOG for whatever IOR classes were appropriate. The poor state of the economy–and the introduction in 1975 of 25% rate of VAT on boats and boating equipment by a government hostile to yachting–was reflected in the absence of sponsors for a British team to defend the Southern Cross trophy. Even Arthur Slater, an indefatigable worker in raising sponsorship funds for British teams racing abroad, failed to find anyone. A team was nevertheless selected in the hope that sponsorship would be forthcoming and the winning 1975 Admiral's Cup team–Ron Amey's *Noryema X*, the top scoring yacht in the series; John Prentice's *Battlecry*; and Robin Aisher's *Yeoman XX*–was nominated.

Still no sponsor came forward, so *Noryema X* was shipped at her owner's expense and two other yachts were chartered locally and raced by Chris Dunning and Arthur Slater. But the Trophy that year went to New Zealand with the British team third.

Nor was sponsorship forthcoming for the British team for the 1976 Onion Patch series. One of the team, *Synergy*, owned by D.W.H. McCowen, was going to be in American waters anyway; the owners of the other two boats, *Noreyma X* and *Marionette*, had to pay their own way. The RORC-organised Transatlantic Race which followed the series, in which the British team came third, was won by a club member from Germany, Dr Lubinus, in his yacht *Duva*.

The failure to find sponsors for these two important international series showed that, like everything else, approaching large companies for sponsorship was becoming a professional business, and that organising overseas challenges required long and detailed planning. To arrange these challenges Don Parr, who was to succeed Nick Greville as vice commodore in 1977, headed a small committee to raise money for overseas challenges, and this found a sponsor, Overseas Containers Ltd., for the British team for the 1977 Southern Cross series.

During the early part of 1975 Dunhill's had indicated their intention to withdraw their sponsorship from the Admiral's Cup series and so Heath's navigator, Anthony Churchill, who was a club member, had invited Gérard de Ayala, an executive of Champagne Mumm, to give away a few bottles at the 1975 Admiral's Cup prizegiving. This prompted Alan Green to visit Paris that winter to persuade the chairman of Champagne Mumm, Baron de Gunzberg, who was himself a keen yachtsman, to take over from Dunhill's. It proved to be the start of a long and profitable partnership between the club and the *firm.

At the beginning of 1976 Owen *Aisher stood down after holding the office of admiral for seven years. In his 20-year stint as hon. treasurer he had guided the club with all the financial acumen he had shown in his highly successful business career as well as being one of the great postwar patrons of yachting. He, and later Robin Aisher, built and raced a whole succession of yachts and metre boats called *Yeoman*, 29 so far.

Owen Aisher was succeeded by the commodore, Maurice Laing, who will be well remembered by older members for his long and successful ownership of *Loujaine II* (ex-*Prospect of Whitby*). Built in 1971, he altered her extensively and she proved over and again that whatever the disadvantages of the IOR the rule wasn't just about building new every season and that it treated old boats who were campaigned well more than fairly.

Another recommendation of John Roome's working party had been for the club to experiment with new races and a second working party, chaired by

Nick Greville, studied the possibilities of a suggestion of Roome's to hold a race round Britain and Ireland in 1976. The British Islands Race, as it was called, proved a popular idea but some owners wanted to race the 1,860 miles non-stop while others only wanted to take part if they were allowed into port en route to change their crews and re-stock with food and water.

It thus became a two division race. Division I, racing non-stop with a minimum of five crew, attracted 15 starters; Division II, in which the eight starters had to have a minimum crew of four, had three pit stops, at Crookhaven, Stornoway, and Blyth. Both divisions started and finished at Southsea. The start, on 5th June, was in light airs and fog and after struggling as far as Dartmouth the navigator of John Roome's *Flycatcher*, which was racing non-stop, calculated that if they continued at the same average speed they would not finish before 17th March 1977!

However, the wind picked up and *Flycatcher* for one did not have to make a single tack before finishing twelve days later. *More Opposition*, skippered by round-the-world yachtsman Robin Knox-Johnston (Sir Robin from 1995), who joined the club the following year, took Division I line honours in a time of 10days, 23hrs, 53min., but was pushed into third place on corrected time by *Electron II* and *Flycatcher*. In Division II one of the club's rear commodores, Rodney Hill, finished first on elapsed time in *Morningtown*, but on corrected time the prize went to Britannia Royal Naval College's *Hindostan*.

For the 1977 season Beta Division was renamed the Restricted Division which was open to bona fide cruisers whenever built. It was a sign of the times that the owners of all boats in this division had to sign a declaration that they would not race with the object of furthering trade or business.

A race in the English Channel was organised by the club to celebrate the Queen's Jubilee—it was marred by the loss of a crew member off *Charlatan V*, one of the 63 starters—but the main event was, of course, the Admiral's Cup series, to which had been added another inshore event of 30 miles, raced the Thursday before the start of Cowes Week. Nineteen nations took part but the trophy was retained by the British team of Chris Dunning's latest *Marionette*, Jeremy Rogers' *Moonshine*, and Robin Aisher's *Yeoman XX*.

The series, now wholly sponsored by Champagne Mumm, was the most difficult the club had ever staged for there was little or no wind and races had to be postponed or resailed. The 1973 and 1975 Fastnets had been slow but the 1977 one was even slower. Some entries ran out of food and water, and it took even the fastest boats 3½ days to reach the Rock. The race was won by an American Admiral's Cupper, Dave Allen's *Imp*, an innovative Ron Holland design which, in the words of Bob Fisher, 'made all the other ocean racers obsolete from the moment that she was launched.'

Griffin III covered a lot of ocean in the first two seasons of the decade. In 1970 she had entered the Middle Sea Race before cruising back to home waters, and in 1971 she had raced from Falmouth to Gibraltar, and then cruised back. After the 1974 season she was sold and there was some discussion as to whether the club, in the adverse economic climate that then prevailed, should have a boat at all. The committee decided it should, and in February 1975 Maj-General Woods, the chairman of the Griffin committee, bought a 'short-term' boat, a Morgan 36 called *Liz of Lymington* which was renamed *Griffin IV*. She did not prove entirely satisfactory and was sold early in 1977, and was replaced by a Nicholson 33 called *Golden Guinea*, which rated in Class IV. Renamed *Griffin V* she did not have a successful summer, and had to retire from several of the hard weather races because she was leaking. Perhaps this prompted the committee in the autumn to make a fundamental change to how the club boat was operated.

The first three *Griffins* had served the club well and the system of chartering them to members, and racing them with a reasonable mix of experience and 'keen ignorance', meant that any member who wanted to could sail in them. In the past, to use Mary Pera's felicitous analogy, the club boat had been used as the nursery slopes for ocean racing, but it was now becoming more and more difficult to run one economically and effectively. The old-style, rather happy-go-lucky approach had become less practical as offshore boats had become more complicated to handle.

'It appears to your committee,' John Roome commented at the 1977 AGM, 'that throwing newcomers to our sport aboard a lively Class IV yacht late on Friday evenings for a thrash round the channel is perhaps not the best method of training.'

It was decided to pick up on the idea of one member, Colin Turner, to have an offshore racing school by chartering *Griffin V* to the National Sailing Centre which would run a six-day course culminating in an offshore race. The scheme worked well. *Griffin V* performed creditably in several offshore races, and introduced a hundred eager young yachtsmen to the sport. Also, thanks to a grant from the Sports Council, much of the financial burden was lifted from the club. In 1978 Tony Mark–who had taken over as Griffin secretary in 1970–stepped down and was replaced, in due course, by John Hoare.

However, hard racing produced such a high level of wear and tear aboard *Griffin V* that at the end of 1978 a new club boat, which rated in Class III, was ordered for the 1979 season. This was an OOD34, designed by Doug Peterson and produced by Jeremy Rogers' boatyard. One of the first Offshore One-Designs[1] to hit the water, the OOD34 was the result of a general reaction against the IOR which was reducing the life of successful boat designs, according to one yachting writer, to weeks instead of years.

1 Peter Johnson, in January 1976, had been the first to propose an offshore One-Design class and the idea had taken off

both photos Beken of Cowes

In May 1978 Mary Pera stepped down as secretary but she was promptly co-opted onto the main committee, and in the following years served on several sub-committees, before being elected vice commodore in 1981. It was during her time as secretary that the club's dress code became more relaxed as 'I maintained that it was not for a mere woman to tell men what they were to wear.' A suit and tie were no longer *de rigeur*. Instead there were 'New Zealanders barefoot in September, going home after the Admiral's Cup; Californians in exotic colours; highly paid match-racing helmsmen passing through in sailing gear.' It made life much more interesting and lunch was always enjoyable 'because one met everyone who was anyone in the sailing world, from America, Australia, or wherever.'

As a barrister, Pera was also a valuable addition to the various international juries she served on in the 1980s, including the Admiral's Cup jury which she chaired. In 1993 she was made a Councillor of Honour of the ORC in recognition of her many years as a councillor and committee chairman. She was replaced as secretary by Alan Green, who had been appointed her deputy in 1974, while Janet Grosvenor, who had joined the club in 1969, became Green's deputy.

LEFT: *Griffin IV* (ex-*Liz of Lymington*), a Morgan 36 which the club bought in 1975 RIGHT: *Griffin V* (ex-*Golden Guinea*), a Nicholson 33 which the club bought in 1977

Green was soon in the thick of what was to become *the* controversial issue of the 1980s when he received a race entry form for a boat called *The State Express* with the sail number 555. For some years owners had been given dispensation from the IYRU's Rule 26–which had been introduced in 1969 to stop any form of advertising on boats or crew clothing–to use brand names for their sponsored boats in the various trans-ocean events. But this type of advertising was beginning to infiltrate into offshore racing, and the combination of sail number and name seemed to be too much of a coincidence, and Green wrote to the owner saying so.

The owner denied there was any sponsorship of his boat by the cigarette manufacturers whose product was identical to his boat's name and sail number, but after speaking to the secretary agreed to use another name. The secretary's action was endorsed by the committee. Discreet sponsorship of races was one thing; blatant advertising quite another. However, as the commodore was to point out at a later date, the fuss caused by taking action often gave a brand name more publicity than it would have received if the matter had been ignored. Catch 22, but the committee was determined to protect the amateur status of ocean racing, come what may.

Certain forms of advertising in *Seahorse* were also frowned upon, and when an advertisement for a sailcloth manufacturer appeared in the club magazine adorned with unclothed beauties the magazine's publisher was sent 'a firmly worded letter'.

But the immediate problems of IOR and the increasing commercialisation of the sport were to be completely overshadowed in the summer of 1979 by a disaster unparalleled in the club's history.

Chapter Twelve

FASTNET DISASTER–AND AFTER

THE 1979 Fastnet began rather as the two earlier ones had done, in a Force 3 to 4 from the west, and it could be that some of the 303 starters –a new record–had become lulled into a false sense of security by the absence of heavy weather. If so, they were soon to be disabused when a freak *storm hit the fleet in the southern Irish Sea and for many competitors it quickly became a struggle for survival. As usual when the weather was bad, the smaller boats caught the worst of it.

Only 85 starters completed the course, and 15 lives were lost. Some were thrown overboard when their boats were knocked down, and were swept away and drowned when their safety lines snapped; others became victims of hypothermia when their liferafts capsized or disintegrated. Many were rescued from the water, or from their water-logged boats, by 13 RNLI lifeboats whose volunteer crews spent over 170 hours at sea; by various ships in the area–including the Dutch frigate, HNLMS *Overijssel*, the fleet's guardship–and by helicopters from RNAS Culdrose.

Morningtown, the Oyster 46 owned and skippered by Rodney Hill, also played a conspicuous part in the rescue operation. She was the junior radio-relay vessel for the Admiral's Cup teams and those aboard her kept a continuous radio watch in the worst possible conditions that led, in the words of one official RAF rescuer taking part, 'to the rescue of about 20 survivors as well as saving the RAF and the Royal Navy many hours of vital search time.'

Twenty-three boats were abandoned, but only four sank. One of those lost was the club's *Griffin VI*, skippered by Neil Graham with Stuart Quarrie as mate. While under bare pole some 35 miles from the Rock the boat was rolled completely over by a rogue wave. The washboards protecting the main hatchway dropped out, the sliding hatch was thrown back, and the sea poured in.

When *Griffin VI* righted herself the crew below managed to reach the deck, but with the cabin full of water there was only three feet of freeboard and Graham gave the order to abandon ship. The crew climbed into the liferaft and were eventually rescued by another competitor, the French boat *Lorelei*. The rescue took almost two hours in mountainous seas and darkness. It was a brilliant piece of seamanship on the part of the French skipper, Alain Catherineau, and he was subsequently made Yachtsman of the Year in Britain, a popular choice.

Ashore, at Plymouth, the RORC organisers only slowly became aware of the scale of the disaster. By late Monday afternoon it was obvious that, with the strength of the wind, the maxi[1] yachts would be arriving well ahead of schedule, and Alan Green went out to the breakwater to set up the finishing line early. By evening Green's deputy, Janet Grosvenor, found it hard to walk against the rising wind and by the morning the first reports of boats retiring began to come in.

At nine o'clock on Tuesday morning Grosvenor received a message to ring Johnny Clothier, a RORC rear commodore, and the only flag officer not taking part in the race as his wife was expecting their second child. He had heard the forecast and was very concerned, and his concern increased when Grosvenor told him that the weather was so bad that Green and his finishing team were stranded on the breakwater. Clothier immediately decided to join Grosvenor, and by the time he arrived two hours later confused reports were pouring in from the Coastguard of boats seeking assistance and of crew members lost overboard.

Many boats were unaccounted for and accurate information was almost impossible to obtain as the organisers had no direct radio link with any of the competitors. 'The first problem we had,' said Janet Grosvenor afterwards, 'was with the reports of people being lost. For example, a man was lost overboard from *Festina*, but we didn't know which *Festina*, there being three of them in the race. There was no means of finding out quickly. Our phones were completely blocked with people ringing in so our chances of ringing out to get information we needed badly were hampered.'

The GPO, which then ran the telephone system, quickly put in extra telephones and reorganised the ones already there. GPO operators and naval ratings manned the extra lines to feed the race organisers with accurate information on the whereabouts of each boat; the police arrived to sort out the situation at the docks which had become packed with cars and people; and overnight the computer was reprogrammed to print out the latest whereabouts of each Fastnet competitor. This was used not only by those handling incoming calls but by the Land's End Coastguard co-ordinating the rescue operations.

1 the first maxi boat home, Bob Bell's *Condor of Bermuda*, established a new record of 71hrs,25min.,23secs

1979 Fastnet Race Disaster

The damage done to the cockpit of *Camargue* (right) which had been abandoned after being rolled completely over. The crews of most crippled yachts stayed aboard and either managed to reach harbour or were taken in tow by lifeboats. Here *Casse Tete V* (below), which lost her rudder, is being taken in tow by the Courtmacsherry lifeboat, *Sir Samuel Kelly*, after her crew had rigged a spinnaker pole to steer with

Ambrose Greenway

A *Yachting World* photographer records Neil Graham (above), the skipper of *Griffin VI* which foundered during the race, receiving a half-model of her from the magazine's assistant editor, John Driscoll, at the clubhouse while committee member Brian Saffery Cooper looks on

Offers of help were gratefully received by the exhausted organisers to answer calls now flooding in from all over the world. The club's flag officers were given little respite after finishing the race and were deployed on various tasks, one of which was to debrief the crews as they arrived. A Serious Incident Unit was established by Keith Ludlow, who had replaced Matthews as the rating secretary in 1977, and Sir David Mackworth Bt, and this handled the flood of enquiries about yachts which were known to have suffered casualties.

Green, after returning from the breakwater on Tuesday afternoon, fielded the twice-daily press conferences. A strict regime was imposed where any questions could be asked at the conferences but no interviews whatever were granted outside them, a successful policy which saved the organisers much time despite the many efforts to persuade them to talk 'out of court'. Initially, only the yachting correspondents were there but later the world's press descended in droves. After Janet Grosvenor's office had been invaded by a TV crew, Jean-Louis Fabry, one of the club's foreign rear commodores, lent a member of his crew to act as a bouncer. Questions were asked in the House of Commons and Green came under great, and sometimes hostile, pressure to explain why the race had not been abandoned. Green, in measured tones, explained that it remained, as it always had done, the irrevocable responsibility of the individual owner to start, and continue, in a race, and that to cancel a race once it had started was impractical and pointless.

The rescue operations continued throughout Tuesday and Wednesday, and into Thursday, and after the race an official inquiry was opened. Run jointly by the RYA and the RORC, its principals were Maurice Laing, Hugh Forbes, and Lt-Col. James Myatt, and they received a Report drawn up by a working party, which included Green, Grosvenor, and the RYA's Bill Anderson, and was chaired by the club's vice commodore, Chris Dunning. Three copies of a detailed *questionnaire were sent to each skipper with a request that two should be passed on to responsible members of his crew, and one of the club's bedrooms was turned into an office to collate the 530 which were returned from the crews of 235 boats. The Report was published on 11th December 1979. It made certain recommendations about the organisation of the race, boat construction, sails and equipment, particularly safety equipment, and the identification of competitors. 'The Fastnet is a supreme challenge to ocean racing yachtsmen in British waters,' the Report concluded its findings. 'In the 1979 race the sea showed that it can be a deadly enemy and those who go to sea for pleasure must do so in the full knowledge that they may encounter dangers of the highest order. However, provided that the lessons so harshly taught in this race are well learnt we feel that yachts should continue to race over the Fastnet course.'

The club's first reaction to the Fastnet report was to refer it to its technical committee to look into stability and associated design aspects relating to offshore racing. It also acted quickly in the face of considerable public criticism, some of it ill-considered, by introducing crew qualifications for its non-stop British Islands and Lymington-Bayona Races held in 1980.

New Special Regulations were introduced to improve watertight integrity by dealing with matters such as loose companionway washboards and the separation of bilge pump outlets from cockpit drains; trisails and VHF radio became mandatory for the Fastnet; qualifications for competing were introduced; and the number of starters was limited to 300. There were also investigations as to why some boats were knocked down while others were not. Though they reached no conclusion as to why this should have happened, recommendations were made to the ORC to amend the IOR rule, and many of these came into force internationally on 1st January 1981. For a period thereafter the rule, to everyone's relief, entered a period of little change.

~

The early 1980s saw the introduction in large numbers of fractionally rigged boats. Only 5% of the 1979 *Admiral's Cup fleet had been rigged in this way; by 1985 it had risen to 68%. The 1980s also saw the increasing use of such exotic materials as Kevlar and titanium, and an ever-increasing level of sophistication in constructing what by then had become known as 'Grand Prix' yachts. But the relentless pressure for design advances, and the lack of requirements by the IOR for interior accommodation, sometimes reduced the resale value of these yachts to less than half their original cost.

The decrease in size of boats in the Admiral's Cup series during the 1980s was also quite marked and reflected the move towards smaller boats generally:

The British Admiral's Cup team with the Admiral's Cup which they were defending in 1979. The Australians won, the British team came sixth. From left to right: Jeremy Rogers (*Eclipse*), Rt. Hon. Edward Heath (fifth *Morning Cloud*, captain), and Ernest Juer (*Blizzard*). Behind them hangs the painting of Venice by Edward William Cooke RA (1811–1880) which two members rescued during the Blitz only 17% of the fleet had ratings lower than 31ft in 1979, in 1985 it was 58%. In 1979 32% of the fleet rated higher than 34.6ft, in 1985 only 4% did.

For the elite top segment of the fleet the perpetual search for lightness combined with strength continued, with one-off hulls now being more often constructed with composite laminates, not aluminium. But lower down the scale production boats continued to be overwhelmingly popular and by 1986 only 10% of the IOR-rated fleet were one-offs. So when it came to replacing the club yacht which had been lost in the Fastnet the decision was made to go for another production boat.

The OOD34 had been criticised in some quarters as two had sunk in the race and nine of the 11 taking part had suffered knock-downs beyond the horizontal. But the Griffin sub-committee, having studied the facts very carefully, could not agree with those who thought the OOD34 unsuitable for seagoing. Time was too short to make a decision to buy for the 1980 season so an OOD34, *Allamanda*, was chartered for the National Sailing Centre.

Efforts to buy an OOD34 for the 1981 season failed but Robin Aisher came to the club's rescue by lending it his Hustler 36 for the summer. With the help of a grant from the Sports Council, this was purchased from him and on 18th March 1982 she was renamed *Griffin* by the wife of the new commodore, Audrey Dunning.

Griffin was raced quite successfully, but was badly holed during a port and starboard incident in May 1983 when she had right of way. She was sold in 1984 when the National Sailing Centre acquired a Sigma 41 which, with the club's agreement carried the name of *Griffin*. She was sailed mostly by committee member, Stuart Quarrie, and in 1986 she won the Somerset Memorial Trophy as the RORC's Yacht of the Year. The club supported the Centre by encouraging provisional membership, awarding prizes to students, and sponsoring two or three students each year for a Griffin course from the Griffin fund, but it could no longer afford to own a club boat.

With the country in the grip of a recession the number of starters taking part in the club's programme in 1980 dropped to 346, the lowest since 1972. Off the water inflation raged—it was over 20% in May—and like most other organisations the club's finances suffered accordingly. But membership kept creeping up and by the end of 1981 numbered 3,216 which included 1,285 overseas members and 109 provisional ones. At the end of the year, after 11 years in office, the hon. treasurer, Peter Green, stepped down and was replaced by a past rear commodore, Tony Greener.

The pressure on the IYRU's Rule 26 relating to advertising was unrelenting. Up to 1977 the national authority had had the right to alter the rule to meet its particular requirements, but in an attempted clampdown this right was rescinded by the IYRU in January 1977 when permission had to be sought and was not always granted. A revised rule came into force in January 1981. This allowed, in exceptional circumstances, for organisers to apply through their national authority to the IYRU, for boats to be named after their sponsors. It also allowed advertising matter on crew clothing provided permission was sought from the crew's national authority and from the national authority of any country in which they raced. In March 1981 the Australian Yachting Federation submitted a formal request to the RYA for the 1981 Australian Admiral's Cup team to be allowed to display the name of its sponsors on crew clothing. By 10 votes to 2 the RORC committee agreed to suggest to the RYA that for the Admiral's Cup series there would be no objection to consent being given provided the names 'are not displayed on clothing between a period two hours before the start of a race and two hours after the individual yacht finishes.' Quite how anyone was going to enforce this was anyone's guess and it is possible to sense, reading such a ruling now, the pressure for change that was being exerted on those defending the sport's amateur status.

Another restriction which was increasingly becoming an anomaly in the early 1980s was directly related to the club's aim of fostering and encouraging the study and practice of navigation and seamanship. This was the use of linked electronic aids in RORC races in home waters (they had been allowed in the Financial Times Clipper and Parmelia Races). Following the 1979 Fastnet, in which some of the boats in distress had given the rescue services inaccurate positions, the club knew it needed to improve safety. So when it was seen that linked electronic aids had not affected the quality of the racing elsewhere all restrictions were at last lifted–some would say not before time–in 1983.

The highlight of the 1981 season was the victory of the British Admiral's Cup team: Peter de Savary's *Victory of Burnham*, Brian and Pam Saffery Cooper's *Dragon*, and *Yeoman XXIII*, sailed by Robin Aisher who captained the team. It had a convincing win over the United States and the other 14 teams, but when *Victory*, which had by then changed hands, took part in the Southern Ocean Racing Conference (SORC) in early 1982, and very nearly won it, her rating was found to be 1.4 feet higher than shown on her certificate.

The problem of incorrect ratings had by then reached almost epidemic proportions. Fur had flown at the SORC in 1981 when it had been found that three boats had raced with the wrong rating; the same year two had been found to have incorrect ones at the Sardinia Cup (inaugurated in 1978 along the lines of the Admiral's Cup series), as a result of which two yachtsmen were banned for cheating[1]; and the owner of the Class V winner in the 1981 Solent Points Championship had withdrawn his boat from the series after it was found that it had been rated incorrectly.

1 cheating was not a new phenomenon–in 1971 Ron Amey reported that 'he had seen a yacht being inclined when a piece of lead was lying on its shelf'–but the scale of it was

With *Victory* the committee of inquiry, set up immediately by the RORC, found no evidence of fraud or malpractice, but it did find that the boat had not been properly prepared at the time of her original measurement and that she had only been partly remeasured for the Admiral's Cup trials. The notes on her original measurement had been routinely destroyed but it was thought possible that an error in transcription had been made. Though some thought it unnecessary, Keith *Ludlow resigned at the end of the season–he was later appointed the ORC's deputy chief measurer–and was replaced in the spring by M.G.A. MacDougall. These scandals and other related problems shook many yachtsmen's confidence in the IOR, but *Victory's* incorrect rating did not affect the results of the British team's triumph in the 1981 Admiral's Cup.

The 1981 season ended with the club's first Caribbean Pursuit Race which started on 8th November from Cowes with 13 entries divided into an IOR and an Open Division. The race was under the patronage of the King of Spain, a RORC member in his own right, and at the end of the first leg, at Las Palmas, the competitors received a great welcome. The second leg started with an additional eight boats and ended at Antigua. But though this *inaugural race was declared a success only seven entries were received for the subsequent race in 1983, and it was postponed until 1985 when entries started from either Falmouth or Barcelona.

Recession in 1982 caused the number of starters in club events to drop to a ten-year low. Even such a prestigious event as the One Ton Cup had to be cancelled through lack of entries; and for the first time the club was unable to assemble a British team for the 1982 Onion Patch series. Instead, the Americans allowed an EEC team to take part which comprised two boats belonging to foreign members–Dr K. Fischer's *Hamburg*, from Germany and Peter Vroon's *Formidable*, from Holland–and one, *Nick Nack*, owned by a British member, Nick Langley Pope. It finished seventh.

The recession did not prevent four past club commodores, and the serving one, Chris Dunning, taking on five past UNCL presidents in a match off the Mediterranean island of Cavallo. Sponsored by Champagne Mumm, it was the best of three races in half tonners. UNCL, skippered by Jean-Louis Fabry, was the victor in all three but the Entente Cordiale was the real winner. Known as the Coupe des Présidents, it became a biennial affair and it took a decade for the RORC commodores to chalk up their first victory.

In 1983 sponsorship for the Admiral's Cup series was renegotiated with Champagne Mumm by Green and the new hon. treasurer, Tony Greener. A ten-year deal was struck and the series became known as the Champagne Mumm Admiral's Cup (CMAC). The opposition to sponsorship, advertising, and professionalism had by now melted away for the committee voted unanimously to accept the deal. The club's relationship with the firm was excellent and after all, one committee member consoled himself, it was the series which was going to have its name changed not the cup itself.

But sponsorship was slow to be accepted by the membership. After the committee unanimously approved the commodore's idea of having a division for sponsored boats in the 1984 British Islands Race a quorum could not be mustered at an Extraordinary General Meeting in December 1983 to approve it, and those present opposed it.

In 1983 the Admiral's Cup was defended by Graham Walker's *Indulgence*, Brian and Pam Saffery Cooper's *Dragon*, and Dixon Atkinson's *Black Topic*. They had been chosen after yet more trouble with ratings when two of the boats competing for a place in the team were found, at a late stage in the trials, to have incorrect ones. Both had previously belonged to Continental owners and the procedures for vetting certificates originating from outside Britain had to be strengthened. In a wind-starved series the British team finished eighth, its poorest placing ever, with the series going to Germany.

The economy was in better shape in 1984. Yet the number of boats participating in the club's domestic programme during even numbered years remained stubbornly static and the British Islands Race had to be cancelled through lack of entries. To increase numbers shorter courses were organised for the smaller classes and were opened to boats rated by the new Channel Handicap System (CHS) which had been introduced that year on an experimental basis.

By now IOR had become extremely expensive and CHS was a cheap, simple rule which did not need a measurer for a certificate. Originally devised[1] by UNCL, the RORC had helped develop it. The Sail Training Association, with which the club had been associated ever since Illingworth had helped found it in 1956, had a simple rating rule which it kept secret, and Green's suggestion that CHS should also remain under wraps to prevent it being breached by designers was accepted as being a sensible move to prolong its life. Even so, at the time, no one thought it would last more than five or six years.

The policy of shortening courses was continued in 1985 when the club's traditional 200-mile triangular races in the Channel were curtailed or dropped in favour of less lengthy, more interesting events, with starts on Saturday morning instead of Friday evening. Dunning told those opposing this change that if the club continued to run only longer races then more and more people who wanted to race in its programme would not be able to do so as neither they nor their crews had the time. Of those who did have the time, many wanted to spend at least some of it off the water relaxing. This change of emphasis needed some careful liaison with JOG[2] to minimise overlap.

1 the principals involved were Robin Aisher, Alan Green, Jonathan Hudson, Jean-Louis Fabry, and the French measurer, Jean Sans

2 JOG, which now accepted larger boats for longer events, was by the 1980s just one of several organisations to hold offshore races that competed with RORC ones

Chris Dunning's last report as commodore at the 1984 AGM further emphasised the pressure of modern living. He recalled that the Seine Bay Race that year had made the record books by being so devoid of wind that every single starter had retired. 'To have finished,' he said, 'would have meant staying out until Monday at least, and these days *bosses don't respond to poetic appeals which involve you having been becalmed like a painted ship on a painted ocean. If you're not at your desk on Monday morning he'll put someone else there!'

There was pressure, too, on the rating office, which had moved to a new location in Lymington. CHS soon doubled the rated fleet but unfortunately the office had neither the staff nor the equipment to cope, and there was a large backlog of work. A senior measurer, Commander Tony Ashmead, who took over as rating secretary, did not mince his words when he reported to the main committee in November that 'it was an unpalatable fact but if the rating office was to change from being run in an amateur way to a professional way this required equipment and qualified people to run it.'

Robin Aisher, the incoming commodore, had a lot on his plate administratively for he not only sat on the ORC and IYRU, but had RYA commitments too. But the rating office was quickly on its feet, which was just as well as in November 1985 another rating rule was adopted by the ORC as an alternative to the IOR. This was the International Measurement System (IMS) which had been transferred by the American authorities to the ORC, and the rating office had to grapple with its complexities before IMS divisions were introduced into the club's events in 1988.

IMS employed a Velocity Prediction Programme (VPP) to assess the potential speed of a boat when its hull measurement and rig data were fed into a computer. The data was obtained by measuring the hull with an electronic wand and transmitting it to a mini computer. This in turn sent it to a mainframe computer so that the VPP could produce on screen the entire geometrical shape of the hull. From this, and the aerodynamics of the rig, the VPP calculated the boat's potential speed in a variety of wind speeds and directions. It was all a far cry from Ray Barrett and his bits of string and calico tape.

The economic pressures that existed during the mid-1980s had sent a series of shock waves through even the most conservative recesses of society. Along with much of London clubland, they had rocked the RORC and during 1985 the main committee was much exercised as to how to ride them. It formed working parties and held special meetings to discuss the impact of advertising on the sport which was reaching crisis proportions, and the internal problems of an overworked secretariat. One solution was to take advantage of the club's commercial opportunities. The income derived from this would result in more

The crew of Richard Loftus' *Desperado* celebrate rounding the Rock in fine style during the 1991 Fastnet Race

Pasquale Landolfi's *Brava Q8*, a member of the winning Italian Admiral's Cup team in 1995

Mayhem! A race during the first Mumm 36 world championships in 1994

Brian Stewart's *Zulu*, used regularly as the club's committee boat, during the 1995 Admiral's Cup series

Start of the 1998 North Sea Race

This photograph of Commodore Terry Robinson's Swan 48, *Assuage,* was taken in 1997. When Robinson became commodore that year he donated the Assuage Trophy for a RORC mini series. Fittingly, *Assuage,* sailed by a Royal Naval crew, won the Trophy after taking honours, class, and overall in the Cherbourg Race

The Sydney 40, chosen by the club to be the Class 2 boat for the 1999 Admiral's Cup series, seen here during trials on the Hamble, October 1998

and better paid staff, and in 1986 two limited companies were formed, a tax efficient way of channelling all the club's growing commercial interests.

The problem of advertising and sponsorship was more complex. Aisher commented that the club was at a crossroads. He suggested forming a 'Grand Prix', or open, division for professional yachtsmen where advertising would be permitted. It would compete over the same courses at the same time as the other divisions but for separate prizes. This idea was adopted and in due course the IYRU, with the concurrence of the ORC, granted the Admiral's Cup management committee permission to allow sponsored boats, and teams, into the 1987 CMAC series. The club's sailing rules that required crews to be amateur was repealed as unenforceable.

~

The 1985 season proved to be particularly successful for the club. Though the British Admiral's Cup team of Lloyd Bankson's *Phoenix*, Larry and Debbie Woodell's *Jade*, and Peter Whipp's *Panda*, failed to retrieve the Cup–which the Germans won again–they came a very creditable second. *Phoenix* was jointly campaigned with Graham Walker, whose crew moved across to her after Walker's *Indulgence* hit an obstruction off the Isle of Wight during the De Guingand Bowl Race and sank. This combined effort resulted in *Phoenix* being awarded the title of best individual boat in the series, the first time ever it had been awarded to a production boat. *Panda* did well, too. Sailed and navigated by Peter Whipp, she won a tough and testing Fastnet in which 68% of the fleet of 222 retired. However, except for the maxi *Drum*, which lost her keel, no competitor had to seek assistance. In a largely reaching race Marvin Green's 80ft sloop *Nirvana* set a new course record of 60hrs,41min.,15secs.

Another success for the club in 1985 was *Jade's* victory in the One Ton Championships; and at the end of the year three other top one tonners–Peter Whipp's *Panda*, Irvine Laidlaw's *Highland Fling*, and Mike Peacock's *Cifraline 3*, which had been chartered by Chris Griffiths–were shipped to Australia to take part in the Southern Cross series. At Melbourne they were delayed by a strike and it was only the resourcefulness of their manager, June Clark, and the co-operation of the Australian authorities, which enabled the boats to be transported overland to Sydney in time to tune up in good time for the first race. However, their efforts were rewarded and the British team won the series.

A letter sent to the commodore by Nick Greville and another member, Peter Vroon, about the growing disillusionment with the IOR was debated by the main committee at the beginning of 1986. The letter expressed concern that the club was not using its influence in the ORC to alter the rule radically for 1987. Greville and Vroon felt that boats built to the IOR 'were unseaworthy not only in shape but in construction' but that anyone wishing to be competitive was forced to build such a boat. Aisher reminded the committee that the ORC had recently introduced scantling rules which at least went some way to providing safer-built boats, and that to make a radical change to the rule would make many of them obsolete overnight. The committee agreed, but both they and Aisher must have known that the writing for the IOR was on the wall.

Politics of another kind intruded when the committee had to decide whether to accept a challenge from South Africa for the ¾-ton championships which the club was to organise in 1986 at Torquay. The Gleneagles Agreement, which laid down the sanctions then imposed on the South African apartheid government, did not cover yacht racing, and though there was some concern that, with anti-apartheid feeling running high, there was risk of the series being disrupted it was decided by 12 votes to 4 to accept the challenge. It was held without hindrance, and was won by Graham Walker's *Indulgence*, his first world title after eight years of competition. However, the club's joy was not unconfined as the absence of a sponsor left a large hole in its racing accounts; but its funds were bolstered by a rise in its membership, which now totalled 3,446, with many of the new members qualifying by completing the latest Whitbread Round-the-World Race.

Robin Aisher steering *Yeoman XXI*, July 1981

Alastair Black

British teams competing in the Sardinia Cup had never performed particularly well. Indeed, their results had become progressively worse–they had finished 4th, 7th, 9th, and 11th in earlier series. But in 1986 the team of Chris Dunning's *Marionette*, Stephen Fein's *Full Pelt*, which was the highest point scorer in the series, and Martin Gibson's *Pocket Battleship*, achieved a notable victory over the Germans who had been in the ascendancy in offshore racing for several years.

The 1985 Admiral's Cup had been dominated by one tonners so the club stipulated that for the 1987 series the three-boat teams, while still racing within the 30ft-40ft rating band, would have to have an aggregate of at least 95ft. As three one tonners only added up to 91.5ft, this excluded any more one-ton teams, such as those fielded by Britain and New Zealand. The decision was to make temporarily popular the so-called mid-raters or two-ton class to fill the

Alastair Black

gap between the one tonners at the bottom end of the band and the 50–footers at the top end.

Victory in both the Southern Cross and Sardinia Cup series in 1986 augured well for the British Admiral's Cup team in 1987 which now had Stuart Quarrie as its manager. For the first time it, too, had a sponsor, the stockbrokers James Capel, which had been found by a Public Relations firm, Interaction, working on the team's behalf. But it needed more than PR and sponsorship to win what was still the most coveted prize in offshore racing. Competitive though the team was, Mike Peacock's *Juno III*[1], Alan Gray's *Jamarella*, and Graham Walker's *Indulgence*, could only finish second behind the New Zealanders who, at their sixth attempt, took the trophy for the first time and did so with little of the financial support lavished on other teams. Instead of money they had, as their manager Don Brooke put it afterwards, the support of three million people and 60 million

Peter Whipp's *Panda*, one of the 1985 British Admiral's Cup team, crossing the Royal Yacht Squadron line

1 *Juno III* came second on corrected time in the Fastnet in 1987. But she won the Fastnet Challenge Cup as the winner, *Full Pelt*, racing under the name of *Irish Independent* in the Irish Admiral's Cup team, was a sponsored boat

sheep, while Tim Jeffery remarked that, as in 1985, 'Britain fielded a team of three fine boats, not a fine team of three boats. The distinction is fine yet very telling.'

The 1987 Champagne Mumm Admiral's Cup series was the final competition in the third Champagne Mumm *World Cup series, and it resulted in New Zealand and Britain both scoring the same number of points to share the World Cup trophy. To avoid a repetition of this, the club stipulated that if a tie occurred in future the team with the best aggregate time in the Fastnet would be declared the World Cup winners.

The Admiral's Cup series had been filled with rumours of cheating and a letter was sent by the club to 436 participants asking for any information they might have on the subject, and 77 replies were received. In October 1987 an international jury disqualified *I-Punkt*, which had raced for the Austrian team, for infringing IYRU Rule 22 by transferring water ballast. The RYA then banned the boat's charterer and crew from any event, the charterer for ten years, his crew for lesser periods. The ban on the crew was later suspended and in June 1989 the RYA suspended the charterer's ban from March 1990. He was therefore free to sail in any RYA event from that time provided he did not re-offend.

There were also persistent rumours that the British team had shifted ballast during the series and subsequently at the One Ton Cup held in Kiel. The committee felt it was too close to the problem to judge it dispassionately and an RYA official was asked to chair an inquiry with one of the rear commodores, Duncan Munro *Kerr, and a member of the main committee, James Holman. Besides having the letters from crew members as evidence, the inquiry panel interviewed over 20 individuals and subjected two of them to close interrogation. This must have left no stone unturned as the two RORC members were barristers, but the owners and crews of all four boats under scrutiny were exonerated.

'Bar-talk and poorly substantiated press reports,' the inquiry panel concluded, 'are as damaging to the sport as cheating itself', and recommended that the rules should be published as widely and actively as possible. This the club had already arranged to do after holding an owners' seminar on the problem at the 1988 Boat Show. A 'don't cheat' diagram was included in its programme, a 'don't cheat' sticker was issued to every owner for display on board, and a new Declaration Form was drawn up which all crew members had to sign at the end of a race. One wonders what George Martin would have thought of it all.

In September 1987 the club was left a two-year-old Briand-designed one tonner, *Ritec Poinciana*, in the will of the owner, Mrs Katinka Vinke. It had been thought that the boat might become the new *Griffin* as the name had reverted to the club after the National Sailing Centre had been closed at Cowes earlier that year and the Centre's Sigma 41 sold. Unfortunately, the boat was found to be unsuitable. Instead, the name was lent to Alan Gray's British Performance Sailing (BPS), run by Stuart Quarrie, and its One Tonner, *Sidewinder*, was renamed *Griffin*. The Griffin fund continued to sponsor young people for offshore crew training courses at BPS and at a similar school, Britannia Sailing.

No British boat could be mustered for either the 1987 Southern Cross Series –instead the team chartered in Australia–or for the 1988 Sardinia Cup, but Robin Aisher, Mike Peacock, and Alan Gray did compete for the Kenwood Cup held in Hawaii that year and came a very creditable third overall. At the 1987 AGM the commodore announced that membership now stood at 3,545 and it has maintained that level ever since.

The 1988 racing programme caught the eye of one commentator who noted that like the races described within it it had a new look with a 'bold red RORC logo type appearing under a sparkling picture of a Swan cruiser racer in a fresh breeze.' He added that the crew were obviously enjoying every minute and there was 'not a leg to be seen over the side', an oblique reference to the growing determination amongst racing administrators to find a way of banning what had by now become common practice.

There was indeed a new feel to the domestic programme with 13 races taking place in the Channel as well as the short ones connected with Channel Week. There were also seven other more traditional events which ranged from the 700-mile Round Ireland Race, now sponsored by Cork Dry Gin, to a 430-miler from Lymington to La Rochelle.

The relative merits of the various rating systems was hotly debated in committee in 1988. One committee member reported that Olin Stephens thought IMS should replace IOR. Another, John Dare, had already made a positive step in this direction, for he had just taken delivery of his wooden 36ft Humphreys-designed *Apriori*[1], one of the first custom-built yachts designed with CHS and IMS in mind. Jonathan Bradbeer, who had replaced Aisher as commodore at the start of the year, stated that though IOR had proved to be very effective over the years it had been allowed to stray to produce boats which were unpleasant to sail for long periods offshore, which had no accommodation and which were difficult to sell.

Despite growing disillusionment with IOR the committee decided to stick with it for 'Grand Prix' racing, but agreed that the rule definitely needed a radical overhaul to bolster its flagging popularity. The committee therefore lobbied ORC Councillors to amend the IOR. Among other improvements, it wanted boats that possessed greater inherent stability, were moderately narrower and had less flare, had more displacement, and could be used for cruising which would help maintain their re-sale value.

1 she was the club's CHS champion yacht in 1989

Dramatic view of John Dare's *Apriori* taken from the masthead by photographer Rick Tomlinson

These suggestions, dubbed Rule 90 by the committee as it was to be introduced in 1990, were rejected by the ORC which was, however, quite happy for the RORC to develop and test them. But at a special meeting in September 1988 it was decided, though not unanimously, to abandon Rule 90 and to run an IOR division with an unaltered rule in 1989; promote IMS by holding seminars and awarding IMS prizes; continue to offer CHS and to reallocate some of the club's trophies to the CHS fleet.

The differences of approach to racing between the IOR and CHS fleets led to different RORC regulations. One was that boats competing in events run under IOR were permitted advertising, while those in CHS and IMS ones were initially banned from having it. Another was that a recent ORC ban which prevented crews from dangling their legs over the weather side at night was rescinded by the club, but for the IOR fleet only as 'we believe,' Bradbeer stated, 'that those sailing in the CHS classes prefer the excuse to turn in at night, rather than feeling obliged to sit with their legs over the rail.'

In January 1989 David Edwards, who had succeeded Maurice Laing as admiral in 1983, stepped down and was replaced by Don Parr of *Quailo* fame. In 1968 Edwards had become, at 39, the second youngest-ever commodore and had also served as ORC chairman from 1970 to 1978. Throughout this time he had raced at the highest level and scored some notable successes. During the 1980s, at a time when he no longer owned a 'Grand Prix' boat, he continued to race offshore with other members. On one occasion, when invited to crew in Maurice Laing's ¾-tonner *Bathsheba*, he asked what he should take aboard and was advised just to bring a sponge. He asked what he needed a sponge for and was told it was for putting under his chin when he fell asleep on the weather rail! Not at all fazed, he went out afterwards and bought himself a ¾-tonner—and did very well in her, too.

For the 1989 Champagne Mumm Admiral's Cup series the number of races was increased to six with the addition of a long inshore one in the vicinity of the Nab Tower. Fears that the series' popularity would falter proved groundless for the same number of teams, 14, competed as in 1987. In fact, it was widely voted the best series yet with designers, builders, owners and crews bringing together a fleet of outstanding performance.

To answer criticisms that earlier British challenges had not been sufficiently cohesive, the club formed a team of three in 1988 to select and coach the British crews: Richard Keeling, the current vice commodore (chairman), Admiral's Cup veteran Harold Cudmore (non-racing captain), and RYA/RORC keelboat specialist, Bill Edgerton (coach). They imposed a strict regime and insisted on the co-operation of all potential contenders. Cudmore put his finger on the problem succinctly: the failures since 1981, he wrote, had been caused by the falling number of trialists, the appearance of professional rivalry between boats and crews, and the lack of any team tactics. The answer was that once selected the final team had to pull together and sail as a team.

Nick Rains

Harold Cudmore, Admiral's Cup series 1989

Because of lack of tuning partners for the most likely contenders the British selectors switched the trials to Kiel Week and the club announced that the team would be selected from those present at Kiel. There was therefore some confusion, and acrimony, when they chose Walker's fourth *Indulgence*, even though she was not at Kiel, but the hard work of the British trio—which also included

Alan Gray's *Jamarella*, the top boat in the series, and Mike Peacock's *Juno IV*–paid off, as they brought back the trophy to Britain for the first time in eight years.

A change in format was called for in the series' 'wash-up' meeting. The Cup's trustees agreed, and from 1991 each team was to comprise three level rating boats at one ton, two ton, and 50ft level. These were maximum limits and the series would be run as a team level-rating event, with a single start for the three classes. This meant there would be three fleet winners each day but no overall top individual boat, a move that returned the emphasis, as the trophy's donors must have wished, to team performance not that of individual boats. This change was followed in November by the ORC freezing IOR for six years, a move which, as will be seen, had the opposite effect to that intended.

For the rest of the RORC fleet the 1989 season, during which the clubhouse was thoroughly refurbished, was the longest in the RORC's history. The programme opened with the Cervantes Trophy Race at the end of April and closed with one from Cowes to Cherbourg, which began on 22 September. But with the selectors encouraging British team contenders to race as much as possible abroad against potential team members from other countries there was a dearth of competition until the inaugural Lymington Regatta in July which was won by Alan Gray's *Jamarella*. Run jointly by the RORC and British Performance Sailing, the regatta was held just before the start of the Admiral's Cup series and proved very popular with the crews of the 54 competing boats, of which 37 were Admiral Cuppers.

At the end of 1989 a general manager, Leslie James, joined to oversee the clubhouse and the club's finances. Alan Green was appointed to the new post of director racing and special events and Tony Ashmead was given the new title of director rating and measurements. Janet Grosvenor remained Green's deputy and also took on the task of Griffin secretary from John Hoare who had filled the post for the previous seven years. Reorganised and revitalised, the secretariat was now geared to face what was to be the most challenging decade in the club's history.

Chapter Thirteen

INTO THE NEW MILLENNIUM

B Y 1990 the RORC had become big business—and it had to be run as such if it was to continue to provide the social facilities and standard of racing its members had come to expect. For some years it had spread its talents and its expertise to foster offshore racing by holding seminars and lectures, running week-end training courses for race officers, continuing to encourage—as it always has—*youngsters into the sport, and organising special international events as well as its domestic programme. All this cost time and money, and the 1990s was markedly short of both.

The club's most marketable asset was the Champagne Mumm Admiral's Cup series, but with the IOR in decline, the costs of campaigning escalating alarmingly, and with the economy about to be plunged into the deepest recession since the Second World War, this financial cornerstone of the club's activities appeared to be under threat.

'The RORC owns and promotes the Admiral's Cup, and is now running the business as a joint venture with Champagne Mumm,' was how two committee members expressed the situation later, 'but we hold 100% of the shares. The time has come for the shareholders to tell the operators to introduce a new product, to enhance the image and enlarge the customer base, because in our view the market is still there, but the product is very jaded.'

To tackle the demands that the new decade was likely to bring John Dare, a current rear commodore who succeeded Bradbeer as commodore in 1991, wrote a paper called *The Years Ahead*, which posed a number of questions about the club's future direction; and the vice commodore, Richard Keeling, also contributed one about the future selection and management of British Admiral's Cup teams. These, and a paper written in March 1990 by committee members Tom Jackson, Tom Sperrey, and John Mansfield, about the club's increased involvement in sponsorship, and about race planning and management, proved valuable signposts for the club as it approached its 75th anniversary.

There was also the ever-present responsibility of maintaining the clubhouse. During the postwar decades it had established itself in the affections of thousands of men and women who ocean raced, and it remains the heart and soul of the club. But it needed—and still does—constant attention. In May 1990 a fire spread from a neighbouring house into No.19. Members of the secretariat and staff acted promptly and effectively to minimise the damage, but a subsequent survey found that extensive repairs had to be made to the roof and other parts of the building.

The dilemma which faced the main committee was whether to implement a plan which would update the electrics, plumbing, and kitchen facilities, and keep the fabric in good repair; to revamp the whole interior so that members had a 'state of the art' clubhouse; or whether it would not be cheaper and more convenient to move to a more appropriate building.

Whatever was decided would surely affect the future of the club and the new general manager, David Minords, who had joined in December 1990, made a detailed analysis of these alternatives. The main committee decided that the first option was the only really viable one, but the funds had to be raised to implement it. One of the ways was to issue debentures, and this was duly approved at the 1992 AGM; and in October 1992 a five-year maintenance plan was started.

The decline in the IOR was also a major cause for concern. The difficulty facing the club was that its rating office, which was now a self-supporting company called Seahorse Rating Ltd., had been founded on IOR, there was a large investment in it, and IOR—compared with IMS—was the easiest and by far the most cost effective rule for the club to administer. Yet the decline in IOR numbers was such that it was only likely to remain active as a level rating Grand Prix rule, and then only because nothing better was available. The matter was further complicated because on the one hand IMS was not proving popular—only 472 UK boats were rated under it in 1990—while on the other any further increase in the 3000 CHS rated boats might make it difficult for the rating office to maintain its standards in administering CHS.

Iain Macdonald-Smith, vice commodore 1990-92, proposed that IMS should be used for the Admiral's Cup series from 1993 onwards which would mean the series returning to cruiser/racers and being opened up to more people. The series, he believed, was too important to the club for it to be left with an IOR system that was more or less defunct. The committee agreed, but thought that an IOR division should be retained for some domestic races in 1991. At the same time it must continue to promote IMS, while CHS would remain as an inexpensive system for those competing at a lower level. However, Don Parr, who was the chairman of the Admiral's Cup management committee as well as the club's admiral, was doubtful about introducing IMS to the Admiral's Cup series as quickly as 1993, and the change was delayed until 1995.

The 1990 racing season reflected the state of the economy. Though the club organised 21 races there was a staggering overall reduction of 44% in the number of starters. The worst hit was the Channel Race. Where there had been 95 starters (excluding Admiral's Cup, Class A and Whitbread starters) in 1989 there were only 12 in 1990. Only the short cross-channel races (Cowes-Ouistreham, Ouistreham-Cowes, and Cowes-Cherbourg) saw small increases in the fleet. This underlined the popularity of shorter events which ended somewhere interesting and where an owner could guarantee to get home on Sunday evening before, in Bradbeer's heartfelt phrase, 'the traffic grinds to a halt'.

International events such as the Sardinia and Kenwood Cups were also hit by the worldwide recession. Choosing teams for these, and similar,

Jamie Lawson-Johnson

Barry Pickthall

ABOVE: Start of Brent Walker Challenge from Brighton on 21st July 1990
LEFT: crew of Richard Keeling's two-tonner, *Spartan*, the winner of the race

events was now handled by the newly formed British Offshore Sailing Squad (BOSS), which Keeling had proposed in his paper and was run by Iain Macdonald-Smith. A strong team was assembled for the Sardinia Cup, but not even a European team could be found for the Kenwood Cup.

The biggest domestic event in 1990 was the Brent Walker European Challenge, a race owned by the sponsors but run by the RORC. An 1,100-miler from the marina in Brighton to the one in Puerto Sherry (Cadiz) in Spain—both owned by Brent Walker—it attracted 60 starters. Designed also as a feeder race for that year's Sardinia Cup, it will probably be remembered by competitors and officials alike for the fabulous parties at the start and the finish. The overall winner was Richard Keeling's two-tonner, *Spartan*, and the CHS winner, Peter Johnson's *Highwayman*, won the club's Silk Cut Award for his performance in the race.

With a few exceptions, the number of starters in the club's long-established races in 1991 returned to pre-1990 levels. The season kicked off with a new event based at Cowes, the Red Funnel Easter Challenge, a series of four inshore races. Organised from committee boats, it was the club's first all-inshore regatta. Twenty-two boats took part and one of the highlights was the provision of coaching support. This was supplied by Bill Edgerton, the coach the club shared with the RYA for some years, who gave entertaining and instructive talks each evening accompanied by videos of the racing. This, and the debrief that followed, proved popular—as did Janet Grosvenor's[1] chocolate eggs that were awarded as prizes —and the regatta became a regular fixture. So did the eggs.

A special flexi[2] course, where the course was only announced just prior to the start, was laid on for IOR boats and the UK Admiral's Cup trialists. It proved to be a tough and testing one, but fickle breezes again affected some events, all but 18 of the 64 starters in the Myth of Malham Race to Fécamp, a new destination for the Club, having to retire when they ran out of wind. However, those that did make it were given a warm welcome by the local yacht club which stayed open all night selling cognac, lager—'and a lot of black coffee.'

The North Sea Race, which now ended at Scheveningen, attracted a large entry of 23 British, and 39 Dutch and Continental, boats. The number of British starters was well up on what it had been over recent years as EAORA had made it part of its points championship. It also counted as part of the Dutch-run Noordzeeweek, sponsored by Group 4, and British and Dutch fleets essentially sailed a separate race as the former raced under CHS while the latter raced under IMS. This was a matter of regret to both and showed how divisive multiple rating systems were.

In contrast to light conditions earlier in the season, the trials for the 1991 British Admiral's Cup team were held in testing conditions with contenders

1 Janet was appointed the RORC's Racing Manager when Alan Green retired as Director of Racing and Special Events, Christmas 1999

2 delaying announcement of the course allowed the race management to take into account the current weather conditions and the latest weather forecasts so that the race's length (in time) could be adhered to

racing in six short races in Christchurch Bay. The series only attracted eight teams, the lowest since 1965, but the quality of the racing was high in what was virtually three level-rating regattas rolled into one. The British team comprised Peacock's Farr 50, *Juno V*, a new one-tonner, *Port Pendennis*, designed by Ed Dubois, and the Farr two-tonner, *Wings of Oracle*. *Juno V* was the only privately owned British boat, though Dubois arranged for *Port Pendennis* to be campaigned under the British flag before her Turkish owner took delivery, while *Wings of Oracle*, which was plagued by crew problems, was owned by Oracle Software. The team came fourth behind France in a closely fought contest where the final result was not known until half the fleet had finished the Fastnet.

However exciting, the event did not stop the growing criticism that IOR no longer provided the type of boat suitable for what was basically still an offshore series. 'The best part of a week is spent at sea over the Channel and Fastnet Races,' wrote one critic, 'in boats that, to be competitive, are little more than plastic boxes dishing out plastic food'. What's more, freezing the IOR, though with the laudable intention of maintaining rule stability, had really proved a death sentence even at Grand Prix level as one of the costs spiralled in the search for a miniscule advantage in performance.

There were 712 CHS starters in club events during 1991, 246 IMS, and only 105 IOR, of which 63 were Admiral's Cup competitors. This confirmed that IOR was more or less moribund, but as the committee was stuck with it for the 1993 series it urged the new Champagne Mumm Admiral's Cup management committee to change the format to allow *two-boat teams into the series, as the organisers of the Sardinia and Kenwood Cups had already done. When the management committee refused there was something of a furore. The main committee agreed that as a last resort the RORC should declare what the format would be but, as will be seen, such drastic action proved unnecessary.

It was a busy year for Ashmead and his new assistant, John Moon, at the rating office with the computer system being totally upgraded. And when the ORC decided not to become involved in the writing and administration of the new Whitbread Offshore Rule, which would govern the 60ft yachts entering the next Whitbread Race in 1993, the club stepped in. The rating office, with the Whitbread council, drew up the new rule, and from 1997 the event was raced under the club's burgee.

Malcolm White, Yachting World

Michael Peacock, the owner of a series of successful yachts called *Juno*, aboard *Juno V*, Majorca 1987. Standing behind him is the naval architect, Rob Humphreys. The current editor of *Seahorse*, Andrew Hurst, is at the helm

At the end of 1991 the hon. treasurer, Tony Greener, retired and was replaced by Sir Timothy Bevan. In thanking Greener for his excellent contribution to the affairs of the club over the last 20 years, the commodore, John Dare, remarked that it was a credit to the retiring hon. treasurer that despite all the upheavals on and off the water the RORC was in such a solid financial position. Between them Greener and Minords had turned a projected deficit for 1991 into a surplus of £20,000, no mean achievement given the adverse economic climate.

Malcolm White, Yachting World

One of the highlights of the 1992 season was the Rolex Commodores' Cup[1]. Initiated by Dare, this was an international team event run to promote IMS. It was a handicap event using the Ton-Cup style of regatta of three inshore races, a short offshore, and a long offshore. Teams of three boats in three different size bands came from the constituent parts of the UK as well as from all over the world. In 1992 and 1994 only foreign countries were allowed to have two teams, but from 1996 the English, Welsh, Scottish, Irish and Channel Islands were also allowed two.

The series, now established as a biennial event, had originally been envisaged as a fairly low key Corinthian affair. However, it did not turn out quite like that for the series filled an international gap for the IMS fleets and looked as if it might rival the Champagne Mumm Admiral's Cup in popularity. There were 12 teams in 1992, and such was the attraction of the series that a high proportion of the world's top *professional sailors turned up.

Tom and Vicki Jackson, the owners of the highly successful *Sunstone*

In spite of teething problems with IMS—with some yachting journalists thinking extraction the only answer—the regatta did create, as the club's vice commodore commented, the essential 'buzz' which top sailors need to remain interested. There was a good deal of press criticism for the selectors' choice of Tom and Vicky Jackson's *Sunstone* as a member of the English team. Some commentators thought the yacht had a particularly favourable rating; others griped that a 'state of the art' yacht should be chosen, not a heavy displacement S & S design built in 1965 which was used by her owners as their floating home.

1 donated to the Island Sailing Club in 1978 for a similar event, which became defunct, the trophy is on loan to the RORC

When the Jacksons won the first two races on handicap it looked as if the selectors' choice had been vindicated. Unfortunately for them there were problems with the IMS computer programme and when the first two races were rescored *Sunstone* dropped several places, and the English team came a poor sixth.

Despite this hiccup, and the fact that by the end of the regatta some competitors were wearing T-shirts adorned with the phrase '1992 Comedy Cup', most of the 400 plus participants were delighted to have taken part in an excellent series which had drawn such a sizeable offshore fleet. But IMS continued to draw a lot of flak and amongst many yachtsmen the initials came to stand for 'International Mystery System'.

Another highlight in 1992 was a revived Round Britain Race, sponsored by the Teesside Development Corporation, with stopovers at Cork, Lerwick and Hartlepool. It was won by Mike Taylor-Jones' remarkable S & S 34, *Deerstalker*, a veteran ocean racer of 1974 vintage which had chalked up a class win in the previous year's Fastnet and was to become the Class IV champion in 1995.

The great debate on the various rating options open to the club rumbled on through much of 1992. At a special review meeting in the autumn the main committee agreed that it must get the club's fleet together again and not sailing in separate CHS and IMS divisions as it had been doing for the past two seasons. CHS was made the primary system for 1993 and the club's principal trophies were reallocated accordingly, and there was be parallel scoring[1], with dual certificate holders getting two results and an opportunity to compare their performance in each fleet. But IMS classes were retained in the North Sea, Fastnet, Channel, and Transatlantic Races, and the club still held the IMS Nationals. With CHS becoming the primary system a more sophisticated form, designated CHS (E), was developed where certificates were validated, or 'endorsed', by the RORC rating office. 'Endorsed' CHS was used in major events such as the CHS Europeans and the Fastnet, and from 1998 only those with an endorsed certificate were eligible to win a prize.

In late 1992 the worldwide recession combined with the lack of interest in building new boats to the IOR–particularly in the two-ton class–forced the hand of the Champagne Mumm Admiral's Cup management committee. It introduced age allowances to try and encourage the owners of older yachts to compete, and ruled that two-boat teams were eligible provided they were chosen from two of the three classes, which were the same as in 1991. With the two best results in each race for each team counting, this gave the three-boat teams a discard, an advantage which the management committee hoped would persuade competing countries to send three-boat teams if they possibly could. Even with these concessions the commodore, John Dare, had to report to the main committee in December 1992 that, to his consternation, there was no guarantee that a British team could be put together.

1 also known as 'shadowing' in the UK and 'co-scoring' in the USA

These upheavals had not gone unnoticed by the current trustees of the Admiral's Cup, David Edwards and Peter *Green, and they asked the RORC to form a steering committee to consider the future of the series. By then both trustees had become convinced that a development design rule such as IOR and IMS was just too expensive to be acceptable and that one-designs were the way forward. As far as Edwards was concerned 'the issue became, not whether it was possible to continue to run a development rule indefinitely, but whether we should even have tried after the introduction of the use of computers in yacht design.'

The management committee had already launched an international competition to find an appropriate one-design for the Class 3 slot. It proved to be one of the club's most important achievements during the 1990s as it had been responsible for producing the original specification which was dispatched to designers and builders world-wide, and in the spring of 1993 it set about bringing the new class to fruition. By then the serious contenders had been narrowed down to six. David Minords and Stuart Quarrie, the project's manager, then visited each of the boatyards and designers to assess their proposals, and

The veteran *Deerstalker*, winner of the 1992 Teesside Round Britain Race, with owner Mike Taylor-Jones and crew after their victory

both photos Barry Pickthall

reports were written on each with no recommendations being made. In July the international selection committee met at Cowes and judged Farr International's 36ft one-design the best package. This included the idea that four builders, in the USA, New Zealand, Argentina, and France, should be contracted to build the yacht. Each had its own geographical market, though the UK remained open so that British owners could order from any of the builders.

In recognition of all the support Champagne Mumm had given the club over the years the boat was called the Mumm 36. A new company, Seahorse Yachts Ltd., and a management group, with Minords as its chairman, were formed to oversee the project and to look after the class. From the first the aim of the management group was to have very strict control over the fleet which was backed up by vigorous inspections. This ensured that all the boats were identical, and persuaded those sailing them that they were.

'We therefore reached the situation where people were not concerned about other boats they were racing against, but concentrated on the sailing and the sailors they raced against,' said Minords. 'This of course was one of our aims right from the beginning.' This achieved, the management group gradually withdrew to allow the owners' association to take control of the class. The steering committee, on which competitors and designers as well as the RORC were represented, met three times and one of its decisions, rather against the RORC's better judgment, was to adopt the new ILC 40 as the middle-sized boat for the 1995 series. A product of a new ORC Grand Prix Rule, the International Level Class Rule, the ILC 40 fitted well with the existing 40ft IMS class which had sprung up during the early 1990s. But as there were insufficient level rating boats on the water for the big-boat slot it was decided to make this an IMS handicap class in the 44ft-50ft category. This meant that Classes 2 and 3 would race level while Class 1 raced on handicap with each class having its own separate race results.

Contrary to the prediction of some gloom mongers the 1993 Champagne Mumm Admiral's Cup series proved an unqualified success. 'As newsworthy events go,' wrote Andrew Preece in *Yachting World*, 'it delivered the goods: boats sank, boats crashed, boats lost crew overboard at night and, at the end, the winner [Germany] won by less than one point.' Seven full teams competed, with Holland also appearing with a two-boat team, though only 15 yachts out of the 23 entered finished the series which encountered some heavy weather.

The British team was organised by Graham Walker's Crusade Yacht Club, Britain's challenger for the 1995 America's Cup. Two of the team were chartered yachts from Turkey with some of their Turkish crew retained aboard. The third yacht, Walker's *Indulgence* (ex-*Juno V*), topped the Admiral's Cup fleet in the Fastnet, but the British team finished sixth.

The prototype Mumm 36 was the splendidly named *Pigs in Space*. Racing for the winning American White Team, she dominated the 1994 Rolex Commodores' Cup, and only missed being the series' top boat when she lost her rig in the fifth race. The first Mumm to race in European waters was Alan Gray's *Jamarella* in the Hamble Winter Series in October 1993, with the class's inaugural regatta being held at Key West, Florida, in January 1994. By March 1994 orders worldwide for the Mumm 36 had topped 100, way beyond anyone's expectations; by June 1994 the rating office—which by 1993 had issued 3,000 rating certificates while dealing with seven different rules—had issued 55 Mumm 36 One-Design certificates; and that July the club ran the inaugural Mumm 36 world championships, sponsored by Ancasta, with on-the-water umpiring being used for the first time in fleet racing.

Apart from the Rolex Commodores' Cup regatta, which attracted nine national teams, the other leading domestic event for the club in 1994 was the Teesside Round Britain Race which reestablished its eminence in Corinthian long distance offshore races. It attracted 15 starters and was won by one of the club's foreign rear commodores, Hans Peter Baum from Hamburg. But although the domestic programme was interesting and varied, the number of entries into club events dropped from 622 in 1992 to 456 in 1994.

After the poor showing of all the British national teams in the 1994 Commodores' Cup the British National Coach, Bill Edgerton, said British teams should be selected by the RYA not the Club. Subsequently, the RYA proposed an independent chairman for the committee electing the 1995 British Admiral's Cup team, and Robin Aisher was appointed.

In July 1995 the club organised the second Mumm 36 world championships which drew 23 entries and was again sponsored by Ancasta. It proved to be the most spectacular regatta of the season, with the world's top sailors competing in high winds and big tides, and the team of on-the-water judges had a tough time of it, too. 'It was an event that proved that, for the sailor looking for racing of the tightest kind, there is nothing better around,' wrote Andrew Preece. 'It's short, sharp and vicious, with absolutely no room at all for mistakes. And the boats are exciting, too. Upwind in the groove they are sensitive and lively, downwind they're a handful and they catch out even the best in the world. For yacht racing in boats with keels, this is where it's at.'

After the regatta the Mumm 36, *Group 4 Mumm*, was selected for the British team's Class 3 slot, but the lack of interest in Grand Prix IMS by British yachtsmen meant there were no competitive boats available for the Big and Middle boat slots, and at the last moment Robin Aisher flew to Germany to try and charter them. Hans-Otto *Schumann, the veteran German Admiral's Cup campaigner and a past club rear commodore, generously lent him *Rubin XIV*, renamed

Group 4 Seahorse, for the Class 1 slot; and the RORC chartered an ILC 40, *Group 4 Seahorse Astro* (ex-*Aerosail Astro*) for the Class 2 slot with Cudmore at the helm.

The series again drew eight teams to Cowes. For the first time, one from Scandinavia was accepted, though this altered the original concept of national teams to include ones linked by consanguinity. However, it was decided that a similar entry in future would be at the absolute discretion of the management committee—a Scandinavian team was again allowed in 1997—and that any such challenge must come from a body recognised for the purpose by the constituent national authorities of the nations concerned, in this case the Scandinavian Yachting Association.

Not surprisingly, the last minute scramble to form a British team brought poor results, though *Group 4 Seahorse* topped the Admiral's Cup fleet in the Fastnet. In a series now upped to nine *races—during which it was reported to the Admiral's Cup management committee that some boats were not meeting the spirit of the IMS rule with regards to accommodation, and some were meeting the spirit only—the British finished last with Italy gaining its first win. The Italian team's *Brava Q8* put in an outstanding performance with her 68-year-old owner, Pasquale Landolfi, one of the current rear commodores, sitting on the weather rail non-stop for 22 hours to bring his boat home first in her class in the Fastnet Race. This made her the top-scoring boat and she was subsequently awarded the Somerset Memorial Trophy.

The RORC, with Rear Commodore Clare Wardle in charge, decided to form its own team for that year's Southern Cross series. It was the first appearance of a British team 'down under' for several years and, with the series requiring an IMS racer, an IMS cruiser, and a 'vintage' boat with an age date of 1st January 1986, or older, chartered boats were used. One of them was skippered by Hans Peter Hensel, a club member and a member of the German Admiral's Cup team, and another by Clare Wardle. A team was also put together for the 1996 Onion Patch series.

To simplify the complexity of scoring under IMS the club had announced before the 1995 season that it would use a time-on-time single-number system, called TMF (Time Multiplication Factor), worked out by Alan Green, to calculate race results in all its races except the Admiral's Cup series. This was introduced, in the words of one member, 'to combat distrust/fear/loathing/ incomprehension of/indifference to the IMS's Performance Curve Scoring.' It also gave competitors what they wanted: an idea while racing how they were faring against others and a quick result when the race was over.

The club's domestic programme also began to reflect the RORC's determination to encourage the amateur side of the sport. In 1995 a new CHS amateurs-only regatta was introduced, run on the same lines as Cork Week, which included two days of inshore racing, followed by the Cowes-Dinard-St Malo Race. The following year the Rolex Commodores' Cup, expanded to nine races, banned all but a token representation of professionals. They were not allowed to steer and only two were allowed on big boats, one on the medium ones, and none on the small ones, an idea also borrowed from Cork Week. The series attracted 15 teams from nine countries, seven of the teams coming from the UK. In a series which gave cruiser/racers a fair crack of the whip, by giving them a whopping 1.5% time allowance, England's Green Team were the victors.

Youth was also targeted, with the club organising two Teachers Round Britain and Ireland Races in 1995 and 1996 in which the emphasis was on the young gaining experience in offshore racing. Both events, which was raced in three stages, involved ten identical Jeanneau 36s with experienced skippers and mates, and young, relatively inexperienced crews.

Regattas were also proving popular and in 1995 the club organised the Heligoland Regatta. This comprised the 50th anniversary North Sea Race (Harwich-Scheveningen) and then one to Heligoland, the first time the club had used that island as a destination since 1938. In a drive to promote IMS, and to bring together the British and Dutch fleets in the race, the Club measured without charge every UK entry in the North Sea Race.

The Myth of Malham weekend mini-regatta held the same year was unusual in that it took the fleet, over 50 strong, on a hard inshore course with lots of short legs and deck work, and was followed–without going ashore–by a 24-hour offshore race over a testing flexi course.

Another innovation in 1995 was to change the course *during* an offshore race. Initially called a variable course as opposed to a flexi course–or a pre-planned one such as the Fastnet–variable courses are now a type of flexi course. These have proved, if proof were needed, that far from making the navigator redundant, as some opponents of electronics had feared in the previous decades, he or she remains a vital part of the afterguard.

Already common practice for inshore races round the buoys, the variable course has two particular advantages: it allows the race management to make the course more interesting if there was an unexpected shift of wind and the length can be altered to achieve a given average speed or elapsed time target. The Channel Race was one of three events in which variable courses were used in 1995. This had a target duration of 36 hours, and when against all the forecasts the wind did not die at dusk the course for the 80-strong fleet, which included 50-footers, maxis and Whitbread 60s, was lengthened by 50 miles.

In September 1995 35 sailors, who represented several yacht clubs and associations, attended a seminar at the Royal Overseas League to discuss the future of offshore racing in the UK. Papers were presented by John Bourke–a five-times competitor for Ireland in the Admiral's Cup who had taken over as commodore in 1994–by Don Moreton, one of the rear commodores and chairman of the programme & race sub-committee; by Alan Green; and by John Warren who had been appointed the director of rating after the retirement of Tony Ashmead in 1993.

As a result of this seminar, and a growing unease with how IMS was being administered by the ORC, the technical committee formed a sub-committee–chaired by one of the rear commodores, Paul King, and comprising John Warren, three naval architects and Mike Urwin, the club's technical manager–to work on a new rule which would be accepted internationally and come into force at the start of the new Millennium. The aim was to use it for international offshore events such as the Admiral's Cup and Commodores' Cup series instead of IMS which the committee now believed was not being as well administered by the ORC as it should have been. However, when the ORC accepted the club's single-figure scoring TMF system for the 1996 season, the crisis of confidence in IMS temporarily abated, and in the autumn the new rule was put on hold.

Don Parr, appointed an Admiral's Cup trustee in 1993, stepped down as admiral at the end of 1995. He was replaced by Sir Timothy Bevan whose post of hon. treasurer was taken by Terry Robinson.

In 1996 the 14 competitors in Chay Blyth's BT Global Challenge, each with RORC in gold on its transom, was started by the club. The race included another innovation by Alan Green, the e-mail jury. Instead of a jury being present at each of the starts, any protests were sent immediately by satcom to race headquarters. This asked the yacht being protested for its comments before sending all the facts to jury members scattered across the world, and they e-mailed their opinions to the chairman who then delivered his verdict. Infinitely cheaper than flying juries around the world, this method of judging could be in common use in the new Millennium.

The season also saw a 20% increase over 1994 in the number of starters (622) in club races showing that at long last, after a period of some turmoil, the club

Press Association

Pete Goss with the club's trophy for outstanding seamanship. He was awarded the trophy–he is only the fifth person to receive it–in April 1997 for his rescue of fellow competitor Raphael Dinelli during the single-handed Vendée Globe Race. He keeps the trophy until it is awarded again was back on the right track with its domestic programme. The five-race Red Funnel Easter Challenge, with Harold Cudmore in charge of the coaching, attracted a fleet of 40 boats which competed in light breezes; the Cervantes Trophy had 43 starters; and *multihulls made their reappearance in an RORC event when some took part in the Myth of Malham Race.

However, the five-day regatta for the CHS and IMS nationals was disappointing. They drew only 17 starters for the former and six for the latter though the flexi-course De Guingand Bowl, which was part of it, attracted another 19. Perversely, when short courses were all the rage, the Round Ireland Race had 61 starters, the largest ever, and was won by D.T. Cullen's *Big Ears*, the second time a J-35 had taken the overall trophy.

At the start of 1997 Terry Robinson replaced John Bourke as commodore and David Aisher, grandson of Owen, became hon. treasurer. Robinson donated the new Assuage Trophy for a RORC mini series which included the Fastnet, St. Malo, Channel, Cervantes Trophy and Cherbourg Races. Fittingly it was won by his Swan 48, *Assuage*, sailed by a Royal Navy crew, after she had won line honours, class, and overall in the Cherbourg Race.

The British Admiral's Cup team was announced early with Graham Walker's *Corum Indulgence* (44–50ft), Tony Buckingham's *Easy Oars* (ILC40), and Tim

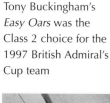

Tony Buckingham's *Easy Oars* was the Class 2 choice for the 1997 British Admiral's Cup team

Malcolm White, Yachting

Barrett's *Bradamante* (Mumm 36) being selected. For the first time, all three yachts had been designed and built outside the UK. The team's captain, Rear Commodore Richard Matthews, worked closely with Graham Walker and Peter Morton to make sure the team was competitive and the British were the only ones to have a full Admiral's Cup team at the Key West Regatta.

After protests from abroad about using single-number scoring for the 'Big Boat' slot in the Admiral's Cup, IMS Performance Curve Scoring was retained. Only seven teams were present, but it was a high quality series with the Americans taking the trophy for the first time since 1969. The British team finished 5th.

courtesy Terry Robinson, photo Leslie Coney

With a large fleet of 245 taking part in the Fastnet, including multihulls, maxis, and Whitbread 60s, a safety factor was added which altered the traditional Fastnet course. After rounding the Rock all competitors had to round the Pantaenius buoy to port which had been positioned five miles south-west of the Rock by the Commissioners of Irish lights. Sponsored for the first time by Champagne Mumm, it was a light-weather race. Not surprisingly, the first home was the 60ft multihull, *Primagaz*, with Laurent Bourgnon at the helm. She took just under 45hrs,44min.,44secs to cover the multihull's course, which was 50 miles longer than the normal one. The maxi, *Banque in Luxembourg (BIL)*, skippered by Ross Field, won line honours and the Kees Van Dam Memorial Trophy for the first CHS boat on corrected time, and the Fastnet Challenge Cup was won by *Morning Glory* for the first IMS boat on corrected time.

After the Champagne Mumm Admiral's Cup series the Club dropped a bombshell when it announced that, in collaboration with UNCL, it was producing a new two-level rule, IR 2000. The lower level, known as IRC, took over existing CHS yachts at 'club' level in January 1999. The upper level, known as IRM, using measured elements, provides a new, straightforward, published high-level rule which, after all the difficulties with IMS, the RORC perceives is much needed. It was launched in July 1999 and came into force in January 2000.

The 1997–98 Round-the-World Race, raced under the club's burgee, was the last sponsored by Whitbread. To commemorate this, an inscribed artillery shell was presented to Southampton's Deputy Harbour Master at the finish of the race, 24th May 1998, by the commodore, Terry Robinson (left). He later presented identical ones to the Chairman of Whitbread and to the commodore of the Royal Southern Yacht Club, the organisers of the finish of the race. The inscription reads: RORC 1997/8 Whitbread, The Final Round, Fired by 289 Cdo Bty RA(V)

The Admiral's Cup Management Committee also produced its own bombshell. In a determined attempt to meet the sponsor's target of ten teams at the next event, it announced that the 1999 series would have an entirely different format. It would be run in July before Cowes Week and take two weeks not three. The Fastnet Race—which would remain part of the club's domestic programme—would be replaced by a race of about 450-500 miles around the Wolf Rock. There would also be a new Channel race, a flexi-course lasting around 44 hours, and six inshore races which would revert to taking place in the Solent[1].

The Big Boat slot was again to be filled by the IMS 50ft handicap class and the small one by the Mumm 36. However, it was decided that the Middle Boat slot should also be a one design, and Bashford Boats' Sydney 40 was chosen. As part of the deal a number of these new designs would be available for charter for the series at £1 each, plus sails.

The 1998 domestic season comprised 18 races compared with 15 in 1997 and 14 in 1996, and these attracted 619 starters, an increase of 15% on 1996. Especially pleasing were the increase in entries for the Red Funnel Easter Challenge and the CHS Nationals, but it was the Rolex Commodores' Cup which dominated the domestic programme with the German Red team chalking up an impressive win.

The club's 1999 race calendar was a packed one with 21 events, and included the first IRC championships, which attracted 80 entrants and was sponsored by Independent Insurance, and the first Sydney 40 World Championships.

The Fastnet, despite no longer being part of the Admiral's Cup, proved as popular as ever, attracting 213 starters. For the first time the Fastnet Trophy was lifted by a woman when Catherine Chabaud from France, sailing her Open 60, *Whirlpool-Europe 2*, finished in the best IRC corrected time of 82hrs, 47min.,50secs; and Ross Field's Maxi One Design, *RF Yachting New Zealand*, established a new monohull elapsed record of 53hrs,08min.,51secs. The multihulls sailed the same course as the monohulls and *Fujicolor* covered it in an elapsed time of 40hrs,27min.

However, the highlight of the 1999 season was, of course, the Champagne Mumm Admiral's Cup. Its Management Committee widened the concept of consanguinity, and this encouraged the participation of two new teams—Europe and Commonwealth—as well as ones from Australia, France, Germany, Italy, Holland, Great Britain and the United States. It was, as one commentator noted in *Yachting World*, 'a new era of Admiral's Cup racing—new boats, new races, new teams and new courses.'

The Europe team came about because Pasquale Landolfi decided to build a new 50-footer, *Brava Q8*, too late to take part in his country's selection races.

1 When raced, because of the forecast weather conditions, the flexi-course lasted about 29 hours (211 nautical miles), and only the 50-footers turned at the Wolf Rock, over a course measuring 389 nautical miles from Cowes and back. The other two classes sailed about 50 miles less, turning at the Lizard

He therefore applied for, and was granted, permission to enter a team under the flag of the European Union. He was joined by two fellow Italians: Marco Greggio, who had been campaigning his Sydney 40, *Merit Cup*, since the Sardinia Cup, and Vincente Honorato's Mumm 36, *Moby Lines*.

The Commonwealth team emerged when, at the last minute, the planned Channel Island team failed to materialise. So the one firm member of it, Simon Henning's Mumm 36, *Alice* (ex-*Group 4 Mumm*), joined forces with the 50-footer *Chernikeeff*, whose owner, Peter Harrison, was sponsoring the British team. The third team member, and a moving force behind the Commonwealth challenge was David Walters, a well known RORC owner. He chartered a Sydney 40, *Turbo UK*, skippered by Jonty Sherwill with a 'hard core' Hamble team.

The series began with a row that broke out over the rating of the French team's 50-footer, *Krazy K-Yote Two*. The boat had a free-standing mast with no spreader or shrouds which managed to exploit the IMS rule which calculates the windage on a yacht's mast. The ORC refused to certify her provisional rating issued by the RORC. The French were offered a compromise which provided dispensation for the mast during the series if they accepted a less favourable rating. They refused and the French team withdrew, but later the two other team members decided to race.

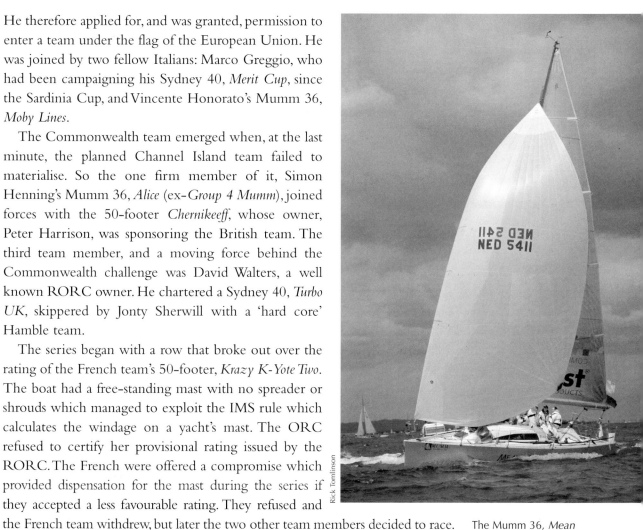

Rick Tomlinson

This hitch apart, the series was a resounding success. The outcome, as it normally did, depended on the final race. The British team were in the lead at the start of the Wolf Rock Race, which carried a 3.5 points multiplier, but one of its boats failed to perform. This let in the Dutch, who have been competing since 1959, and they proved worthy first-time winners.

This history of the club's first 75 years should not be concluded without mentioning that Terry Robinson, as the club's commodore, 1997-1999, and chairman of the Admiral's Cup Management Committee, must be given great credit for pushing through the changes to the Admiral's Cup, and for the introduction of IR2000. With these in place the club, and indeed the whole sport, can face with optimism and enthusiasm the challenges the new Millennium is bound to bring.

The Mumm 36, *Mean Machine*, one of the Dutch team which won the 1999 Champagne Mumm Admiral's Cup series. A consistent performer, she won her class in the crucial Wolf Rock Race, finished fourth in the short offshore race, came second in one inshore race, third in three others, and fifth in the other two

Competing Teams And Winners

YEAR	TOTAL NUMBER OF TEAMS	ARGENTINA	AUSTRALIA	AUSTRIA	BELGIUM	BERMUDA	BRAZIL	BRITAIN	CANADA	COMMONWEALTH	DENMARK	EUROPE	FINLAND	FRANCE	GERMANY	HOLLAND	HONG KONG	IRELAND	ITALY	JAPAN	NEW ZEALAND	NORWAY
1957	2							1ST														
1959	3							1ST						3RD		2ND						
1961	5							2ND						5TH		3RD						
1963	6							1ST						5TH	6TH	4TH						
1965	8		2ND					1ST						5TH	8TH	3RD		7TH				
1967	9		1ST					2ND					6TH	4TH	5TH	7TH		8TH				
1969	11	9TH	2ND		10TH		3RD						6TH	7TH	5TH	8TH		4TH				
1971	17	4TH	3RD	16TH	12TH	8TH	10TH	1ST					15TH	9TH	5TH		11TH	7TH		14TH		
1973	16	6TH	2ND		14TH	8TH	10TH	3RD		13TH			11TH	7TH	1ST	5TH		16TH	9TH			
1975	19	12TH	9TH		19TH		15TH	1ST	18TH				11TH	2ND	4TH	8TH	7TH	17TH			5TH	18TH
1977	19	10TH	7TH	14TH	17TH		12TH	1ST					6TH	4TH	11TH	3RD	8TH=	5TH	18TH			12TH
1979	19	5TH	1ST		14TH		19TH	6TH	18TH				7TH	11TH	13TH	3RD=	8TH	3RD=	12th			
1981	16		7TH=		15TH	16TH		1ST	6TH				11TH	3RD	10TH	14TH	4TH	7TH=			5TH	15TH
1983	15		4TH	10TH	13TH			8TH	5TH				12TH	1ST	7TH		11TH	2ND	15TH	6TH		
1985	18		4TH	8TH	18TH		14TH	2ND	16TH		5TH		7TH	1ST	11TH		10TH	12TH			3RD	
1987	14		3RD		13TH			2ND			7TH		8TH	5TH	10TH		4TH	11TH		1ST		
1989	14	14TH	5TH					1ST			2ND		4TH	8TH	10TH		13TH	9TH	7TH	3RD	11TH	
1991	8		8TH					4TH			6TH			1ST	5TH			2ND	7TH			
1993	8		2ND					6TH						3RD	1ST	8TH		7TH	4TH	5TH		
1995	8							8TH						3RD		7TH	6TH	1ST				
1997	7		4TH					5TH						2ND			3RD		6TH			
1999	9		7TH					3RD		8TH		2ND	9TH	4TH	1ST			6TH				

Of The Admiral's Cup 1957–1999

PAPUA NEW GUINEA	POLAND	PORTUGAL	SCANDINAVIA	SINGAPORE	SOUTH AFRICA	SPAIN	SWEDEN	SWITZERLAND	USA	WINNING ADMIRAL'S CUP TEAMS			
·	·	·	·	·	·	·	·	·	2ND	BRITAIN	*Myth of Malham*	*Uomie*	*Jocasta*
·	·	·	·	·	·	·	·	·	·	BRITAIN	*Griffin II*	*Ramrod*	*Myth of Malham*
·	·	·	·	·	·	·	4TH	·	**1ST**	USA	*Windrose*	*Figaro*	*Cyane*
·	·	·	·	·	·	·	3RD	·	2ND	BRITAIN	*Clarion of Wight*	*Outlaw*	*Noryema III*
·	·	·	·	·	·	·	6TH	·	4TH	BRITAIN	*Quiver IV*	*Noryema IV*	*Firebrand*
·	·	·	·	·	·	9TH	·	·	3RD	AUSTRALIA	*Mercedes III*	*Balandra*	*Caprice of Huon*
·	·	·	·	·	·	11TH	·	·	**1ST**	USA	*Red Rooster*	*Carina*	*Palawan*
·	·	·	·	·	6TH	·	13TH	·	2ND	BRITAIN	*Prospect of Whitby*	*Morning Cloud II*	*Cervantes IV*
·	·	15TH	·	·	12TH	·	·	·	4TH	GERMANY	*Saudade*	*Carina III*	*Rubin*
·	·	·	·	·	13TH	6TH	14TH	10TH	3RD	BRITAIN	*Noryema X*	*Yeoman XX*	*Battlecry*
·	9TH	·	·	·	·	8TH=	16TH	15TH	2ND	BRITAIN	*Moonshine*	*Yeoman XX*	*Marionette*
·	17TH	·	·	16TH	·	10TH	15TH	9TH	2ND	AUSTRALIA	*Police Car*	*Impetuous*	*Ragamuffin*
·	·	·	·	·	·	12TH	9TH	13TH	2ND	BRITAIN	*Dragon*	*Victory of Burnham*	*Yeoman XXIII*
9TH	·	·	·	·	·	·	14TH	·	3RD	GERMANY	*Pinta*	*Outsider*	*Sabina*
15TH	·	17TH	·	·	6TH	·	13TH	·	9TH	GERMANY	*Outsider*	*Rubin VIII*	*Diva G*
·	·	·	·	·	·	·	12TH	·	6TH	NEW ZEALAND	*Goldcorp*	*Propaganda*	*Kiwi*
·	·	·	·	·	·	·	12TH	·	6TH	BRITAIN	*Jamarella*	*Juno IV*	*Indulgence VII*
·	·	·	·	·	·	·	·	·	3RD	FRANCE	*Corum Saphir*	*Corum Rubis*	*Corum Diament*
·	·	·	·	·	·	·	·	·	·	GERMANY	*Pinta*	*Rubin XII*	*Container*
·	·	·	4TH	·	5TH	·	·	·	2ND	ITALY	*Capricorno*	*Brava Q8*	*Mumm-a-Mia*
·	·	·	7TH	·	·	·	·	·	**1ST**	USA	*Flash Gordon 3*	*MK Cafe*	*Jameson*
·	·	·	·	·	·	·	·	·	5TH	HOLLAND	*Innovision 7*	*Trust Computer*	*Mean Machine*

Winners Of The

YEAR	TROPHY	YACHT	OWNER
1925	FASTNET CHALLENGE CUP	*Jolie Brise*	E.G. Martin
1926	FASTNET CHALLENGE CUP	*Ilex*	Royal Engineer Yacht Club
1927	FASTNET CHALLENGE CUP	*Tally Ho!*	Lord Stalbridge
1928	FASTNET CHALLENGE CUP	*Nina*	P. Hammond
1929	FASTNET CHALLENGE CUP	*Jolie Brise*	R. Somerset
1930	FASTNET CHALLENGE CUP	*Jolie Brise*	R. Somerset
1931	FASTNET CHALLENGE CUP	*Dorade*	R. Stephens Sr.
1933	FASTNET CHALLENGE CUP	*Dorade*	R. Stephens Sr.
1935	FASTNET CHALLENGE CUP	*Stormy Weather*	P. Le Boutillier
1937	FASTNET CHALLENGE CUP	*Zeearend*	K. Bruynzeel
1939	FASTNET CHALLENGE CUP	*Bloodhound*	I. Bell
1947	FASTNET CHALLENGE CUP	*Myth of Malham*	J.H. Illingworth
1949	FASTNET CHALLENGE CUP	*Myth of Malham*	J.H. Illingworth
1951	FASTNET CHALLENGE CUP	*Yeoman III*	O.A. Aisher
1953	FASTNET CHALLENGE CUP	*Favona*	Sir M. Newton
1955	FASTNET CHALLENGE CUP	*Carina II*	R. Nye
1957	FASTNET CHALLENGE CUP	*Carina II*	R. Nye
1959	FASTNET CHALLENGE CUP	*Anitra*	S. Hansen
1961	FASTNET CHALLENGE CUP	*Zwerver*	W.N.H. van der Vorm
1963	FASTNET CHALLENGE CUP	*Clarion of Wight*	D. Boyer and D. Miller
1965	FASTNET CHALLENGE CUP	*Rabbit*	R.E. Carter
1967	FASTNET CHALLENGE CUP	*Pen-Duick III*	E. Tabarly
1969	FASTNET CHALLENGE CUP	*Red Rooster*	R.E. Carter

Fastnet Race 1925–1999

YEAR	TROPHY	YACHT	OWNER
1971	FASTNET CHALLENGE CUP	Ragamuffin	S. Fischer
1973	FASTNET CHALLENGE CUP	Saga	E. Lorentzen
1975	FASTNET CHALLENGE CUP	Golden Delicious	P. Nicholson
1977	FASTNET CHALLENGE CUP	Imp	D. Allen
1979	FASTNET CHALLENGE CUP	Tenacious	R.E. Turner
1981	FASTNET CHALLENGE CUP	Mordicus	Taylor and Volterys
1983	FASTNET CHALLENGE CUP	Condor	R.A. Bell
1985	FASTNET CHALLENGE CUP	Panda	P.T. Whipp
1987	FASTNET CHALLENGE CUP	Juno	M. Peacock
1989	FASTNET ROCK TROPHY, BCT IMS	Diane	R. Schwartz
	FASTNET CHALLENGE CUP, BCT IOR	Great News	R. Short/Jones/Forbes
1991	FASTNET ROCK TROPHY, BCT IMS	Iona	N. Brown
	FASTNET CHALLENGE CUP, BCT IOR	Passage	G. Isett
1993	FASTNET ROCK TROPHY, BCT IMS	Encore	J. Dolan
	FASTNET CHALLENGE CUP, BCT IOR	Indulgence	G. Walker
	KEES VAN DAM MEMORIAL TROPHY, BCT CHS	Eagle	A. Todd
1995	FASTNET CHALLENGE CUP, BCT IMS	Nicorette	L. Ingvall
	FASTNET ROCK TROPHY, BCT IMS non Admiral's Cup	Nicorette	L. Ingvall
	KEES VAN DAM MEMORIAL TROPHY, BCT CHS	Nicorette	L. Ingvall
1997	FASTNET CHALLENGE CUP, BCT IMS	Morning Glory	H. Plattner
	FASTNET ROCK TROPHY, BCT IMS non Admiral's Cup	Royal Blue	G. Ekdahl
	KEES VAN DAM MEMORIAL TROPHY, BCT IMS	BIL	Maxi fleet
1999	FASTNET CHALLENGE CUP, BCT IRC	Whirlpool-Europe 2	C. Chabaud

— PATRON —

Her Majesty The Queen

Officers Of The Club

— PRESIDENT —

1925–1926
Major Philip Hunloke, CVO

— ADMIRAL —

1927–1934
Major Sir Philip Hunloke, KCVO

1935–1946
Lieut Cdr E.G. Martin, OBE, RNVR

1947–1956
R. MacLean Buckley, MC

1957–1968
Sir Myles Wyatt, CBE

1969–1975
Owen A. Aisher

1976–1982
Sir Maurice Laing

1983–1989
David Edwards

1989–1995
T.D. Parr, CBE

1996–
Sir Timothy Bevan

— COMMODORE —

1925–1934
Lieut Cdr E.G. Martin, OBE, RNVR

1935–1937
Major T.P. Rose Richards

1938–1947
Michael H. Mason

1948–1950
Captain J.H. Illingworth, RN

1951–1952
Robert Somerset, DSO

1953–1956
Myles Wyatt, CBE

1957–1960
A.V. Sainsbury

1961–1964
P.J.F. Green

1965–1968
W.M. Vernon

1969–1972
David Edwards

1973–1975
Sir Maurice Laing

1976–1978
J.W. Roome

1979–1981
T.D. Parr

1982–1984
C.A.F. Dunning, MBE

1985–1987
R.A. Aisher

1988–1990
J.L. Bradbeer

1991–1993
John A. Dare

1994–1996
J.O.P. Bourke

1997–1999
T. Robinson

2000–2002
Peter Rutter

Chapter Notes

One: THE KING OF SPORTS

Page 10: in April 1924 *Northern Light*'s owner asked Martyr to help sail her back to New York from Nova Scotia, where she had just been built. Martyr then wrote an article in *Yachting* about the vicissitudes of this maiden voyage and the problems that had arisen in the schooner's construction. The following year he began a series of articles in *Yachting World*, later published as a book, about a British-registered schooner called *Southseaman* which he had had built in Nova Scotia. These articles are obviously an expanded version of the story of *Northern Light*, and the two schooners have identical dimensions. As there is no record of *Southseaman* ever being registered in Britain (or in Canada, or the United States), it must be assumed that Martyr's *Yachting World* articles and book were what is nowadays called 'faction'.

Page 10: The gentleman owner who left everything, or nearly everything, to his professional crew did not, of course, disappear entirely from the offshore racing scene. Ralph and Geoffrey Hawkes, of the Boosey and Hawkes music business, joined the club in the mid-1930s. They owned the 40-ton cutter, *Firebird X*, which had a professional crew of four: the skipper who ran the yacht, a paid hand, a cook, and a steward. A current member who sailed aboard her in the 1938 Dover-Kristiansand Race remembers the cuisine as being superb but the racing as being, well, comfortable more than competitive.

Page 12: at the RORC's 1932 Annual General Meeting Nicholson, who died in 1953, was unanimously elected an honorary member and in January 1951 he became a life honorary member. He was, without doubt, the greatest yacht designer of his era and right up to the 1970s he or his descendants ran the firm of Camper & Nicholson which was in the forefront of designing and building every kind of racing yacht. For a detailed history of the firm up to 1939 see William Collier's thesis lodged at the University of Liverpool in 1997.

Page 12: over the decades the RORC rule was subject to numerous alterations and revisions before its demise in 1970. For more detail see Phillips-Birt's *British Ocean Racing*. For a historical perspective on the subject of rules and ratings, including the RORC rule and the IOR, see *Yacht Rating* by Peter Johnson.

Page 12: since 1989 the Fastnet lighthouse has been controlled from the shore and a RORC crew now man it for the race.

Page 22: The idea of a seahorse certainly came from Martin but Iorys Hughes told Nick Greville that it was Dick Maclean Buckley's wife, a commercial designer, who had been asked by the committee to design the club's emblem. When the committee saw that the tail was curled the wrong way round they wanted to change it. However, because it had already been used to print the club's programme 'they decided to be eccentric and remarkable, so let it stand.' In the early 1950s the seahorse was redesigned by Bridget Livingston, a postwar owner of *Maid of Malham* and *Myth of Malham*.

Two: THE BLUE WATER BADGE

Page 23: A naval architect by profession, Phillips-Birt became a member in 1951 after qualifying in G.P. Pattinson's *Jocasta* in the 1950 Santander Race. He was the author of numerous books on maritime subjects. They include *British Ocean Racing* which was published in 1961 and traces the development of the sport, and of the RORC, during the club's first 34 years. Phillips-Birt died in 1978.

Page 27: Loomis became a life member in 1927 and took part in 17 Bermuda Races and 11 Fastnets. His book on the sport, *Ocean Racing—The Great Blue-*

Water Yacht Races, 1866–1935, is a classic of its kind. For many years his column 'Under the Lee of the Long Boat' appeared in *Yachting*. He died in 1968.

Page 27: this was W.S. Tallman who later, on Peverley's say-so, became a member for a short while, despite Peverley's comment to the club secretary that 'no amount of money could induce him [Tallman] to go in for another race'. Tallman himself wrote that he was somewhat bashful about joining as he thought the club 'was open only to expert hands and that trailing alongside in the Irish Sea did not provide sufficient qualification'.

Page 30: Miss Wield's work was so appreciated that she was made a life member in 1935 when she retired.

Page 34: Martyr continued to record the ocean racing scene for the yachting press, and earn his living as a writer, but it seems he took no further part in helping to run the club. He crewed in the 1928 Fastnet Race but by then he was no longer listed as a member. He was re-elected in November 1931 and eventually became a life honorary member. He died in 1966.

Page 35: Hoyt was probably the most able American yachtsman of his generation and was an outstanding 6-metre helmsman. He took part in many international events including the America's Cup. It was to Hoyt that Vanderbilt gave the wheel of *Rainbow* at a crucial moment in the defence of the America's Cup in 1934. Hoyt published his memoirs in 1950 and died in 1961.

Three: ROYAL ASSENT

Page 40: by the 1970s the days had long gone when the handful of competitors anchored off the Dinard Yacht Club where the dinner and prize-giving traditionally took place. Instead, competitors always went to the marina in St Malo, though the prize giving remained at Dinard. For various reasons this proved unsatisfactory and caused conflict between the two communities. This came to a head in 1977 when the St Malo Yacht Club put up a notice saying it could not post the race results as the Dinard Yacht Club had refused to let them have them! So in 1978 all activities related to the race were moved by the commodore, John Roome, to St Malo and the fixture was renamed the Cowes-Bay of St Malo Race. Much to the annoyance of Edward Heath, the winner that year, Dinard refused to hand over the King Edward VII Gold Cup and he was not presented with it until the club's prize giving in December. When Don Parr succeeded Roome as commodore in 1979 he tactfully renamed the event, the Cowes-Dinard-St Malo Race.

Page 41: initially the club had a room in the offices of *Yachting World* at 35 Albemarle Street free of charge. From June 1932 a rent of £40 was paid until the building's lease expired the following June.

Page 42: born in 1901, Laurent Giles took an engineering degree at Cambridge. He then worked as an apprentice at Armstrong Whitworth's naval yard before qualifying as a naval architect at Durham University. He set up his own yacht design company in 1927, was a member of the RORC's technical committee from 1933 to 1953, and was one of the most influential yacht designers of the immediate post-war period. He died in 1969. Details of his life and designs can be found in *Laurent Giles: An Evolution of Yacht Design* by Adrian Lee and Ruby Philpott.

Page 42: When Edith Dorrien-Smith resigned in 1947 the secretary was asked to find out if she was the first lady member. He subsequently replied that so far as he could discover she was, and she was granted life honorary membership. Though this was not strictly true, it was a well deserved honour.

Page 44: 'Drake was working independently as a yacht broker,' Olin Stephens wrote later, 'selling used boats, and he had an informal arrangement with an older yacht designer, Roger Haddock, to whom he would send new boat clients. Haddock was retiring and Drake wanted a new association and we agreed to work together for a year, sharing design fees, until I became of age. If it didn't work out we would part; if it did we would continue under a more formal arangement.' Work out it did, and later Rod joined his brother in the partnership.

Page 44: from Waldo Howland's *A Life in Boats*. Uffa Fox who was also aboard tells a different version in his *Sailing, Seamanship, and Yacht Construction*. '*Lelanta*,

Ralph Peverley's schooner, came out to greet us with the news that *Dorade* had sailed the northern course, and had been in Plymouth two days, and as we sailed in, there she was out for an afternoon sail.' The two accounts aren't completely contradictory as Hammond might well not have believed those aboard *Lelanta*–and who could blame him!

Page 46: from the first Fastnet onwards a committee meeting was held at Plymouth after the race, a tradition continued until 1975.

Page 46: in fact, the Haaks Race was held but it attracted only four entries and was replaced in 1933 by the Heligoland Race with the Haaks Cup as the main prize. The Maas Race had many more entries and was an annual fixture (except for 1935) until 1937.

Page 51: 62 designs were submitted to compete for several prizes in two categories, 55ft and 35ft, and they came from all over Europe and three from the United States. The best 29 designs, which included ones from Harley Mead, Laurent Giles, Charles A. Nicholson and Olin Stephens, were published in

1933 by Ernest Day under the title *A Book of Designs of Deep Sea Racing Craft*. The prizewinners were John Read from England, who won the prize for the best designer under 30, Alfred Pyszka from Germany, and H.W. de Voogt from Holland.

Page 55: Nina eventually found an owner who cherished her when, in 1935, she was bought by DeCoursey Fales, a future commodore of the New York Yacht Club. He raced her successfully for decades, so successfully that she won the 1962 Bermuda Race, and, under another owner, is still competing today. 'By many,' Waldo Howland wrote in *A Life in Boats*, 'she is now held second only to the yacht *America* as a racing schooner'.

Page 56: King, a solicitor by profession, was a highly decorated officer in the First World War. Although not a Gunner himself, he presented *Rose* to the Royal Artillery Yacht Club when he had *Ortac* built, and from that time the Gunners have always been enthusiastic supporters of the Fastnet. In the summer of 1939 King had a nervous breakdown and resigned as vice commodore and as a member.

Four: THE DESIGN REVOLUTION GATHERS PACE

Page 58: Bell, a member from 1935, was, apparently, one of the greatest elephant hunters of all time. His steady eye and nerve were certainly a great aid to him when, caught in a fog with a dicey compass, he took *Trenchemer* into Aberdeen harbour. 'He sailed us straight in until the lookout shouted "breakers ahead",' wrote one of his crew after the war, 'The breakers were the seas pounding the Aberdeen break-waters, and we proceeded without slackening speed into that narrow gap as if we had the latest radar'.

Page 58: Bell belonged to a long line of American yachtsmen who have been based in Britain and joined the club. He was MFH of the Galway Blazers, the Kilkenny and the South and West Wilts and became famous in the hunting world as a hound breeder. After being crippled in a riding accident, he took up ocean racing and was soon elected to the club's committee after he became a member in 1935 and was subsequently made a life honorary member in 1954. He died in 1964.

Page 59: the inter-club points championship for the Martin-Illingworth Trophy ceased after 1994, and from 1995 it was awarded to the best IMS club team in the Fastnet Race. From the same year the John C. West Trophy was awarded to the best CHS club team in the Cowes-Dinard-St Malo Race.

Page 59: From a very lengthy, undated memo in the club's archives it is clear that it was Ray Barrett who did most of the work on the new time scale.

Page 61: the youngest sailor to apply for cadet membership was Huey Long's son. Long, who owned a succession of highly successful ocean racers called *Ondine*, applied for his son to become a member in April 1967 as he had sailed with his father in the 1963 Fastnet. The application was rejected because the minimum age for a cadet member was 15. By way of recompense the committee had a gilt RORC plaque engraved and sent to the boy. It read: 'Russell Long. Aged seven. *Ondine*. Fastnet race 1963'. He must surely be the youngest person ever to have taken part in the event.

Page 62: Elizabeth McCaw was the first to round the Rock in the 1937 Fastnet Race. At that time there was no prize for this achievement so afterwards her owner, Dick Reynolds, donated the Elizabeth McCaw Trophy, and a number of identical replicas, as an outright prize for the first boat around it in future races. After the last replica was won by Marvin Green's *Nirvana* in 1985, Green gave a new outright prize, the Catherine Green Trophy, with additional replicas. It is now awarded to the first non-CMAC CHS boat to round.

Page 62: it was with *Ortac* that the 28-year-old Clark really established his reputation as a designer. A man of quick, mordant wit he became a member in 1937 and followed up the success of *Ortac* with a whole string of well-known ocean racers, such as *Erivale*, *Lara*, and *Favona* which he designed for members before and after the war. 'He was a good sailor himself,' wrote his obituarist in *The Times* when he died in 1988, 'striking in his manner, and with great presence. His individualism made him not always the easiest person with whom to work; and his eccentricity manifested itself, for example, in a tendency never to pay bills until the last minute'.

Page 62: the names of many of Illingworth's yachts had Malham in them, the word deriving from Malhamdale a valley in north-west Yorkshire where he lived as a boy. He initially shared *Maid of Malham* with another member, Norman Jones, who then became her sole owner in 1939. After the war *Maid* was owned by a succession of club members, most notably Brigid Livingston who raced her with great success, topping the fleet in 1946 and winning the Trenchemer Cup.

Page 65: Sailorman, published in 1933. It was illustrated with Martin's own water colours and sketches, and covers the time he spent aboard the Thames barge *Vigilant*. The following year he published a slim volume called *Helmsmanship*.

Page 69: not being able to finish at Heligoland must have been a disappointment to members for it was a popular fixture. The Germans always laid on lavish entertainment and there were plenty of places of entertainment including a bar called the 'Lustful Seal'. In 1938 Jim Smellie, a future flag officer who raced aboard that year's winner, *Ortac*, had his bagpipes with him. 'He took the island by storm,' another member wrote. 'One night he played all the way from Pinkus up the 270 steps to the Oberland, followed by a great crowd of Germans with their trousers rolled up, their coats tied round their waists as kilts, all doing what they thought was the Highland Fling'. A Gordon Highlander, Colonel E.B. Beedle, in whose memory the Battler Beedle Quaich was given as a Fastnet trophy in 1969, was another member who liked to take his bagpipes sailing with him.

Page 69: Baldenweck was another of the club's talented amateur designers and *Aile Noire*, which had first appeared in the 1937 Dinard Race, was a development of his earlier yacht, *Isis*. She had a chamberpot in her main cabin which impressed the young Mary Blewitt as being *very* French. After the war René Levainville, the founder of the Union Nationale des Croiseurs (UNC), gave *Aile Noire* to UNCL as its club yacht.

Page 72: Known to a whole postwar generation of members as 'Uncle', Rouse, who died in 1969, often skippered the club's boat during the 1940s and 1950s, helping to introduce many young yachtsmen to ocean racing. After Harrison Butler died, *Yachting Monthly* rated Rouse as being possibly 'Britain's most important amateur designer', and he had over 40 vessels, ranging from dinghies to 100-ton South Sea Traders, to his credit. Besides his 14-ton cutter, *Golden Dragon*, which he had built in Hong Kong in 1939 and raced after the war with considerable success, his designs included the Admiralty yacht, *Tai-Mo-Shan*, and *Tzu Hang* in which the Smeetons made their well-known series of cruises in the 1950s and 1960s.

Five: THE RORC AT WAR

Page 73: a veteran of the 1914–18 war, Peterson is remembered as a man of great charm, warmth and wit, and an accomplished raconteur. He was a competent helmsman but his outstanding contribution

during a race was his cooking. He died in 1983.

Page 73: inevitably, feelings hardened as the war continued and at the December 1942 AGM a motion that the names of all German members be removed from the list of members was carried by 16 votes to 2. An amendment, which proposed that their membership be suspended until the end of the war, was defeated by 12 votes to 8, an unusually narrow majority.

Page 75: both 19 and 20 St James's Place stand on part of the gardens of Cleveland House, a mansion erected by Charles II for his mistress, Barbara Villers, Duchess of Cleveland. In 1690 the site was acquired by the Marquis of Halifax on a 61-year lease and nos 17–20 St James's Place were constructed for him by a local building family, but none has survived to the present day in any recognisable form. No.20 passed through many hands, the last being Sir Edgar Vincent, Viscount D'Abernon (1857–1941). The club leased the house from his widow.

Page 77: a Scot by birth, Helen Cattenach was universally known to everyone as Nellie. Older members remember her as a much loved institution who ruled the clubhouse with homely charm. For many years after the war lunch was quite a formal affair as many members worked in Whitehall and had the time for several pink gins before lunch and to linger over the cheese after it. Nellie provided a set menu for each weekday which never varied. The meal always started with lentil soup, and ended with the steward, Owen Hinton, intoning, as he proffered the cheese board: 'cheddar, cheshire, gorgonzola, or Port Salut–*sir*.' Nellie

retired in 1970 aged 70 and Owen shortly afterwards.

Page 80: Each of the 19 entries which eventually arrived before the 1st July 1944 closing date was assessed by Malden Heckstall-Smith. His reports and the designs were then passed to the committee which in May 1945 awarded first Prize of £50 to F/Lt Welch, then confined in the famous high-security POW camp, Colditz Castle, with F/Lt Hill and Lt Bruce RM second and third respectively. None of the winners was a member at the time, though Bruce was elected in July 1946.

Page 81: most notably the sub-clause 'to study and encourage the design, building, navigation and sailing of sailing vessels in which speed and seaworthiness are combined by any means including scientific research and practical demonstration' was added to clause 2 which delineated the objects for which the club had been formed.

Page 82: Somerset was awarded the DSO during the First World War when he served in the Army and then the Royal Flying Corps which became the Royal Air Force in 1918. He must therefore have been one of very few officers to have served in all three services when he joined the RNVR in 1940. He navigated a Lend-Lease destroyer across the Atlantic, serving in her for a year escorting Atlantic convoys before returning in 1941 to Vospers which he had joined in 1936.

Six: OCEAN RACING RESURRECTED

Page 91: mines continued to be a hazard for several years. In 1946 the Admiralty's displeasure was expressed when competitors in the race passed through a mined area. As late as 1948 there were still minefields in the North Sea which meant rerouting that year's North Sea Race.

Page 93: by the time he died in 1985 Barraclough had been a member for nearly 50 years. He was introduced to ocean racing by John Illingworth who had been his engineer officer in a submarine he commanded between the wars. He skippered Illingworth's *Maid of Malham* in 1938, when Illingworth lent her to the RNSA, and won the Class I championship in her. A very large man he was nicknamed 'Snow White' after his mass of white hair.

Page 96: Ewen Southby-Tailyour records in his biography of Hasler that *Tre Sang*'s crew–almost always fellow Royal Marines officers–were given strict joining instructions which reflected postwar austerity as well as the owner's dress code. 'Bring either a ration card or your own supply of butter, cooking fat, bacon, sugar, tea, plus...spirits or wines for drinking purposes.' Banned were suitcases, felt hats, yachting caps, pyjamas, uniforms, or spare sailing clothes, though an old suit or 'grey bags' and a jacket were permitted for visiting yacht clubs.

Page 96: Hughes, an architect and structural engineer by profession, was 'a splendid seaman, an experienced navigator, and a formidable racing opponent.' Apart from the Mulberry Harbour, he was associated with many notable projects including the Wembley stadium and the Hyde Park Corner underpass, and the dock in which the *Cutty Sark* rests at Greenwich was his design. He joined the RORC in 1938 after racing in Owen Aisher's first *Yeoman*. He died in 1977.

Page 99: It is not altogether clear whether he was referring to the 1947 North Sea Race or the 1946 one which is recalled by Mary Blewitt as she then was: 'It was my qualifying race. The Royal Maas gave us a fantastic reception, as if we had won the war just by ourselves. Rotterdam had just painted all its post boxes red to show solidarity with the British. One of the starters, a West Mersea boat called *Corinna*, piled her decks with bicycle tyres and set out to sell them in Rotterdam. At one stage, the crew got into a nightclub where one of them (a solicitor whose name escapes me) sold a string of brothels in Colchester to a black marketeer. The solicitor also had what he thought was a suitcase full of cigarettes, but other crew members had substituted dirty pyjamas and he had to escape through the window of the Ladies loo. Things went from bad to worse when the nightclub band played *Deutschland Uber Alles* instead of the National Anthem, but I confess that after over 50 years my memory of what was from its inception a complicated story, is not too good. We certainly drank more than we should have done.' Blewitt, author of the evergreen *Celestial Navigation for Yachtsmen*, married Gianni Pera, an Italian naval officer and keen yachtsman, in 1957 and she captained the first Italian Admiral's Cup team in 1969.

Page 99: Heckstall-Smith was a close friend of Charles E. Nicholson and in his thesis on Camper & Nicholson William Collier relates how Nicholson relied on Heckstall-Smith to underpin his own weak mathematical skills. He 'was a wonderful worker in a team of the sort which the Club set to solve its problems,' wrote a fellow member of the technical sub-committee, 'with an ever-open ear for the foibles, ideas and arguments of others.' He was made a life honorary member in 1943 and continued to advise on the club's rule until he died, aged 90, in 1955. As a young man he worked in several shipyards where he showed himself to be a very talented amateur designer. From 1921 to 1926 he was editor of *Yachting Monthly*.

Page 105: Sandison, who died in 1970, worked in the Bank of England. He joined the club in 1947 and subsequently wrote an entertaining book about ocean racing called *To Sea in Carpet Slippers*. When he was past working on the foredeck he became a cook which made him as much in demand as a crew member as did his talent as a raconteur. His book related his times aboard such boats as *Bloodhound*, *Foxhound*, and *Fandango*. 'I remember the first time I sailed with Sandy,' wrote his obituarist in *Seahorse*. 'After a middle watch I retired to my bunk and about 7.45am was woken by a rather hoarse voice singing "Jesus wants me for a sunbeam", and a hairy arm hovering by my shoulder with a steaming cup of tea and the information that it had been "fortified" to give me strength to face the day. What a shipmate!' Sandison also organised the annual dance, which was held every year from 1951, always a successful event.

Seven: THE 'DREADFUL, SHAPELESS, ENDLESS BOXES' ARE BROUGHT TO HEEL

Page 109: In 1971 only 3.7% of contenders for the British team were built in aluminium; in 1973 this had risen to 27%; by 1975 to 60%.

Page 111: *Jocasta* was mahogany built with steel frames. To save weight she had aluminium fastenings, and she was given copper paint on her bottom. This proved a horrendous combination and, according to Iorys Hughes, when she was launched 'she fizzed just like an Alkaseltzer'. She had to spend the winter in an acid bath to remove the copper paint and was then refastened using conventional materials.

Page 112: Mason sold *Latifa* to Jack Salem in 1955. In 1966 the club asked Salem to relinquish her sail number, 121, as her rating was no longer valid. Salem's answer and the club's reaction to it is recorded in the committee meeting minutes of January 1967. Salem 'replied that he had a beautiful model of *Latifa*, and if the club would like to have it, he would be delighted to present it to us. Agreed to accept the model and leave the sail number with him.'

Page 116: one of the starters in the 1953 Fastnet was the *Schlussel von Bremen*, the first German yacht to take part in a club race after the war. Her participation followed the readmission of Germany and Japan to the IYRU (now the International Sailing Federation) in November 1951, though the club stipulated that any prewar members of Axis countries would have to requalify to be re-elected.

Page 120: one memo included the first mention of the use of computers in offshore racing. Dated 25th February 1955, it was written by a committee member, F.W. Morgan. 'Since drafting these notes I have received a provisional offer of the use of an "electronic brain" for working out ratings and preparing analyses, etc.'. By the start of the 1966 racing season all RORC ratings were calculated by computer.

Page 124: The 'Windfalls' were seized largely on the initiative of Brigadier W.E. Fryer, Chief Engineer of 30 Corps, which occupied the Kiel area. The REYC's allotment included two 100sq.metre cutters and a 50sq.metre, and were renamed after the codenames of major Allied landings: *Avalanche*, *Overlord*, and *Torch*. The last was entered in the 1947 Fastnet as *Seamew*, an incorrect translation of her German name, *Seemove*, and her participation ensured that always having a Sapper entry in the race remained unbroken. Not all 'Windfalls' were officially 'liberated'. After the war the Peyton-Jones and Roome families jointly owned *Rebel Maid*, a 50sq.metre 'Windfall' which had been privately acquired. In 1939 she had been taken to neutral Sweden and left in the charge of the German Naval Attaché who rather lost interest in her in 1945. His British counterpart, Captain Henry Denham RN, rang the Peyton-Jones family and they raised a crew and sailed her back from Stockholm. As the Peyton-Jones' yacht had been taken when the Germans occupied the Channel Islands in 1940, this was regarded as a fair exchange.

Eight: WHO REALLY WON THE ADMIRAL'S CUP?

Page 125: the book *Haunted London* relates that the house had long been the home of two spinsters, Anne and Harriet Pearson. When Anne died in 1858 Harriet lived on in the house. In November 1864 she fell gravely ill. Attending her were her housekeeper, two of her nieces, and her nephew's wife. On December 23rd the nephew's wife was left by the sick woman's bedside while the others went to bed. However, the nieces left their bedroom door open, and the lights were left burning on the staircase and landing. About 1am the nieces saw a woman, wearing a shawl and a black cap, go past their door and into the room where the patient lay. One said to the other, 'Emma, get up, it is old Aunt Anne!' and her cousin answered 'so it is, then Aunt Harriet will die today.' The nephew's wife then ran out of the sickroom in great agitation, having also seen and recognised her dead aunt. The three women roused the housekeeper and together they searched the house without finding anyone. Miss Harriet Pearson died at 6am. Before doing so she told them all that she had seen her sister and knew she had come to take her away.

Page 126: It was Cartwright, one of the chief architects of the modern British steel industry, whom Chay Blyth approached during the 1960s with his idea of sailing single-handed round the world 'the wrong way'. The result was *British Steel* which brought the British steel industry invaluable publicity when Blyth accomplished his voyage in 1970-71. Cartwright died in 1998 aged 91.

Page 129: Roome was in charge of *Griffin* in the 1956 Channel Race. He also took part in the 1979 Fastnet Race in his own boat, *Flycatcher*, and is probably the only member to have skippered boats in both events. In his view the seas he encountered in the Fastnet were higher than in the Channel Race but not as steep.

Page 129: A New Zealander by birth, Buckley won the MC in the First World War and became an expert in camouflage. For a time between the wars he ran an airline between England and Scotland with his close friend, Bobby Somerset, and also worked as manager of the school shop at Eton where he himself had been educated. During the Second World War he served as Commandant of the School of Camouflage, with the rank of lt-colonel. When he died in 1960 a member wrote that 'he always seemed to be able to make a simple issue of a problem however baffling, and he is one who has had a great part in building up the Royal Ocean Racing Club into the great institution that it is today'.

Page 131: Traditionally the management committee

has always been dissolved by the trustees after a series and a new one appointed, but some members are now retained to help continuity. Challenging teams have always had the right to appoint someone to the committee and from the 1979 series onwards a minority of overseas members were appointed to it, and ten years later it was enlarged to represent a wide cross-section of participating countries. It comes to decisions by consensus, taking into account the views of the RORC, the policies of the Offshore Racing Council (ORC), and Grand-Prix racing in general.

Page 135: Captain Johnnie Coote RN joined the club in 1949 after serving in submarines during the Second World War. He became friends with Max Aitken and joined his newspaper group in 1959. His career in Fleet Street lasted 15 years, half of which he spent as deputy chairman of Express Newspapers. In the 1979 Fastnet, his thirteenth, he navigated Eric

Swenson's *Toscana* and, in the middle of the storm that hit the fleet, celebrated his 58th birthday with champagne. He died in 1993.

Page 136: Nye, who died in 1988, did not take up ocean racing until after the war when he was 42. He became a member after the 1953 Fastnet. Sandison described him as 'Compact, sturdily built and unemotional...the personification of my idea of the hard-bitten, hard-driving Yankee skipper of a former age'. Besides winning the Fastnet twice, Nye won three Bermuda Races—the last in 1984—and three Transatlantic ones.

Page 137: by the time Hasler entered her for the first single-handed Transatlantic Race in 1960, in which he came second to Chichester, *Jester* was junk rigged. He sold her in 1964 to member Mike Richey. She was lost during the 1988 single-handed Transatlantic Race.

Nine: NO BEARDY WEIRDIES, PLEASE

Page 144: a member from 1959, Primrose died in 1980 when his yacht foundered in a storm off the east coast of the United States. He sold his first boat design when he was 14 and spent all his life designing and building them. The firm which he and Illingworth founded in 1959 was dissolved in 1966 when Primrose became more interested in production boats.

Page 147: starting a race in bad weather has long been a bone of contention between the club and the press. But for many years it has been club policy that starts are only postponed if the line, for some reason, is not clear. As Alan Green points out, if it became club policy not to start a race in, say, a Force 8 or higher, this might encourage designers to design less seaworthy boats—a direct contradiction of one of the club's main objectives.

Page 148: considering her light construction, *Myth's* longevity as a racing yacht was amazing. Under the ownership of another club member, Noel Bevan, she was still taking part in the Admiral's Cup, as a member of the Irish team, as late as 1965. Eventually age caught up with her and she sank off the Brittany coast in 1972.

Page 150: in line with The Queen's wish 'to give an opportunity for young men to gain experience of ocean racing and sailing in one of the bigger yachts' *Bloodhound* covered 7,736 miles during 1963 and was sailed by crews from 32 yacht clubs, including the RORC. But by 1968 she was thought by those taking care of her to be too old to take part in RORC events. The Royal family used her on a number of occasions until they sold her in 1969. She is still raced in classic yacht regattas.

Ten: ENTER THE ONE TONNERS

Page 159: 'Over a span of 40 years, very many men and women learnt about the sea by sailing in Bobby Somerset's crews,' Hasler wrote in *The Times*. 'To them he will remain incomparable for his skill, courage, and wide knowledge, and for his good-natured tolerance of their inefficiency.'

Page 160: The son of Charles A. Nicholson, Peter Nicholson is the current commodore of the Royal Yacht Squadron and has been a RORC member since 1958. As builder, designer, owner, navigator, or helmsman—and sometimes a combination of most, or all, of these—he was involved in many of the top ocean racers between the 1957 Fastnet, when he raced aboard *Cohoe III*, and the 1979 one when he was navigator of *Yeoman XXI*. He took part in just about every ocean race between those dates and regards the period from the mid fifties until the early eighties as 'the golden age of ocean racing' for those competing at the highest level. In those days 'the owners knew a great deal about the technicalities of their boats and about the rating rule. Most of them skippered their own boats and were good seamen. The crews and the owners enjoyed each other's company and were usually great friends both on and off the boat. Today many of the crews compete because they are paid and there is much less socialising. Not many of the owners skipper their own boats and quite a number do not even go to sea in them'.

Page 160: after joining the club in 1957, S.H.R(endall) Clarke owned seven yachts called *Quiver*, the first and last being cruising yachts. He was manager of the British team which successfully defended the Admiral's Cup in 1965 and was rear commodore 1964-66. He died in 1992 aged 82.

Page 164: despite one entry in her log, 'Protests: 1) No vodka, 2) No deep freeze, 3) No morning papers, 4) No Women!', *Griffin II* gave a lot of fun to a lot of people.

Page 164: this new configuration came to prominence in the USA when the Cal-40 *Conquistador*, designed by Bill Lapworth, won the Southern Ocean Racing Conference circuit (SORC) in 1964.

Page 165: A member since 1957, when he took part in his first Fastnet, Snaith, in his series of boats called *Figaro*, was a formidable opponent on the water, particularly when it came to beating his 'dear enemy', Dick Nye. He had the unique record of finishing second overall in the Fastnet no less than three times (1963-67), but the Fastnet Cup always eluded him. After the third occasion he decided the runner-up needed a more suitable reward than a tankard or a plaque. 'As a great artist and head of one of the world's most successful team of industrial designers,' Johnnie Coote wrote of him when he died in 1974, 'it was only natural that he should design what undoubtedly is the most beautiful trophy raced for under RORC rules.' He had it made in the Old Kent Road and named it the Figaro Trophy.

Page 166: at the time he died Wyatt was the chairman of British United Airways, then the country's largest independent airline. He was elected to the RORC in 1937, became a committee member in 1946, and had owned the 9-ton cutter, *Freedom*, and then the 25-ton sloop, *Rosemary IV*, before buying *Bloodhound* in 1947. Just before his death he had been awarded the Royal Cruising Club challenge cup for a voyage in the Arctic Sea in 1967 in his cruising yacht, *Tyger*.

Page 166: when Arthur Slater, a bearded Yorkshireman, lost his left leg as the result of a crash while driving in the 1950 Monte Carlo Rally he turned to ocean racing. He had a false leg fitted but never wore it while sailing. With the help of a bucket swivel seat fixed to the floor of his cockpit he was able to become one of the top ocean racing helmsmen of his era. In his series of boats called *Prospect of Whitby* he represented his country in the Admiral's Cup in 1967,1969, and 1971, in the Onion Patch series in 1968,1970 and 1972, and in the Southern Cross series in 1969,1971, and 1973. He died in 1996.

Page 166: Miller had served as a pilot in the Fleet Air Arm during the Second World War where he picked up the basics in small boat handling and meteorology, and his training in navigation gave him a strong leaning towards instruments. He joined the RORC in 1960 after taking part in a number of races in *Griffin II* and the Lloyd's yacht, *Lutine*. 'Of course he did get across those who were trying to preserve the past system,' Ron Amey wrote of him after he died in 1977, and added that in criticising the Establishment, often quite constructively, Miller perhaps made the mistake of showing that he enjoyed doing so!

Page 167: a Royal Thames Yacht Club trophy donated by John Junius Morgan, the Morgan Cup was first presented for a race first sailed in 1929. From 1958, when it first appeared in the RORC's programme, it has been jointly organised by the two clubs.

Page 170: the son of the Canadian-born newspaper tycoon Lord Beaverbrook, Max Aitken was a highly decorated fighter pilot during the Second World War. After *Drumbeat* he commissioned John Illingworth to design *Outlaw* in 1962. She proved as big a success as *Drumbeat* had been a failure, winning the 1963 Class I championship and many other prizes. Altogether he owned 22 boats in as many years and was twice voted Yachtsman of the Year. He was undoubtedly one of the most distinguished patrons of yachting since the war, launching the London Boat Show as well as the international long-distance powerboat race from Cowes to Torquay. He wanted to bequeath to the RORC what is now the Prospect Museum at Cowes. When he was advised that the death duties would be punitive he gave it to a charitable trust and decreed that the RORC commodore and admiral should always be ex-officio trustees of it. After he died in 1985, the trust acquired an adjoining property called The Disrespect, which included a ground floor shop fronting Cowes High Street. This serves as the museum entrance and is shared with the RORC which uses it as its Cowes headquarters. The bedrooms above the shop are leased to the club which rents them to members.

Eleven: THE IOR RULES, OK

Page 171: the possibility of ocean racing in the Olympic Games was first raised by a RORC committee member in June 1939 when he suggested that it be included in the 1944 Olympics due to be held in the UK. The suggestion received little support. The commodore thought there were ample reason to keep clear of any such participation as there was a danger, judging from the records of other Olympic events, of bad blood being stirred up between the countries concerned which was in direct contrast to the RORC's policy.

Page 173: Amey was one of the club's staunchest supporters from the time he joined in 1960. Between 1958 and 1975 he had ten yachts called *Noryema*, his name spelt backwards. *Noryema VIII*, a glass fibre production Swan 48, was a member of the 1972 British Onion Patch team. Skippered by Amey's friend and navigator, Teddy Hicks, she was the first non-American yacht–and the first production boat–ever to win the Bermuda Race, which that year was one of the toughest ever. Despite suffering seriously from asthma, which often made him very ill at sea, Amey was part of the British Admiral's Cup team in 1963, 1965, 1967, and 1975. He served on the committee for some years, and was a rear commodore from 1969 to 1971. He died in 1995.

Page 176: Wylie's career in ocean racing spanned 60 years. His first race was in *Ilex*, the Royal Engineers' yacht, in 1932, while his last race was in 1982 aboard *Sunstone*, which belonged to his daughter and son-in-law. He was the club's rear commodore in 1967–8 before being elected vice commodore, 1969–71. Between 1967–73 he was one of the selectors for the British Admiral's Cup team which he managed in 1967. He died in 1992.

Page 177: *Seahorse* has undergone several metamorphoses. In 1971 it was transferred to Ocean Publications, owned by member Anthony Churchill, one of the instigators of the 1975 Financial Times Clipper Race, and who, with Guy Pearse, first had the idea of what became the Whitbread (now Volvo) Round-The-World Race. At first *Seahorse* was only distributed to members but later it was put on sale to the public. It was bought by the *Observer* in 1989 and later the same year it started being published every month instead of every other month. It was purchased in 1994 by its present editor, Andrew Hurst, the skipper of several of the British team's Admiral's Cup boats during the late 1980s and early 1990s.

Page 178: Paul died in 1994.

Page 186: the effectiveness of sponsoring the Admiral's Cup series on the sales of Champagne Mumm can be seen in the figures of cases sold annually in the UK before and after the company first became associated with the series. In 1976 they sold 620 cases, in 1977 they sold 1,850.

Page 186: Aisher died in 1993 aged 93.

Twelve: FASTNET DISASTER–AND AFTER

Page 191: several books were later published which cover the disaster in detail. The best is *Fastnet Force 10*, by an American writer, John Rousmaniere, who crewed aboard the Class I *Toscana*. The most recent theories on the storm itself were discussed in an article by D.E. Pedgley, published by the Royal Meteorological Society's magazine, *Weather*, in 1997.

Page 194: one of the questions, B2, asked 'Did you experience a knockdown beyond horizontal including a 360-degree roll?' was answered 'yes' by 77 of those who replied. A 'B2 knockdown' has now become a nautical term.

Page 195: the 1979 Fastnet disaster overshadowed that year's Admiral's Cup series which was won by Australia. Though the British team of Edward Heath's *Morning Cloud*, Jeremy Rogers' *Eclipse*, and Ernest Juer's *Blizzard* could only manage sixth place, *Eclipse* was the top boat in series.

Page 198: Ludlow, a member since 1974, also became a member of the ORC's technical committee and latterly navigated for Maurice Laing in top level competitions. He died in 1993.

Page 198: the RORC's first Caribbean Pursuit Race inspired Jimmy Cornell to found his highly successful ARC (Atlantic Rally for Cruisers) series in 1986. The RORC helped run the ARC in 1998.

Page 200: ocean racers were not popular with an earlier generation of bosses either. 'They always used to say don't employ an ocean racer,' John Roome relates about the 1950s. 'Come Monday morning he's sending a telegram saying he's been becalmed and gets in just before the office closes. On Tuesday he's too exhausted to work; on Wednesday he's ringing round to find out how everyone did in the race; on Thursday he's collecting a crew; and on Friday he's off!'

Page 204: this international team racing championship, which is now defunct, was an idea of Chris Dunning's which the club had launched in 1981. It initially ran over a three-year period to include four major team series worldwide: The Admiral's Cup, the Southern Cross, SORC, and Sardinia Cup. From 1992 the format was changed to a two-year cycle of Grand Prix events worldwide and came under the auspices of the ORC, though the club continued to co-ordinate the series. It concentrated on the Pacific hemisphere one year, and the European-Atlantic the next, each being a separate series.

Page 204: during the inaugural Cowes-Rotterdam Race in 1996, Munro Kerr was lost overboard from *Trocar*, which he shared with his father-in-law Nick Greville. One of the club's brightest and most talented members, he was regarded by many as being a future commodore.

Thirteen: INTO THE NEW MILLENNIUM

Page 209: the agreements with other organisations to promote the work of Griffin petered out in the late 1980s. A new Griffin scheme was launched by Janet Grosvenor in 1992 which helped youngsters gain experience by sailing aboard members' yachts. From 1995 members also lent their yachts for 'Griffin clinics' where teams of youngsters are given professional tuition. In 1998 a new scheme was started in conjunction with the RYA and British Universities Sailing Association.

Page 213: Bermuda and Spain fielded two-boat teams in the 1969 series and New Zealand and Austria one-boat teams in 1971, but teams of less than three boats were banned from 1973 until 1993.

Page 214: a 1991 article in *Seahorse* about budgeting for the Whitbread gives an idea of what professional yachtsmen could earn. The article quoted $100,000pa for a top skipper, $75,000pa for the navigator, and $36,000pa for a regular member of the crew. Performance bonuses were additional to these sums. In 1997 the day rate for a deck hand was in the region of £200.

Page 214: *Sunstone*'s record was a remarkable one. It included an overall win in the 1985 Channel Race against all the Admiral's cuppers, followed by a class win in that year's Fastnet. She won the IMS points championship six years out of seven between 1989–95 and was named Silk Cut Yacht of the Year in 1986 and 1992.

Page 216: a Lloyd's underwriter by profession, Green joined the club in 1949, crewing in boats such as *Bloodhound*, *Foxhound*, and *Lutine*. As Illingworth's partner he won many races in *Myth of Malham*, which won the Class I championship as late as 1961. In

1962 *Myth* was sold to the Livingstons and Green built the Class I *Musketeer* as a 1963 Admiral's Cup contender. She proved disappointing that year but, after a change of rig, topped her class in 1964. He was chairman of Lloyd's 1980–83 and remained an Admiral's Cup trustee until his death in 1996.

Page 218: Schumann first made contact with the British yachting scene in 1954 when he sought shelter from a storm at Cowes. He was immediately attracted to the atmosphere and when it was made plain to him that he would be welcome to take part in Cowes Week he returned in 1956, and came second in that year's Round-the-Island Race. He first competed in the Admiral's Cup in 1963 in the second of his many yachts called *Rubin*, and under his captaincy Germany won the trophy in 1973, 1985 and 1993. He joined the club in 1965 and was made a life honorary member in 1996.

Page 219: Argos satellite data used during the 1995 Fastnet Race allowed, for the first time, a substantially correct picture of team standings calculated in distance-to-finish to be released to the press.

Page 222: allowing multihulls into club races had been intermittently discussed in committee ever since June 1959 when an application to measure a 36ft catamaran was refused, even though the rating secretary said he thought it would be possible. In December 1966 David Edwards reported that the IYRU's catamaran committee had suggested that the club should become involved in arranging races for multihulls, but this, too, was declined. However, by 1974 the Multihull Offshore Cruising and Racing Association (MOCRA) had devised its own rating rules, and its request that multihulls be allowed to race in some RORC events in a class of their own was agreed to if MOCRA was responsible for its own regulations and results. Multihulls were given a starting gun after the RORC fleet, and were also timed in. However, after the crew of the single catamaran shadowing the 1979 Fastnet was lost the club declined to have anything to do with multihulls until 1996.

Sources / Bibliography

SOURCES

PRIMARY

RORC archives which include some correspondence, mainly before and during the Second World War, and minutes of various committees and of the Annual General Meetings

Royal Yacht Squadron archives

E.G. Martin correspondence with H.E. West 1938–44

correspondence in National Portrait Gallery regarding E.G. Martin portrait by the Dutch-born official war artist, Cor Visser

log of *Saladin* for 1925 and 1926 Fastnet

logs of *Jolie Brise* and *Nina* when owned by Robert Somerset

Public Record Office HS1/123: report on *Siderhana Johannis* escape party

log of *Tilly Twin* during 1956 Channel Race

manuscript of memoirs of Capt. E.M.C. Barraclough RN

minutes of Offshore Rules Coordinating Committee

interviews with RORC members and RORC Secretariat

The Yacht Builders: A Study of the History of Camper & Nicholson, 1782–1939 by William Collier. Thesis submitted to the University of Liverpool 1997

SECONDARY

BOOKS

Antrobus, Paul and others: *Ocean Racing Around the World*, Angus & Robertson, 1975

Bruce, Erroll: *From Duck Pond to Deep Ocean*, Boldre Marine, 1997

Bryer, Robin: *Jolie Brise: A Tall Ship's Tale*, Secker & Warburg, 1982

Chichester, Francis: *The Lonely Sea and the Sky*, Hodder & Stoughton, 1964

Coles, Adlard: *Heavy Weather Sailing*, Adlard Coles Nautical, 1980; *Sailing Years*, Granada, 1981

Dear, Ian: *Fastnet: The Story of A Great Ocean Race*, Batsford, 1981; *The Royal Yacht Squadron 1915–1985*, Stanley Paul, 1985; *Champagne Mumm Book of Ocean Racing*, Severn House, 1985

Dixon, Douglas: *The King's Sailing Master*, Harrap, 1948

Duke, Sir Gerald: *The History of the Royal Engineer Yacht Club*, privately published, 1982

Fairley, Gordon: *Minute by Minute: The Story of the Royal Yachting Association (1875–1982)*, Royal Yachting Association, 1983

Fisher, Bob: *The Fastnet Disaster and After*, Pelham Books, 1980; *The Admiral's Cup*, Pelham Books, 1985

Fox, Uffa: *Sailing, Seamanship, and Yacht Construction*, Peter Davies, 1934

Garrett, Alasdair & Wilkinson, Trevor: *The Royal Cruising Club 1880–1980*, privately published, no date

Heath, Edward: *Sailing: A Course of My Life*, Sidgwick & Jackson, 1975

Howland, Waldo: *A Life in Boats*, Mystic Seaport Museum Inc., 1984

Hoyt, Sherman: *Memoirs*, Van Nostrand, 1950. Published in the UK in 1951 by Robert Cross as *Yankee Yachtsman*

Illingworth, John: *The Malham Story*, Nautical Publishing, 1972

Jeffery, Tim: *The Champagne Mumm Admiral's Cup*, Bloomsbury, 1994

Johnson, Peter: *Yacht Rating*, Bucksea Guides, 1997

Kenny, Dick: *To Win The Admiral's Cup*, Nautical Publishing, 1974

King, Stella: *'Jacqueline': Pioneer Heroine of the Resistance*, Arms & Armour, 1989

Kinney, Francis S.: *You Are First: The Story of Olin and Rod Stephens of Sparkman & Stephens*, Dodd Mead, 1978

Lee, Adrian & Philpott, Ruby: Laurent Giles: *An Evolution of Yacht Design*, Nautical Publishing, 1990

Loomis, Alf: *Ocean Racing–The Great Blue-Water Yacht Races, 1866–1935*, Bodley Head, 1936

Luard, W.B.: *Where the Tides Meet*, Nicholson & Watson, 1948

Martin, E.G.: *Deep Water Cruising*, Oxford University Press, 1928; *Sailorman*, Oxford University Press, 1933; Lonsdale Library: *Cruising and Ocean Racing*, Seeley Services, 1933 (part author); *Helmsmanship*, Oxford University Press, 1934

Martyr, Weston: *Southseaman*, Blackwood, 1926; *The Wandering Years*, Blackwood, 1940

Mason, C.F.: *Deep Sea Racing*, Phoenix House, 1953

Mason, Michael: *One Man's War*, privately printed, 1966

Nicholson, John W.: *Great Years in Yachting*, Nautical Publishing, 1970

Phillips-Birt, Douglas: *British Ocean Racing*, Adlard Coles, 1960; *The Cumberland Fleet: Two Hundred Years of Yachting, 1775–1975*, privately published by the Royal Thames Yacht Club, 1978

Plym, Gustav: *Yacht and Sea*, Adlard Coles, 1961

Richards, Brooks: *Secret Flotillas*, HMSO, 1995

Rousmaniere, John: *Fastnet Force 10*, Nautical Publishing, 1980

Royal Corinthian Yacht Club: *A Book of Designs of Deep Sea Racing Craft*, Ernest Day, 1933

Rutherford, Iain: *At the Tiller*, Blackie & Son, 1946

Sandison, A.C.: *To Sea in Carpet Slippers*, Adlard Coles, 1966

Southby-Tailyour, Ewen: *Blondie: A Life of Lt-Colonel H.G. Hasler*, Leo Cooper, 1998

Underwood, Peter: *Haunted London*, Harrap, 1973

MAGAZINES AND NEWSPAPERS

Daily Telegraph

Seahorse

The Field

The Isis

The Times

Yachting

Yachting Monthly

Yachting World

Yachtsman

Index

(pages with black-and-white illustrations are in brackets)